adobe® for fashion: *illustrator*® CS5
The ultimate guide to drawing flats

by Robin Schneider

adobe® for fashion: illustrator®CS5
The Ultimate Guide to Drawing Flats
by Robin Schneider

Find us on the web at: **adobeforfashion.com**

Copyright © 2012 by Robin Schneider
Published by Lulu.com

Notice of Rights
All rights reserved. No part of this book may be reproduced or transmitted in any form by any means, electronic, mechanical, photocopying, recording, or otherwise, without the prior written permission of the publisher. For information on getting permission for reprints and excerpts, contact: permissions@adobeforfashion.com.

Notice of Liability
The information in this book is distributed on an "As Is" basis, without warranty. While every precaution has been taken in the preparation of the book, neither the author nor publisher shall have any liability to any person or entity with respect to any loss or damage caused or alleged to be caused directly or indirectly by the instructions contained in this book or by the computer software and hardware products described in it.

Trademarks
Adobe and Illustrator are a registered trademark of Adobe Systems Incorporated in the United States and /or other countries. All other trademarks are the property of their respective owners. Many of the designations used by manufacturers and sellers to distinguish their products are claimed as trademarks. Where those designations appear in this book, and the publisher was aware of a trademark claim, the designations appear as requested by the owner of the trademark. All other product names and services identified throughout this book are used in editorial fashion only and for the benefit of such companies with no intention of infringement of the trademark. No such use, or the use of any trade name, is intended to convey endorsement or other affiliation with this book.

ISBN 978-1-105-82728-0

Printed and bound in the United States of America.

acknowledgments

This book is dedicated to all of the students that have inspired, challenged and frustrated and me over the years. I may have learned as much from you as I hope you learned from me. Thank you for your encouragement and feedback while I developed this book.

To answer the nagging question of "When is your book coming out?" NOW!

OK, back to the computer...I have a Photoshop® book to write.

Many Thanks
Robin Schneider

A very special thanks to:

Roselani who lit the fuse. Amber, Andy, Angelica, Brooke, Fendi, Jose, Keshia, Kim, Lauren, Stephy, Song, Tephy, and Trixie for allowing me to include their work among these pages. You do me proud!

All the students and faculty of the Art Institute of California - Hollywood who gave me feedback, offered suggestions, voted on the cover design, caught my numerous typos and treated my handouts as if they were gold.

Teresa Becker whose fault it is that I became a teacher instead of a fashion designer. It's the best job I swore I never wanted.

My cheerleaders: Aleta, Stephanie, Miranda, Shideh, Aarone and Athena.

Angee and Anna for their constant crows of encouragement.

Cricket for her unfailing love and support.

And of course Adobe®

table of contents

acknowledgments   iii

introduction   vii

lesson one: getting started   1
WORKSPACE   2
TOOL BAR   4
THE LAYERS PANEL   7
UNDO   8
TERMINOLOGY   9
DRAWING BASIC SHAPES   10
SELECTING OBJECTS   14
USING COLOR   17
PATHS   21
THE PEN TOOL   22
DIRECT SELECTION TOOL   24
ZOOM TOOL   25
HAND TOOL   25
SAVING FILES   27

lesson two: the basics   29
ROTATE   29
REFLECT   31
JOIN   33
AVERAGE   34
PATHFINDER   35
DRAWING FLATS   38
THE BASIC T-SHIRT   39

lesson three: basic flats   45
ADDING THE BACK NECKLINE   45
ADDING SLEEVES   46
THE BACK VIEW   48
ORGANIZING LAYERS   49
ISOLATION MODE   50
EYE DROPPER TOOL   55

lesson four: buttons, collars and cuffs   59
ALIGN   59
DISTRIBUTE   60
DRAWING COLLARS   61
FRONT PLACKET   66
CREATING CUFFS   67
GROUPS   68
BUTTONS   69
SHIRT BACK   70
SLEEVE PLACKET   72

lesson five: skirts and blazers   77
DRAWING SKIRTS   78
PROFILES   82
BASIC BLAZER   83
LAPEL   84
BLAZER FRONT   87

lesson six: brushes and symbols and jeans   93
BRUSHES   93
EDITING BRUSHES   97
CHANGING BRUSH COLOR   98
SAVING BRUSHES   99
LOADING BRUSHES   99
SYMBOLS   102
EDITING SYMBOLS   104
CALLIGRAPHIC BRUSH   109
THE BLOB BRUSH   110
DRAWING JEANS   113

lesson seven: tech packs and time savers — 119

NOTATIONS FOR TECH PACKS	119
DRAWING ARROWS	120
CURVED ARROWS	121
SAVING FOR EXCEL	122
GRAPHIC STYLES	123
CLIPPING MASKS	127

lesson eight: patterns — 131

PATTERNS	131
CREATING PATTERNS	133
SAVING PATTERNS	134
SCALING PATTERNS	136
ROTATING PATTERNS	137
CREATING STRIPES	139
CREATING PLAIDS	141

lesson nine: croqui — 145

DRAWING CROQUI	145
SKIN TONES	146
GRADIENTS	148
DRAWING FACES	149

lesson ten: layouts — 161

LAYOUT	161
ADDING TEXT	166
SELECTING FONTS	167
DOWNLOADING FONTS	167
BACKGROUNDS	168
SAVING FILES FOR PRINT	170

lesson eleven: advanced techniques — 181

USING PROFILES TO ADD FLAIR	181
QUICK & EASY BOLD OUTLINE	182
DROP SHADOW	182
APPEARANCE PANEL	183
LOCATE OBJECT	183
MEASURE TOOL	184
SHAPE BUILDER TOOL	185
THE PENCIL TOOL	187
OFFSET STROKE	188
SCRIBBLE	188
RIBBING	189
BLEND	190
CLIPPING MASK	191
SHADING WITH THE BLOB BRUSH	192
ADVANCED BRUSHES	194
LIVE TRACE	200
LACE	200
COLORING BRUSHES	202
ADVANCED PATTERNS	203
MAKING COLOR GROUPS	206
KULER	207
RECOLOR ARTWORK	208
ENVELOPE WARP	211
WARPING FABRIC FILLS	213
ENVELOPE DISTORT	213

my two cents... — 216

student contributors — 217

resources — 219

Index — 221

introduction

This book is designed to get you up and running in the shortest possible time. It is not a manual for using Adobe® Illustrator®, there are already numerous versions on the market and I will recommend my favorites in the resource section of this book. Illustrator® is an enormous program with unlimited capabilities and tackling it can be a daunting task. My approach is to distil it down to only the tools and techniques relevant to fashion design and present them in an easy to follow format that will allow you to succeed from the start.

This book assumes a basic knowledge of fashion and flat sketching by hand. It focuses only on how to use the computer as a tool to accomplish this in a quick and efficient manor. If you need more detailed information on drawing technical flats, you can find a list of recommended books in the resource section.

Mac versus Windows? Everyone has their preferences and generally the preferred format is the one you first learned on. So stick with what you know and are most comfortable using. The Mac and Windows interfaces for Illustrator® look and function alike so this book will work for both formats. The only thing you need to concern yourself with are the keyboard shortcuts, they differ slightly and I will list both, Windows and Mac throughout the book. Once you gain a basic understanding of the program you should be able to work on either platform as necessary.

You may be surprised to discover that you already know many of the key board shortcuts for Illustrator® especially if you have been using Microsoft word. The commands for Undo, Copy, Paste, New Fle and Save are the same through the Adobe® CS5 suite, so this won't be completely unfamiliar territory for you.

The most important thing is to have fun. The computer is a great tool- it can speed up workflow and allow you the freedom to create. Feel free to experiment; you are only limited by your imagination.

I have created a collection of tutorials organized as I would present them in my classroom. Each exercise builds on the previous one, so to be successful it is important to master each section before moving on to the next. The beginning tutorials will have detailed step by step instructions, but as the book progresses to the more advanced tutorials I will limit the details and focus on concepts and short cuts. Follow along and you'll be drawing CADs like a pro by the end of this book.

lesson one

Why Draw Flats?
Flats are the building blocks of the fashion industry. Drawn to scale, they are the blueprints for crafting patterns and the #1 way of communicating across departments and languages. A flat is a technical illustration of a garment showing all details for production. At a glance, you can determine the design and construction of a garment including placement of trims, buttons, zippers, pockets, stitching and even fabric type. They can be used for forecasting future trends and selling a current product line to buyers before a single sample has been made.

Drawing flats quickly and accurately is critical to the production process. A poorly drawn flat leads to potential pattern problems. The more details included in the illustration, the less the pattern maker can veer from the designer's vision. Remember…any details not indicated on the flat are left for the pattern maker to decide.

Traditionally flats have been sketched by hand- a perfectly good process but slower and less accurate by today's standards. With the introduction of CAD the production process has picked up speed and programs like Illustrator® have become the new standard for drawing flats.

The computer is a terrific tool. It allows the designer to work faster, cleaner and smarter. Since technical flats are often symmetrical, the designer using Illustrator® only needs to draw 1 side of the garment. It can then be copied and reflected to create the other half. Multiple copies can be printed easily from the digital file. Colors and fabrics can be changed and adjusted with the click of a mouse allowing the designer to spend less time redrawing and more time designing.

ILLUSTRATOR® WORKSPACE

It's time to introduce you to the Adobe Illustrator® workspace. The information will be limited to only those tools needed to get started and additional tools will be added as we progress through the lessons. Prepare to learn the Illustrator® tools, how to navigate the workspace, the menu bar and the panels. Understanding these basics will help you to trouble shoot future difficulties.

When you open Adobe Illustrator® the first thing you will see is the welcome screen, you can open a new document by selecting **Create New Print Document** or if you prefer just close it by clicking the little X in the upper right hand corner.

OPEN A NEW DOCUMENT

Let's open a **New Document** by using the keyboard shortcut **Ctrl + N** (Windows) or *Cmd + N* (Mac). A dialog box will open, Select **Print** from the **New Document Profile** drop down menu and the rest of your settings will match the ones below. Click OK.

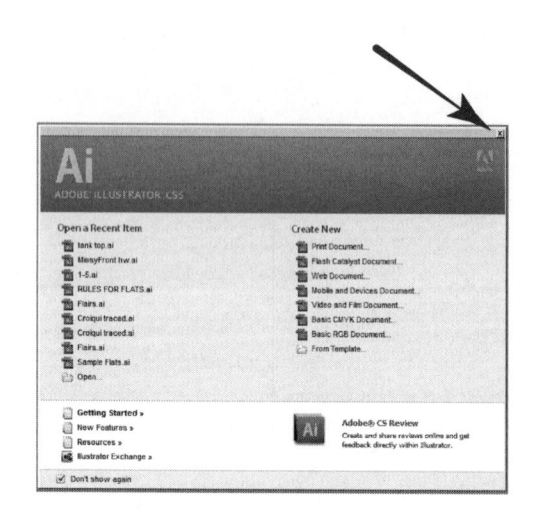

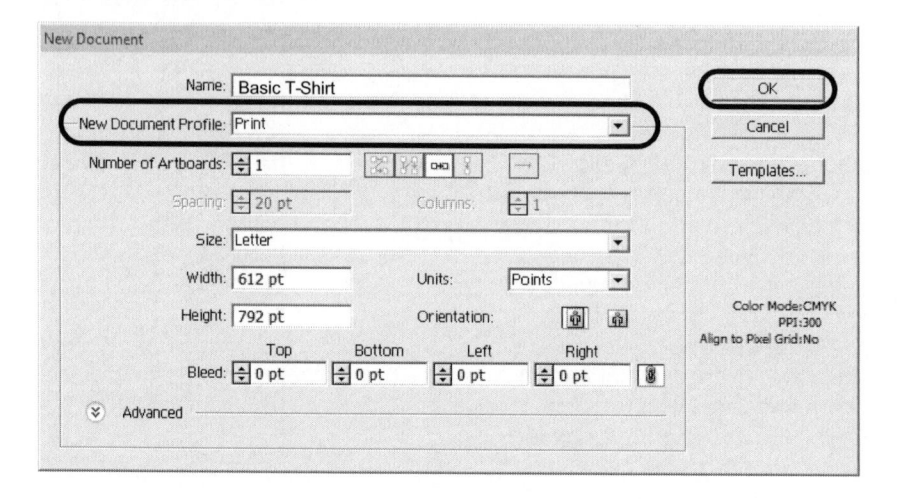

NAVIGATING THE WORKSPACE

The area along the top of the screen is called the **Menu Bar**, clicking on any of the headings will open a drop down menu of additional choices. Just below is the **Control Panel**, a series of tool specific icons that will change as you select different tools from the **Tool Bar**.

The center area of the screen is called the **Art Board**. Its size was determined by the width and height typed in the **New Document Box**. Anything you draw within the boundary of the Art Board will be printable; anything drawn or placed outside of the Art Board will not be printable.
Use it as scratch paper to save copies, colors and images that you might need to refer to later.

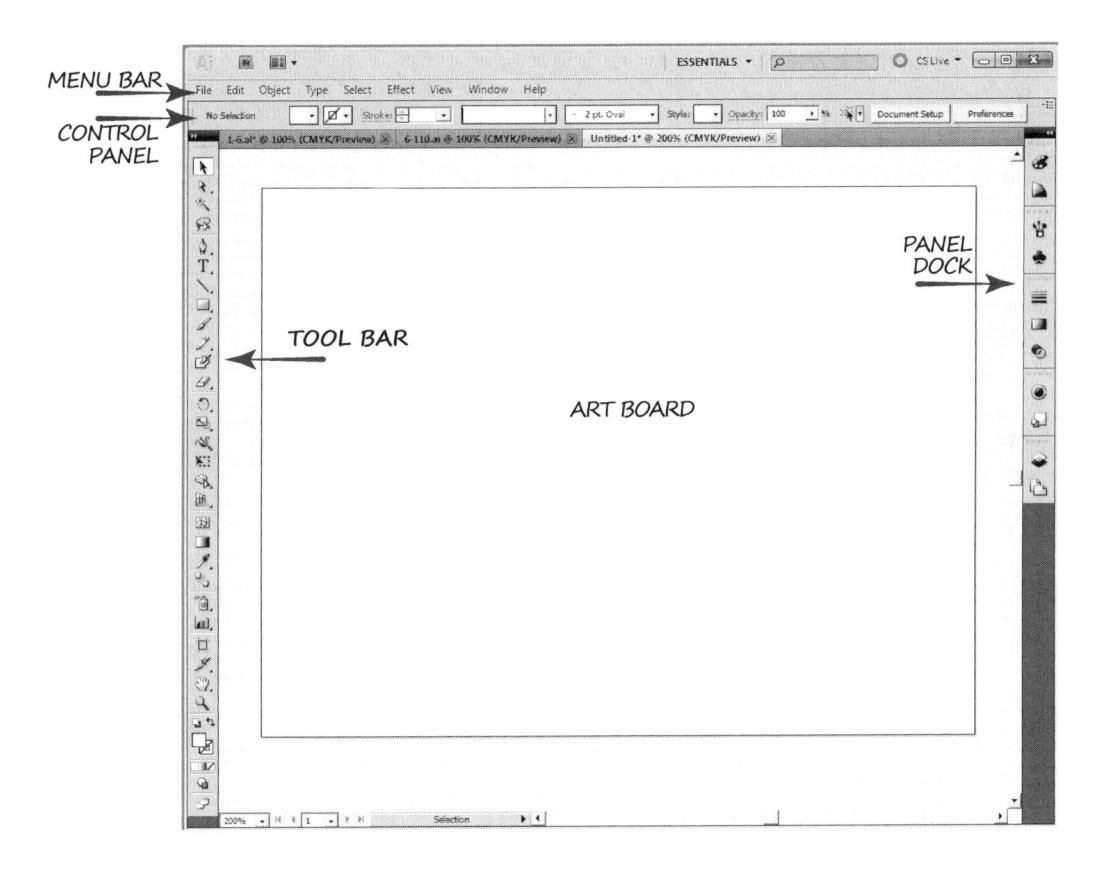

TOOL BAR

Now take a look at the **Tool Bar** along the left side of your screen.

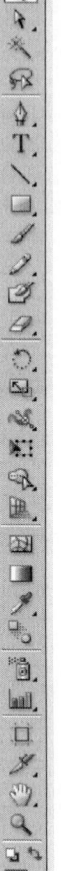

Each icon represents a tool and some of them have a small triangle in the lower right hand corner. This means there are additional icons hidden behind that can be accessed by clicking and holding on the triangle.

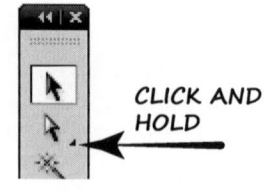

These can be separated from the main tool bar and moved around the workspace for easy access by dragging the cursor to the **Tear off** tab and releasing.

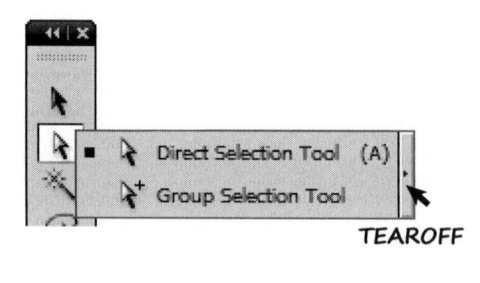

CLICK AND HOLD

TEAROFF

adobe® for fashion : illustrator CS5 | 5

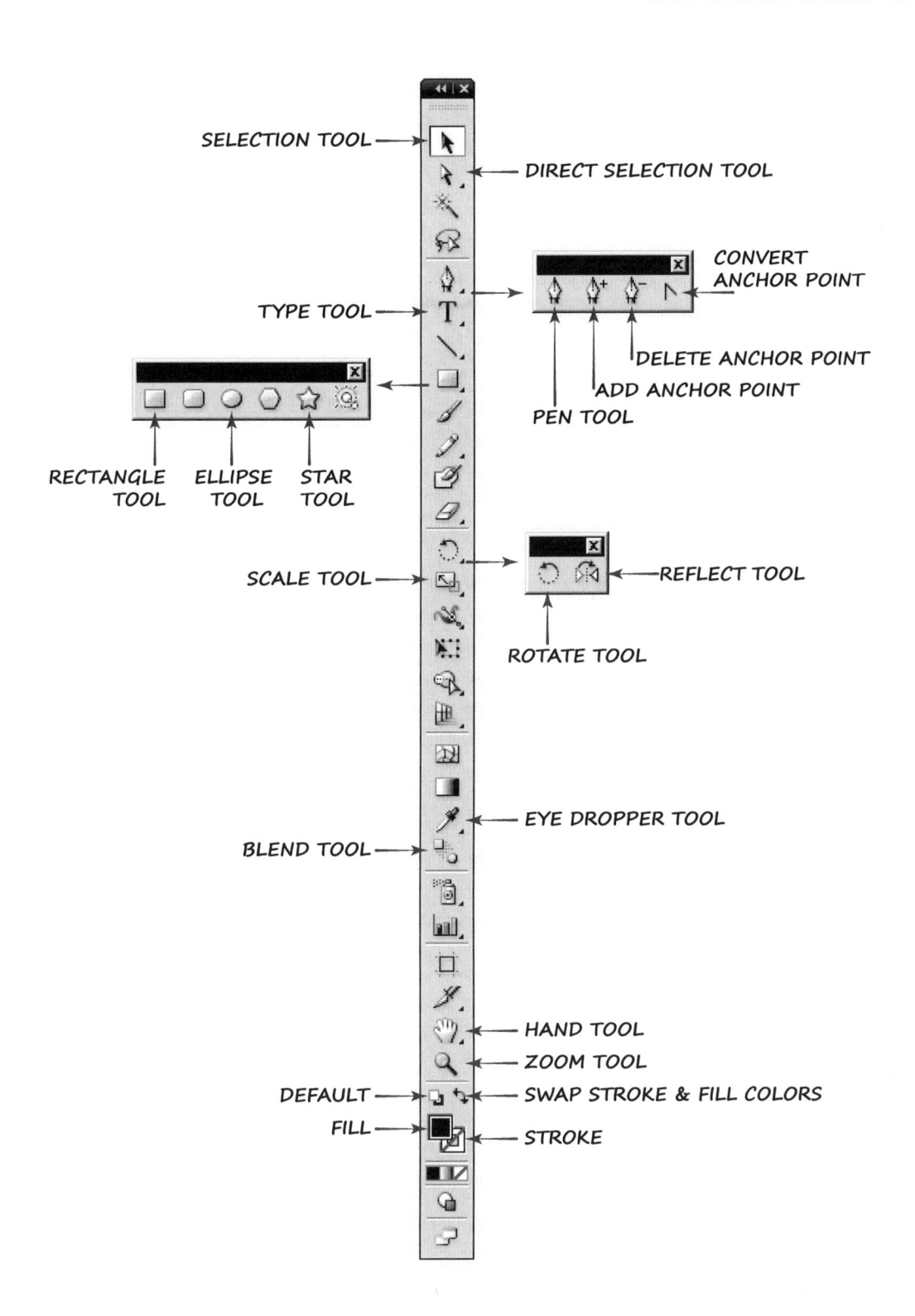

- SELECTION TOOL
- DIRECT SELECTION TOOL
- TYPE TOOL
- CONVERT ANCHOR POINT
- DELETE ANCHOR POINT
- ADD ANCHOR POINT
- PEN TOOL
- RECTANGLE TOOL
- ELLIPSE TOOL
- STAR TOOL
- SCALE TOOL
- REFLECT TOOL
- ROTATE TOOL
- EYE DROPPER TOOL
- BLEND TOOL
- HAND TOOL
- ZOOM TOOL
- DEFAULT
- SWAP STROKE & FILL COLORS
- FILL
- STROKE

Lesson 1: Getting Started

MANAGING PANELS

When you open a new document the default workspace should open with the default panel icons. If no panel icons are visible you can access them by going to the **Menu bar** clicking on **Window** and then the desired panel.

SWATCHES PANEL → Delete → Create new swatch

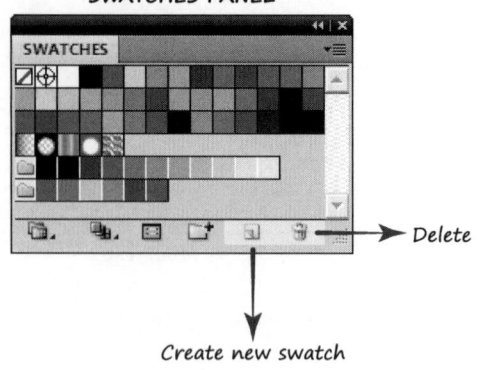

STROKE PANEL

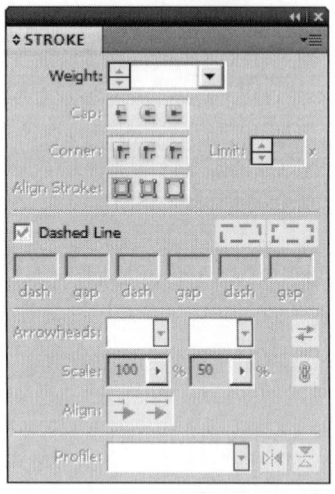

BRUSHES PANEL → Delete → Create new brush

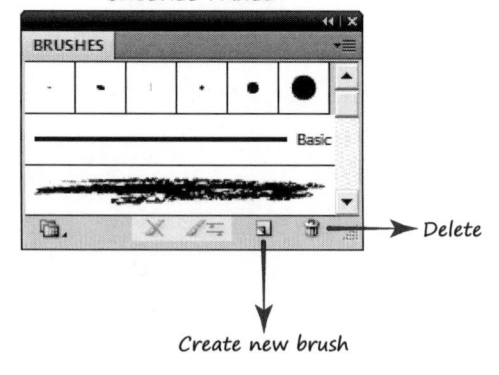

SYMBOLS PANEL → Delete → Create new symbol, Symbol Libraries Menu

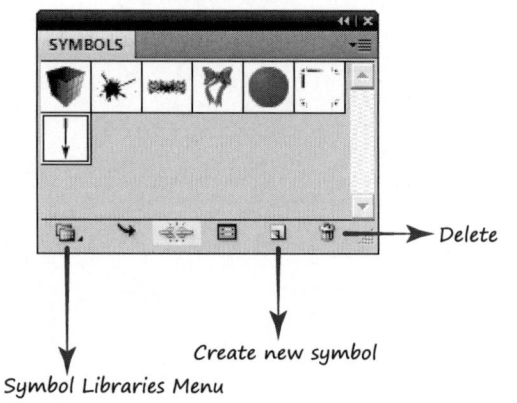

THE LAYERS PANEL

Understanding and using the **Layers Panel** will make it easier and faster to navigate in Illustrator®.

Take a few minutes to understand how the **Layers Panel** works now and you may be saving yourself hours of time scrolling for objects later. Layers can be locked, unlocked, made visible or hidden, duplicated, deleted, selected and reordered.

Organized and labeled layers-like a well organized file cabinet will speed up your workflow by keeping you from wasting precious time hunting for work.

DELETE LAYER
Click and drag a layer into the trash can to delete.

NEW LAYER
Click on the **New layer icon** to add a new empty layer.

LAYER VISIBILITY
Click on the **Eye** to hide the layer.
Click on the **empty box** to show the layer.

LOCK/UNLOCK LAYER
Clicking in the box will lock the layer and show a padlock icon.
Clicking on the Padlock will unlock the layer.

NAMING LAYERS
Double click on the name of any layer to open the Options box. Type in a new name and click OK.

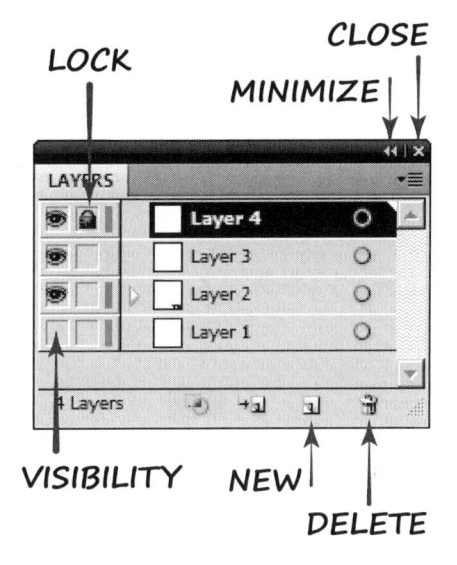

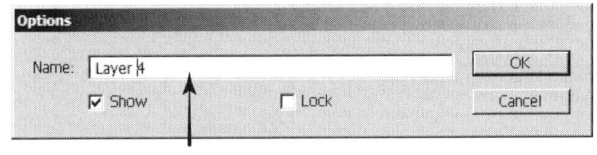

Lesson 1: Getting Started

LAYER ORDER

Think of the layers as a deck of cards that can be shuffled.

Click on a layer and drag it up the stack. When you see two lines with two arrows visible between the layers you can release the mouse to drop the layer into it's new location.

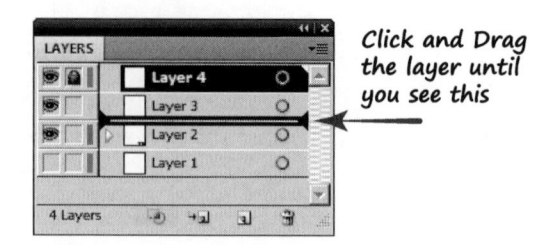

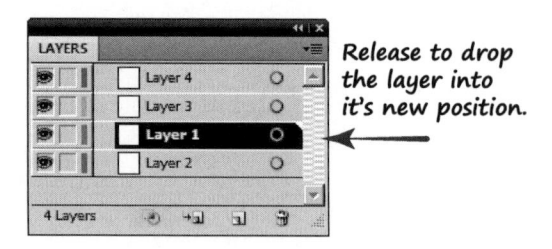

Click and Drag the layer until you see this

Release to drop the layer into it's new position.

UNDO

I want to introduce you to the greatest computer command ever invented, **UNDO** (**Ctrl+Z** /*Cmd+Z*).

If at any time something goes wrong just **UNDO**. Yep, in Adobe® Illustrator® we get do overs. As a matter of fact you get as many undos as your computer's available memory can handle.

Thanks Adobe®!

IMPORTANT:

ONE LAST THING BEFORE YOU BEGIN

TERMINOLOGY

There are a few terms I will be using throughout this book that you will need to know.

CLICK- depress the left mouse button once and release.

CLICK AND DRAG- depress the left mouse button and hold it while you move the mouse. Release the left mouse button.

RIGHT CLICK- depress the right mouse button and release.

LAPTOP USERS

If you are using a laptop it will be helpful to get an external mouse. The techniques in this book are not meant for using a track pad.

SHORT CUT KEYS

I have included both **Windows** and **Mac** commands throughout this book with Windows in **bold type** and Mac in *Italic*.
 ie: **Windows** (*Mac*).

There are three main differences:

Windows	Mac
Control	Command
Alt	Option
Right click	Control click

MAC USERS

You will need to be able to **right click** for many of the functions we are going to be using. You have the option of **Control Clicking**(holding down the Control key while clicking with the mouse) or you can set your preferences to right click which I highly recommend.

SET UP YOUR MAC TO RIGHT CLICK:

1. Go to "System Preferences".
2. Click "Keyboard & Mouse".
3. Click the "Mouse" tab.
4. A picture of the mouse will show up. Click the drop down menu on the right hand side and select "Secondary Button".

Now whenever you click on the right hand side of the mouse, a right click menu will appear

OK, let's get drawing...

DRAWING BASIC SHAPES

We are going to use the **Shape Tools** to draw some basic shapes. You can find them in the **Tool Bar** hiding behind the **Rectangle Tool**.

To release them from the **Tool Bar**, click and hold on the **Rectangle Tool**. Drag your cursor to the **Tear off tab** at the end and release.

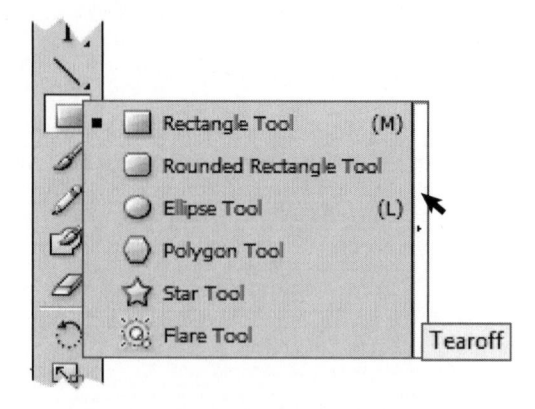

This will create a floating tool bar.

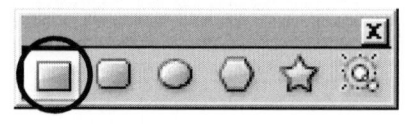

Rectangle Tool

TO DRAW A RECTANGLE:
Select the **Rectangle Tool**.
Click and drag diagonally across the page.
Release the mouse.

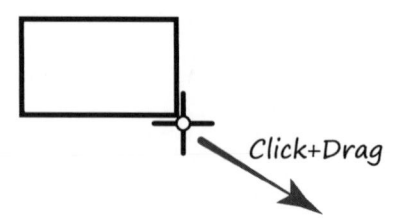

Click+Drag

TO DRAW A PERFECT SQUARE:
Select the **Rectangle Tool**.
Hold down the **Shift** key while you **click and drag.**
Release the mouse first and then Release the **Shift Key**.

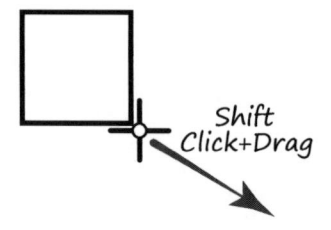

Shift Click+Drag

TO DRAW FROM THE CENTER:
Select the **Rectangle Tool**.
Hold down the **Alt** (*Opt*) key while you **click** and **drag**.
Release the mouse first and then release the **Alt** (*Opt*) Key.

Alt Click+Drag

TO DRAW A PERFECT SQUARE FROM THE CENTER:
Select the **Rectangle Tool**.
Hold down the **Shift and Alt** (*Opt*) keys while you **click and drag**.
Release the mouse first and then release the **Shift and Alt** (*Opt*) Keys.

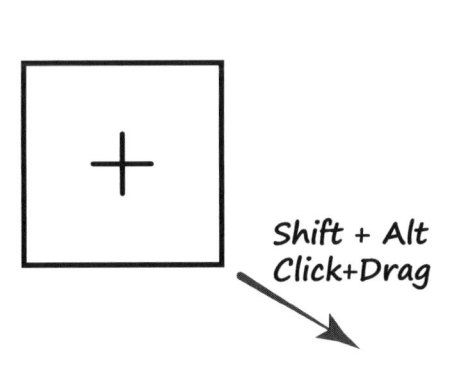

Shift + Alt Click+Drag

TO DRAW A RECTANGLE TO A SPECIFIC SIZE:
Select the **Rectangle Tool**
Click once on the **Art board** to open the Rectangle Options Box.
Type in the width - 2 in (in for Inches)
Type in the height - 1 in
Click OK.

ELLIPSES

You can find the **Ellipse tool** in the **Tool Bar** hiding behind the **Rectangle Tool** or in the **Tear off**.

TO DRAW AN ELLIPSE:
Select the **Ellipse Tool**.
click and drag diagonally across the page.

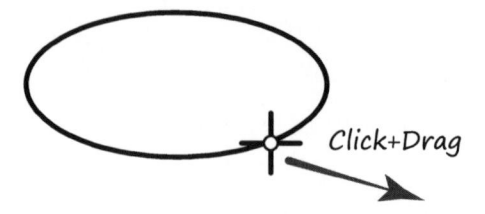

TO DRAW A PERFECT CIRCLE:
Hold down the **Shift** key while you **click and drag**.
Release the mouse first and then release the **Shift Key**.

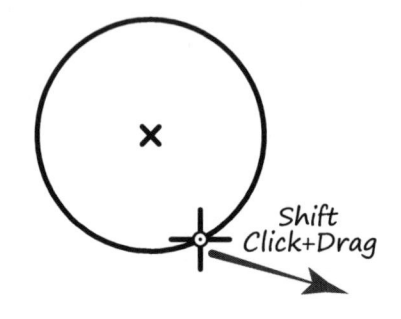

TO DRAW FROM THE CENTER:
Hold down the **Alt** (*Opt*) key while you **click and drag**.
Release the mouse first and then release the **Alt** (*Opt*) Key.

TO DRAW A PERFECT CIRCLE FROM THE CENTER:
Hold down the **Shift and Alt** (*Opt*) keys while you **click and drag**.
Release the mouse first and then release the **Shift and Alt** (*Opt*) Keys.

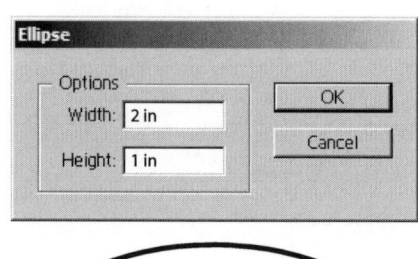

TO DRAW AN ELLIPSE TO A SPECIFIC SIZE:
Select the **Ellipse Tool**
Click once on the page to open the **Ellipse Options Box**.
Type in the width: 2 in (in for Inches)
Type in the height: 1 in
Click OK.

STARS

You can find the **Star Tool** in the **Tool Bar** along with the rest of the shape tools.

TO DRAW A STAR:
Select the **Star Tool**.
Click and drag diagonally across the page.

TO DRAW A PERFECT STAR:
Hold down the **Shift** key while you **click and drag**.

TO DRAW FROM THE CENTER:
Hold down the **Alt** (*Opt*) key while you **click and drag**.

TO DRAW A PERFECT STAR FROM THE CENTER:
Hold down the **Shift and Alt** (*Opt*) keys while you **click and drag**.

TO DRAW A STAR TO A SPECIFIC SIZE:
Select the **Star Tool**.
Click once on the page to open the **Star Options Box**.
Type in the Outer Radius 1: 50 pts
Type in the Inner Radius 2: 25 pts
Type in the number of points: 8
Click OK.

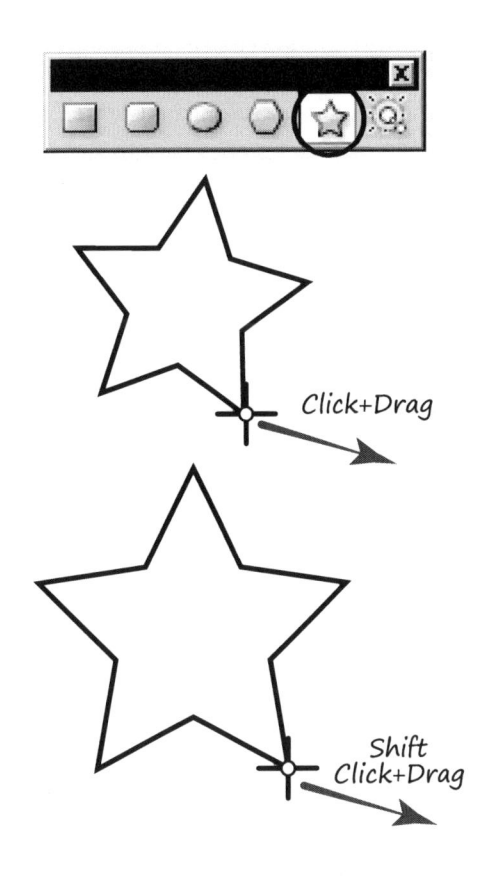

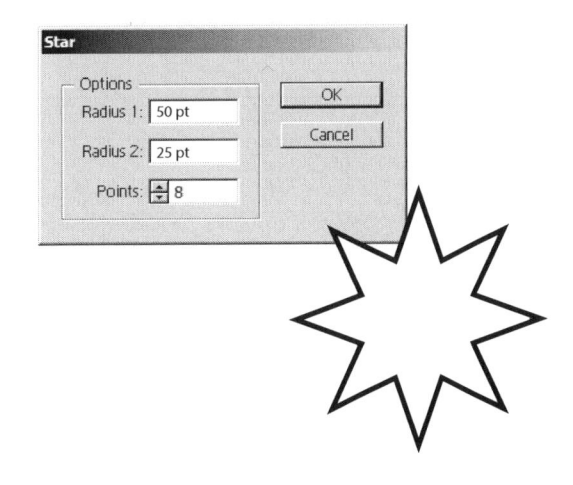

SELECTING OBJECTS

Before an object can be manipulated in any way it must be selected. As smart as your computer may seem at times, it will only do what you tell it to do. The first thing we need to tell it is which object we are going to be dealing with. This is done by making a selection with the **Selection Tool**.

THE SELECTION TOOL

Is used to select the entire object. It is the black arrow located at the top of the **Tool Bar** on the left side of your screen.

There are two different ways to select an object.

1. CLICK TO SELECT: If the object has a **Fill**, you can click directly on it to make a selection.

But if the object has a **Fill of NONE** you must click directly on the outline of the object to select it.

Clicking in the center is equivalent to reaching through an open window-there is nothing there to select.

2. MARQUEE SELECT: Drag across a portion of the object from the outside to the inside to select the entire object.

Because the nature of the Selection tool is to select the entire object you only need to drag across a small portion to select the entire object.

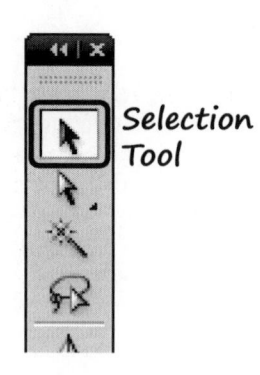

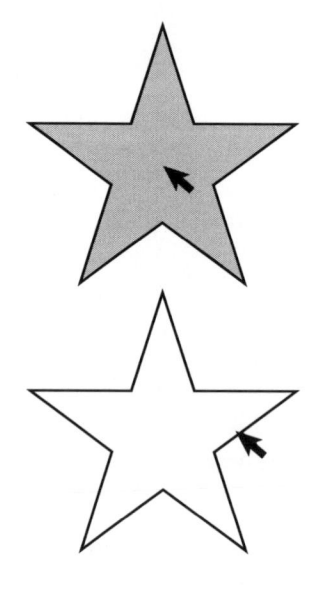

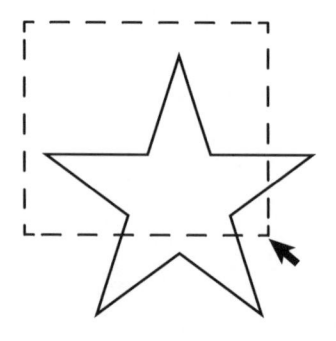

RECOGNIZING SELECTED OBJECTS:

When an object is selected it will have a visible **Bounding Box**. It's **Anchor points** will appear and the path and bounding box will turn a different color. The color will vary depending on what layer the object is on.

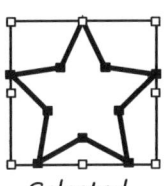

Unselected Object

Selected Object

SELECTING FROM THE LAYERS PANEL:

Click on the **Radial button** to select every object in the layer.

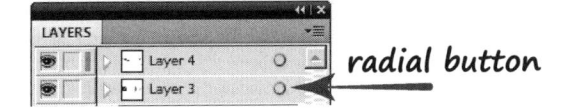

radial button

When every object in a layer is selected a **large square** will appear in the layer.

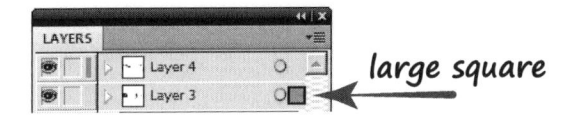

large square

When only one object on a layer is selected a **small square** will appear.

To move an object to a different layer **click and drag** the small square to a new layer.

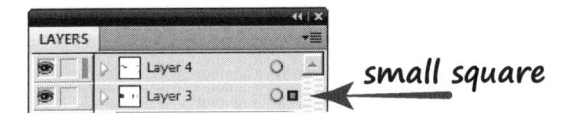

small square

RELEASING OBJECTS

Once an object is selected it can be released in two ways.

1. Click on an empty area of the screen with either of the selection tools.

2. Shift+click on the selected object.

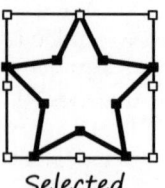

Selected Object

Unselected Object

MOVING OBJECTS

To **Move** an object:
Use the **Selection tool**.
Click and drag the object to a new location. When you have the object placed where you want it, release the mouse button.

It is important to start recognizing when an object is selected and what tool is active at any given time.

USING COLOR

There are many different ways to change the color of an object in Illustrator® and I'm going to focus on three I use most.

Fill Color is the color an object is filled with.

Stroke Color is the color of the object's outline.

The **Default colors** are a white Fill and a black Stroke. But fills and strokes can be any color - black, white or a pattern, They can also have a fill or stroke of None. The icon for None is ⊘ .

When selecting a color it is important to know which area is currently active -the **Stroke** or the **Fill**. This can be determined by looking at the color section at the bottom of the **Tool Bar** on the lower left side of your screen. There you will find Icons for **Fill**, **Stroke** and **Default**. The icons will change to display the current Stroke and Fill colors.

The active icon is the one that is in front and you can switch by clicking on the icon you want to activate.

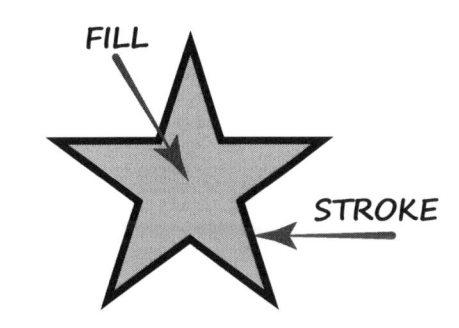

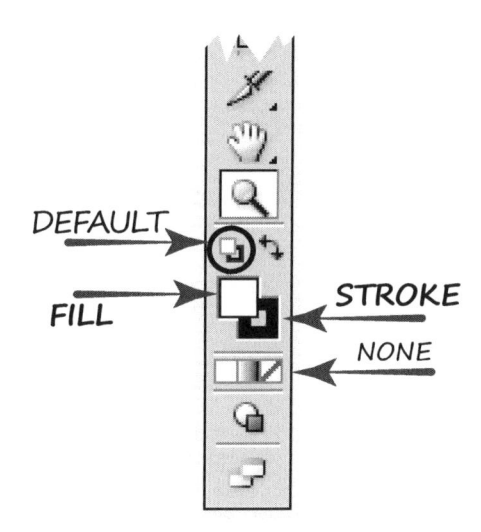

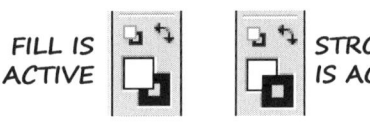

COLOR PICKER

To fill an object with color select the object. **Double click** on the **Fill Icon** at the bottom of the **Tool Bar** to open the **Color Picker**.

Click on an area inside the **Color Picker** to select a color and click OK.
Now your object should be filled with the selected color.

Notice that the color of the **Fill icon** in the **Tool Bar** has changed to the new color.

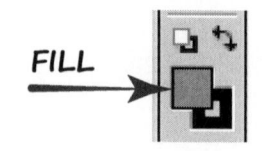

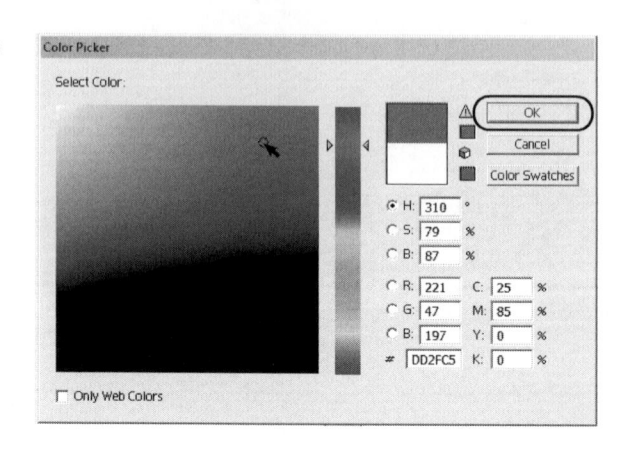

SWATCHES PANEL

A second place you can select color is from the **Swatches Panel**.

You can access the **Swatches Panel** by clicking on the icon from the **Panel Dock** on the right side of the Illustrator® workspace.

(If you don't see it, don't worry. You can access it from the Menu Bar at the top of your screen.)
Click on the Window Drop Down Menu and Select Swatches to open the Swatches Panel.

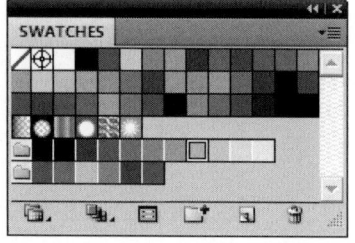

Click on an object with the **Selection Tool**.

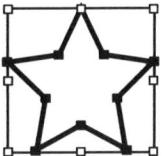

Make sure that the **Fill** is active.
(you can check this at the bottom of the Tool Bar) It should be in front. If not click once on the Fill icon.

FILL IS ACTIVE

STROKE IS ACTIVE

Click on the **Swatch icon** to open the **Swatches Panel**.

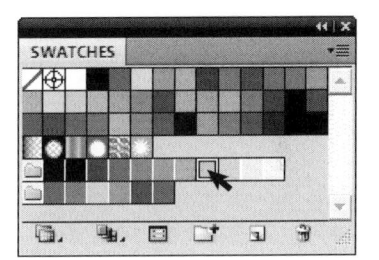

SWATCH ICON

Now click on a swatch to apply it to the selected object.

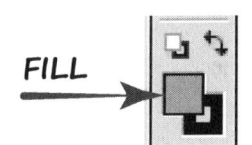

The **Fill** icon in the **Tool bar** will change to the color you just selected.

FILL

TO RESTORE DEFAULT COLORS:

You can restore the default colors any time just click on the **Default icon** in the **Tool bar** or use the "**D**" key on your keyboard.

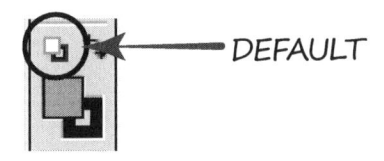

DEFAULT

CONTROL PANEL

The **Control panel** has individual drop downs for **Stroke** and **Fill**.

As long as the object is selected it doesn't matter which icon is active in the tool bar. Just use the drop down for either **Fill** or **Stroke** as needed and click on a swatch.

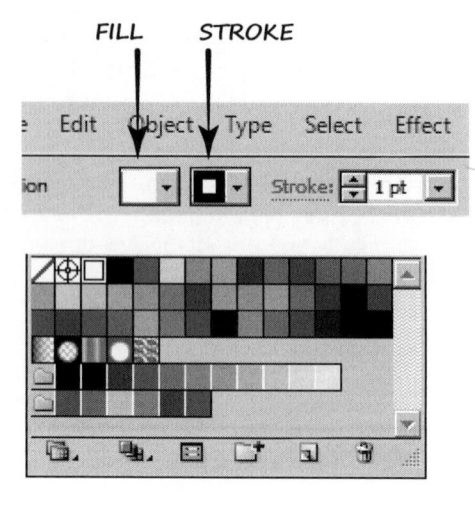

Now you should be able to draw basic shapes, color them and move them around the art board. It's a good start.

PATHS

PATHS are the building blocks of Illustrator®. A **Path** is a series of **Anchor points** connected by **Line segments**. Every shape you draw is a path. It can have as few as two anchor points or as many as you can draw. A path can be open or closed, but until it is given a **Stroke** or a **Fill**, it won't be visible on the page.

A CLOSED PATH is a path that starts and ends at the same anchor point and can easily be filled. These are used for the silhouette of the garment and any piece that needs a fill, including the bodice, sleeves, collars, facings, cuffs, legs and pockets.

AN OPEN PATH is a path whose ends do not meet and should only be used for details like stitches, indicating fullness and shirring.

A COMPOUND PATH is made up of multiple closed paths to create a compound shape like a doughnut. These paths are used for items like buttons and grommets.

The **PEN TOOL** is the tool we will be using most often to create paths. It can be frustrating to learn at first but once mastered you will be able to draw with accuracy and speed. I've broken it down into easy to accomplish steps that will have you up and running in no time.

CLOSED PATHS

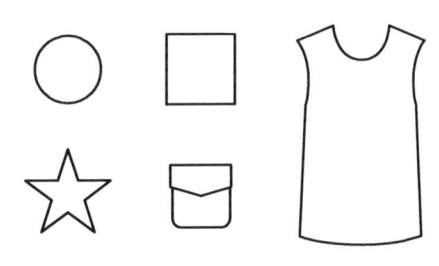

OPEN PATHS

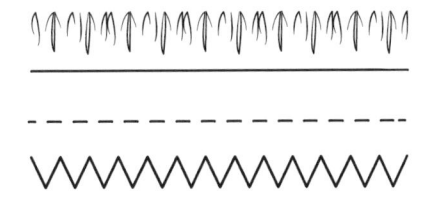

COMPOUND PATHS

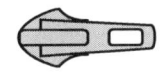

DRAWING PATHS

THE PEN TOOL

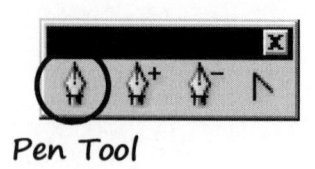

Using the **Pen tool** is like playing connect the dots. **Click** from point to point to point.

Select the **Pen Tool** from the **Tool bar**.

To release the entire group of **Pen Tools** from the **Tool Bar click and hold** on the **Pen Tool Icon**. Drag your cursor to the **Tear off tab** at the end and release.

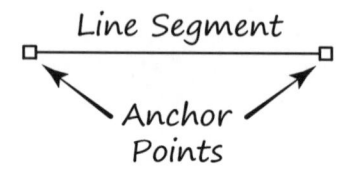

Every time you click on the page with the **Pen tool** it adds an **Anchor Point**. As you click around the page the **anchor points** are connected with **Line segments** to form the path.

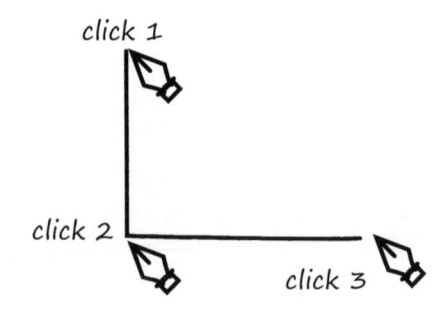

Pen Tool

Line Segment / Anchor Points

To create a **closed path** you must start and end at the same point.

Using the **Pen Tool**
- click point (**1**),
- click at point (**2**),
- click at point (**3**) and
- click back at point (**1**) to close.

*When you click back where you started the **Pen Tool** will show a small circle, if you click now you will close your path.*

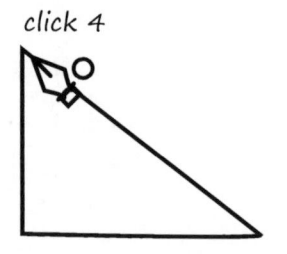

click 1

click 2

click 3

click 4

TO ADD ADDITIONAL POINTS:

Pen Tool
Delete Anchor Point Tool
Convert Anchor Point Tool
Add Anchor Point Tool

Select the path with the **Selection tool**.

Use the **Add Anchor Point tool** to add points by clicking along the path.

TO DELETE POINTS:
Click on existing anchor points using the **Delete Anchor Point tool**.

EDITING PATHS

One of the major benefits of working on the computer is the ability to make rapid changes without needing to redraw the entire garment. By editing points we can turn a crewneck into a V-neck; A shirt into a dress and shorts into slacks.

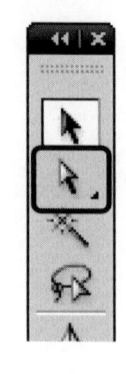

DIRECT SELECTION TOOL

The **Direct Selection Tool** is used to select individual **Anchor Points** or **line segments**. You can find the **Direct Selection tool** (white arrow) near the top of the **Tool bar**.

Use the **Direct Selection tool** to **click and drag** on a **line segment** to move that segment.

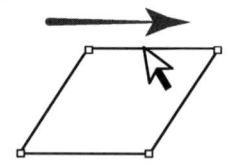

Now use the **Direct Selection tool** to **click and drag** on an **anchor point** to move that point.

NOTE: If you click on an anchor point but end up selecting the entire object just double click on the anchor point to select it and release the rest of the object.

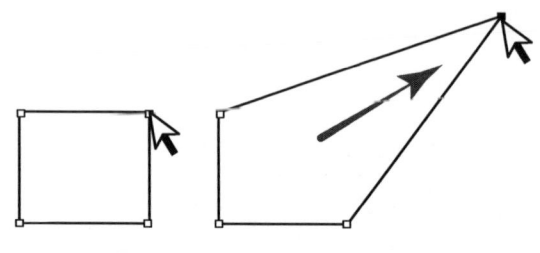

☐ UN SELECTED ANCHOR POINT
■ SELECTED ANCHOR POINT

MOVING AND ZOOMING TOOLS

ZOOM TOOL

The **Zoom tool** is used to zoom in so you can get a closer view of your work.

TO ZOOM IN
Click on the **Zoom tool**, **Marquee select** the area you want to zoom in to and it will fill the screen.

TO ZOOM OUT
Hold the **Alt** (*Opt*) key when you click on the screen with the **Zoom tool**.

TO ZOOM OUT TO FULL SCREEN
Use the keyboard short cut
Ctrl+0 (*Cmd+0*).

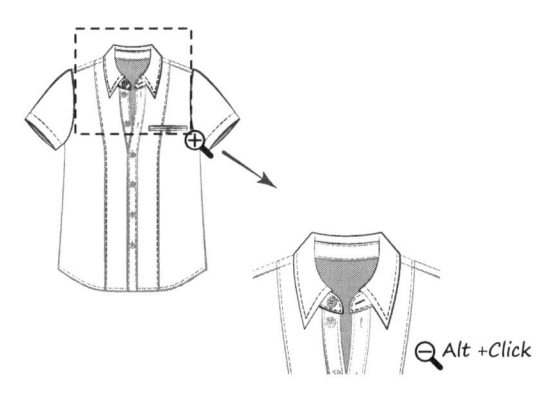

HAND TOOL

The **Hand tool** is used to move the page around while you are zoomed in.
Select the **Hand tool** and **click and drag** on the page to move.

The short cut key is the **Spacebar**.

No matter what tool you are using, if you depress the **Spacebar** it will change to the **Hand tool** . When you release the Spacebar it will return to the previous tool you were using.

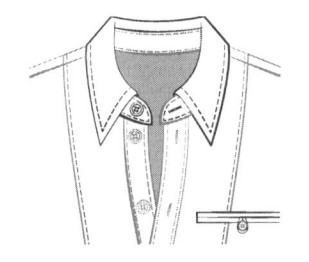

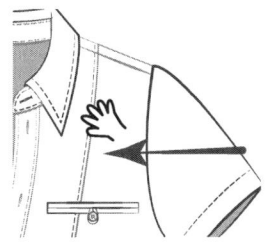

CONVERTING POINTS

Now you have the **Pen tool** skills to draw anything you want - as long as it is made up of straight lines. Obviously we can't design using only corner points and straight lines, we are going to need to make some curves.

Curves are created by converting a **Corner Point** into a **Smooth Point** with handles that will allow us to adjust the arc of the curve.

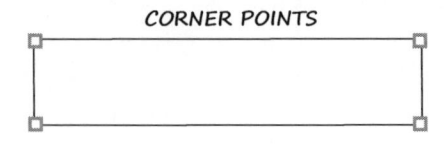

CORNER POINTS

SMOOTH POINTS WITH HANDLES

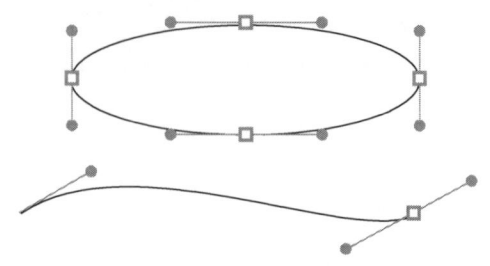

DRAGGING OUT THE HANDLE EFFECTS THE CURVE

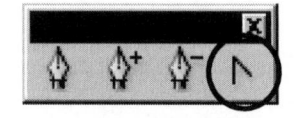

CONVERT ANCHOR POINT TOOL

To convert a corner point into a smooth point use the **Convert Anchor Point Tool**.

Click and drag on the corner point to pull out handles and create a curve.

Click + Drag

If the handles make a loop just drag in the opposite direction to untwist. The handles should always form a tangent to the curve.

To turn a **smooth point** back into a **corner point** just click on it with the **Convert Anchor Point Tool**.

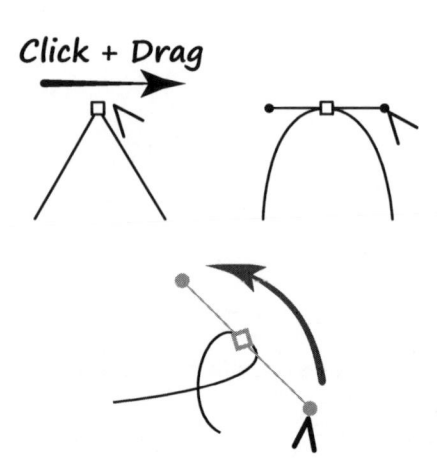

Click

Smooth point

Corner point

It will take some practice to get comfortable using the **Convert Anchor Point tool**.

A good exercise is to draw a few stars and turn them into flowers. This will help you work towards consistency and control.

SAVING FILES

It is very important to stop and save your document frequently. If you don't save you run the risk of losing your work if the computer were to freeze up. Of course this is most likely to happen at the most inopportune time.

FILE > SAVE AS
Name the file
Make sure "**Save as type**" is set to **Adobe Illustrator (AI)**
Click OK.

As you continue to work on this document you can just click **File>Save** every so often to keep the document current.

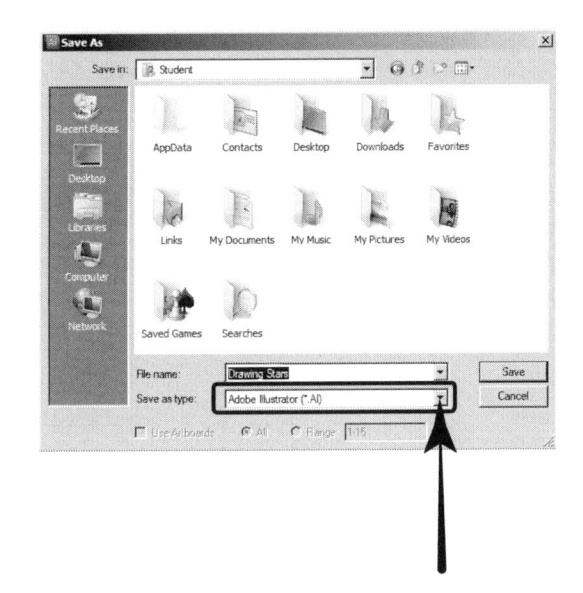

lesson two

By now you have noticed that we often use certain keys to modify the way tools function. For example the **Shift key** constrains the vertical and horizontal movements to allow you to draw a perfect square or circle. These are called **Modifier keys** and there are three of them: **Shift**, **Alt** and **Ctrl** (windows) or **Shift**, **Opt**, and **Cmd** (Mac).

From now on I am going to show you how to maximise the functionality of your tools by using modifier keys.

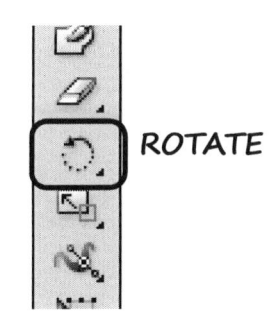

ROTATE

ROTATE

Lets start by drawing an ellipse using the **Ellipse tool**.

Double click on the **Rotate icon** in the **tool bar** to bring up the **Rotate options box**.

Type in an angle and click OK to rotate the ellipse.

Ellipse Rotated 30 Degrees

Try it again but this time click **Copy**.
This will make a **Rotated Copy** of the ellipse.

Ellipse Rotated Copy 30 Degrees

Notice that the rotation point is always the center of the ellipse. But what if you want to designate a different rotation point? Easy- use a modifier key.

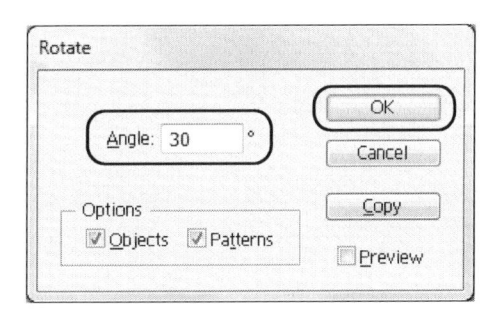

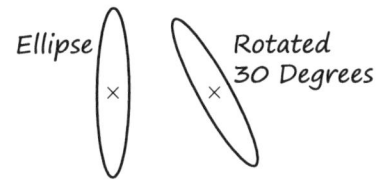

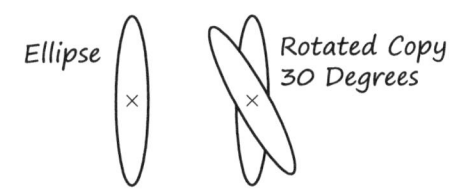

Lesson 2: The Basics

ROTATE AROUND A DEFINED POINT

Draw an ellipse with the **Ellipse Tool**. Click once on the **Rotate tool**.

Alt+click (*Opt+click*) on the page to set the Center point. The ellipse will rotate around the place you **Alt+click** (*Opt+click*).

Alt+Click to set Center Point

When the **Rotate Options** box opens, type in the angle and click **Copy**.

Now the ellipse is rotating around the center point you defined by **Alt** (*Opt*) clicking.

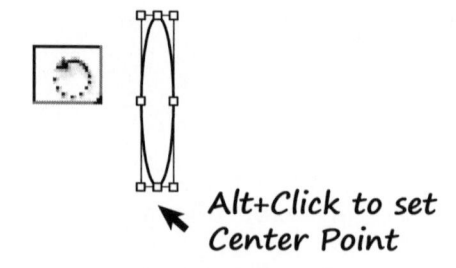

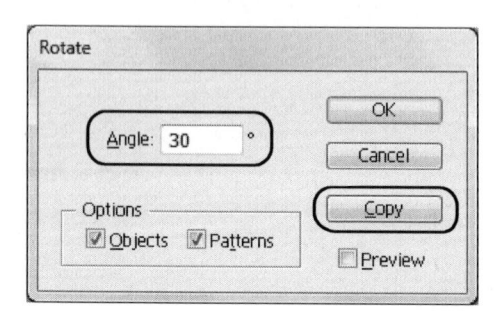

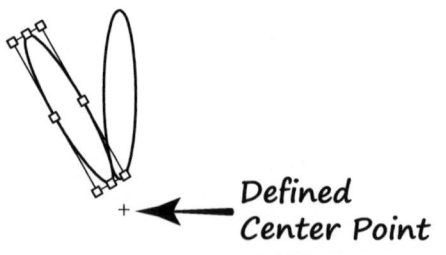

Defined Center Point

DUPLICATE

To repeat the previous command and continue rotating around the defined center point you can use the keyboard short cut **Ctrl+D** (*Cmd+D*) to Duplicate.

You can type **Ctrl+D** (*Cmd+D*) to duplicate an unlimited number of times as long as you do not release the selected object.

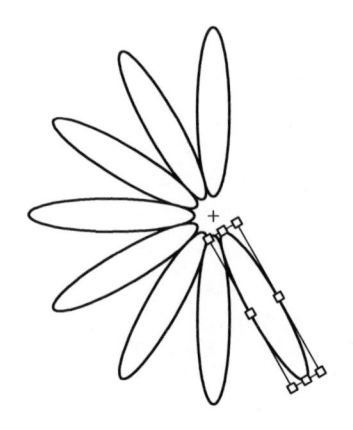

The tool you will find yourself using most often is **Reflect**. Since most flats are symmetrical we can draw one half of the flat and reflect it for the other side. This is an important tool to master.

ROTATE   REFLECT

REFLECT

Select an object using the **Selection tool**. **Double click** on the **Reflect icon** to bring up the Reflect options box.

The **Reflect tool** is hiding behind the **Rotate tool**. **Click and hold** to **tear off** the floating tool bar.

Select **Vertical Axis** and click OK to Reflect the object or click **Copy** to create a **Reflected copy**.

The reflected copy will be placed directly on top of the original object by default. Now you can use the right or left arrow keys on your keyboard to move it over.

Not a bad way to work but not efficient either. Since we will already know where the center line of the flat is, why not use it to define the axis for reflection?

REFLECT USING A DEFINED AXIS

Select an object using the **Selection Tool**. Click once on the **Reflect tool**.
Alt+click (*Opt+click*) anywhere along the center line to define the axis.
When the Options Box opens Select **Vertical** and click **Copy**.

See? Much faster, I may have just saved you an entire 20 seconds- go ahead laugh, but it all adds up and you might really need a coffee break later.

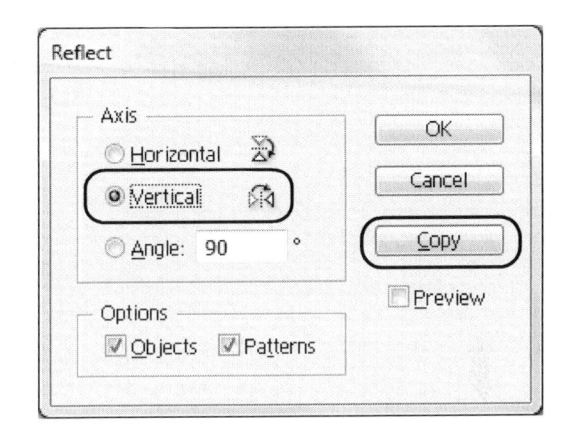

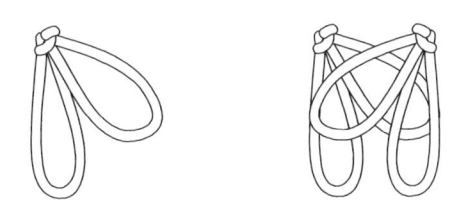

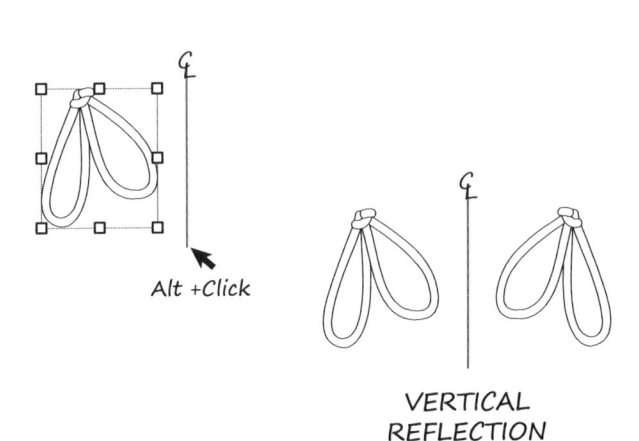

Alt +Click

VERTICAL
REFLECTION

Lesson 2: The Basics

LET'S DRAW A HEART

Start with the **Pen Tool**

- Click on the art board (1)
- Click up and to the right (2)
- Click down and in line with point 1 (3)

Click and drag with the **Convert Anchor Point Tool** to curve point 2.

Use the **Selection Tool** to Marquee select the path.

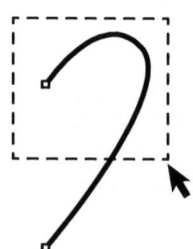

Click once on **Reflect** and **Alt+click** (*Opt+click*) to the left of the path.

Select **Vertical** and **Copy** to make the other side of the heart.

JOIN

The **Join Command** is used to connect two open paths to each other.

With the **Selection Tool** marquee select the two paths.
Right click anywhere on the page to bring up the context menu and select **Join**.

This will create a line segment connecting the two top anchor points.

While the object is still selected **right click again** anywhere on the page and click **Join** to connect the bottom two anchor points.

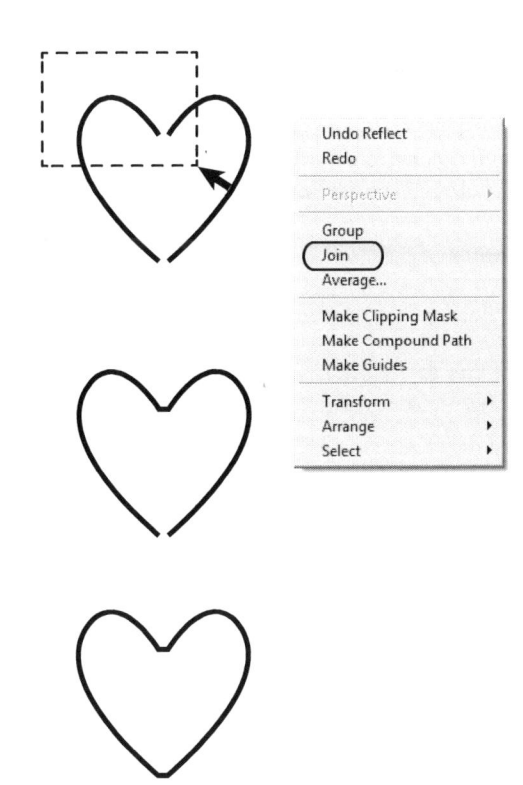

VERSION CS4 AND BELOW

Use the **Direct Selection tool**
Select only the top two anchor points.
Right click anywhere on the page to bring up the context menu and select **Join**.

Direct Select the bottom two anchor points and **right click** then **Join**.

Or you could upgrade to CS6- it's pretty cool!

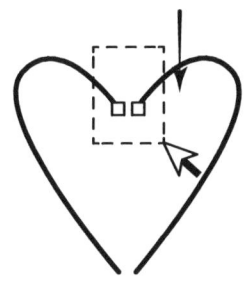

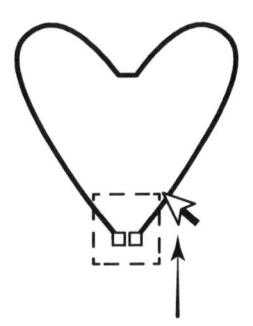

AVERAGE

The **Average Command** is used to average the position of two or more anchor points.

With the **Direct Selection tool** select the two bottom anchor points. You can do this by marquee selecting. *Make sure to drag from the outside of the object toward the inside of the object so that nothing moves.*

Right click anywhere on the page to bring up the menu and select **Average**.

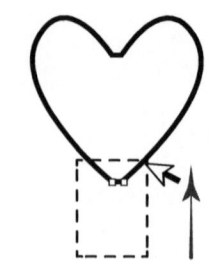

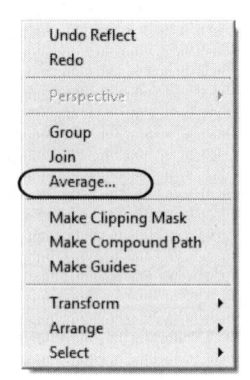

The **Average Options** box will open.
Select **Both** and click OK.
Notice how the two anchor points have averaged into one center point.

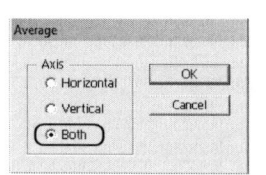

Now do the same for the top.
With the **Direct Selection tool** marquee select the two top anchor points.
Make sure to drag from the outside of the object toward the inside of the object so that nothing moves.
Right click anywhere on the page and select **Average** from the menu.
Select **Both** and click OK.

PATHFINDER

Pathfinder is one of the tools that makes Illustrator® so great.
Pathfinder will allow you to unite multiple objects together, subtract one object from another, create a compound path and divide an object into multiple parts. This can be a bit confusing at first since most of us are not used to drawing by combining shapes in this way. But it is the key to drawing great flats and well worth the time it takes to master.

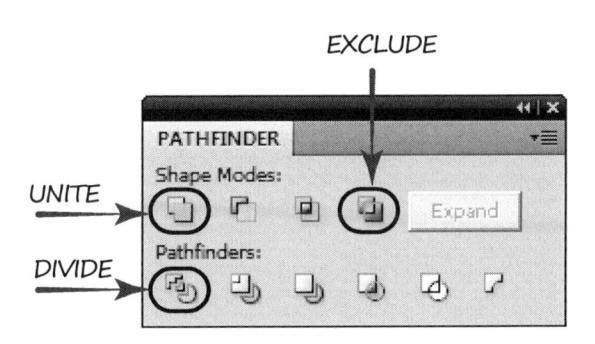

To open the **Pathfinder panel** go to the **Menu Bar** at the top of screen and click **Window> Pathfinder**.

There are ten different **Pathfinder** icons available but I am only going to focus on the main three we will use. Those are **Unite**, **Exclude** and **Divide**.

PATHFINDER UNITE

Pathfinder Unite is used to combine two or more objects into one object. Think of it as sewing pattern pieces together. For this to work the objects must be **closed paths**.

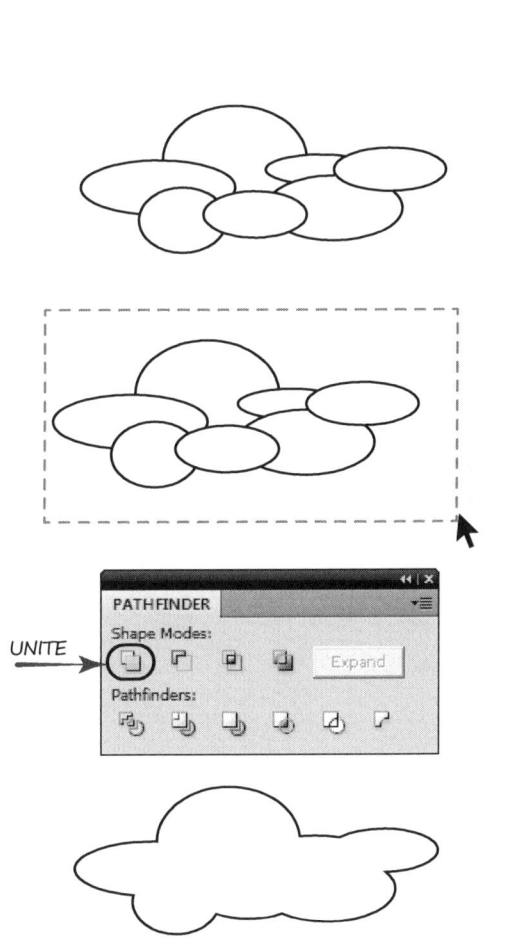

Draw 2 or more closed paths that you would like to combine together. They must overlap for this to work.

With the **Selection tool**, **Marque Select** all of the objects.

Click on **Unite** and your closed paths will be united together into one solid shape.

36 | Lesson 2: The Basics

PATHFINDER EXCLUDE

Pathfinder Exclude is used to create compound paths. A common use for this would be buttons, eyelets, or lace. Think of it as cutting a hole in the fabric.

Draw a closed path.

Draw some additional closed paths that can be to punched out of the first object.
They must all be within the border of the object-not overlapping an edge for this to work.

With the **Selection tool**, Marque Select all of the objects.

Open Pathfinder: **Window>Pathfinder**

Click on **Exclude** to create a compound path. This means the smaller shapes will be cut out of the larger object.

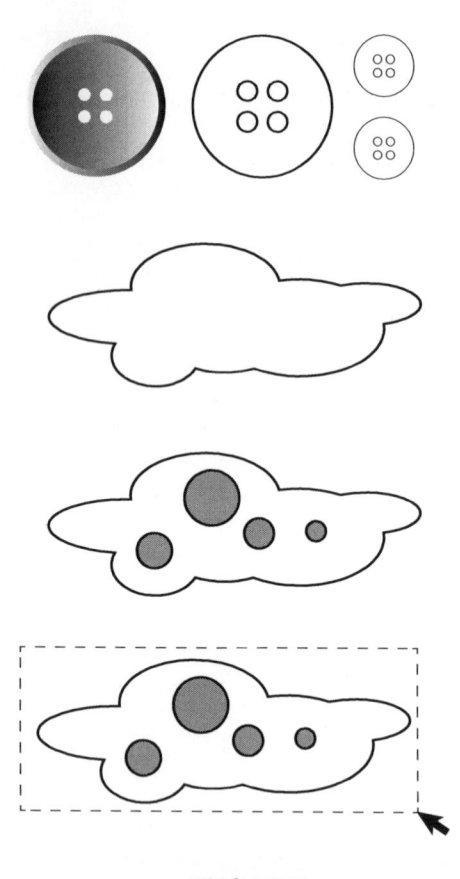

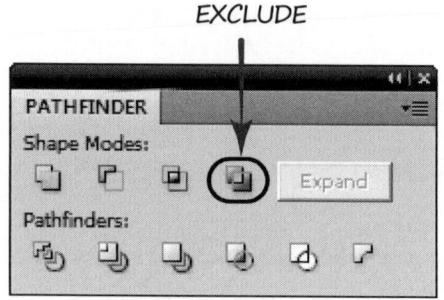

EXCLUDE

PATHFINDER DIVIDE

Pathfinder Divide is used to divide closed paths into multiple pieces. This is often used to create princess seams, color blocking, yokes or cuffs. Think of it as using scissors to cut a piece of fabric into pieces.

Using the **Pen tool** draw a path through the object you want to divide. (this should be an open path).

The path should extend beyond the object in order to make absolutely sure that the path is intersecting the object.

Make sure this path has a **Fill of None** (otherwise you will run into trouble-*trust me on this one*)

With the **Selection tool**, **Marque Select** the object and the dividing path.

Open Pathfinder: **Window>Pathfinder**

Click on **Divide** and your object will be divided into 2 pieces (*note: the lines extending beyond the shape have disappeared*).

Right click and Ungroup.
Click once on an empty area of the page to release the object.
You must always ungroup after dividing.

Now you can click on one of the pieces with the **Selection tool** and move it or fill it with a new color.

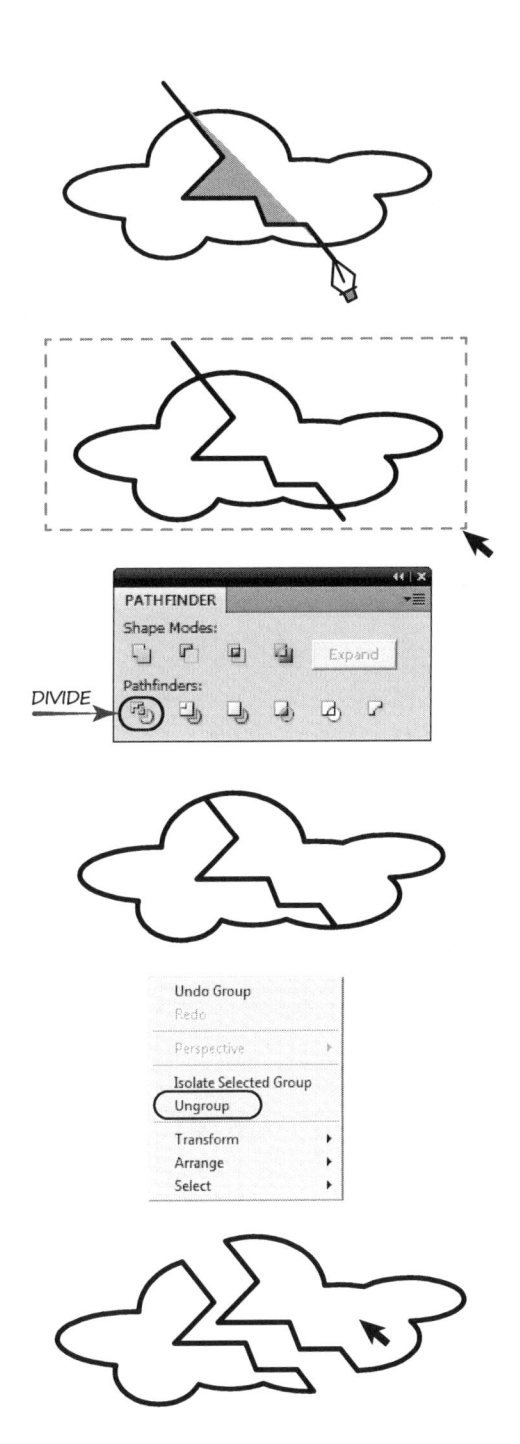

DRAWING FLATS

Now that we've covered the basics it's time to get down to business. Lets draw a flat... The process is simple as long as you follow the steps in order. Once you have gained a comfortable understanding of the process you can experiment on your own.

Before we can start drawing it is important to create a **template**. This will give us the propper proportions to work from and insure consistency throughout the collection of flats.

You can download this template at

www.adobeforfashion.com
under *Free Downloads.*

Download the template file and save it to your desktop for easy access.

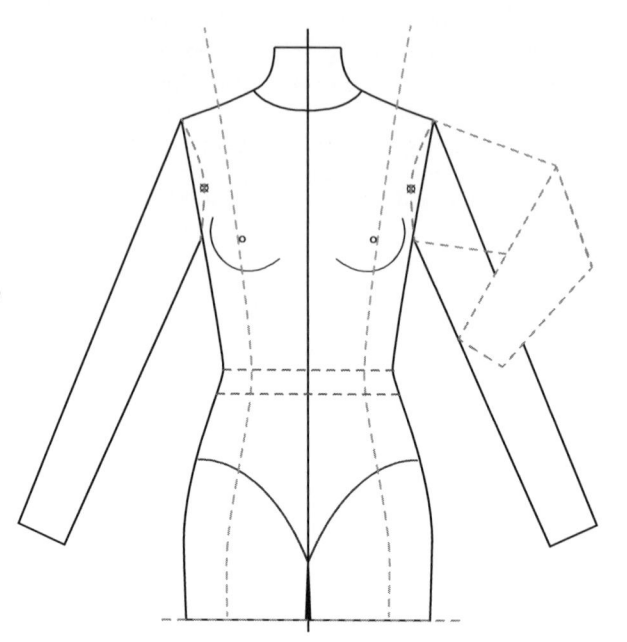

Remember: If anything goes wrong you can always **UNDO! Ctrl+Z** (*Cmd+Z*)

THE BASIC T-SHIRT

Open a **New Document**. Start by selecting **File>New** from the **Menu Bar** to open the New Document Window.
Make sure the **New Document Profile** drop down is set to **Print** and click OK.

In the Menu Bar click on **File>Place** and navigate to where you saved
Flat Template.jpg
Check the **Template box**
Un-Check the **Link box**
and click **Place**.

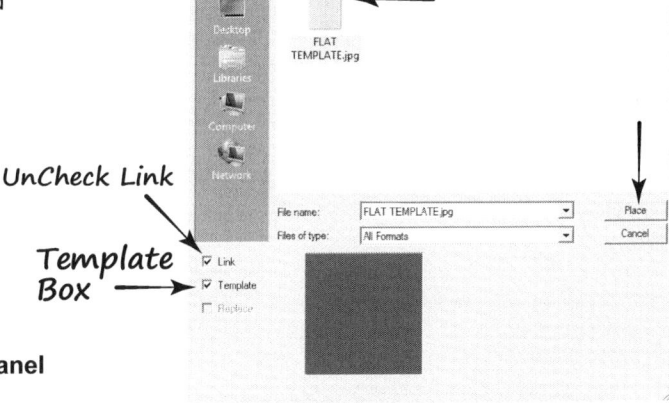

UnCheck Link

Template Box

Now take a look at the **Layers Panel**
You should see 2 Layers.
The top Layer- Layer 1 is ready for business.
The bottom Template layer is locked and the image has been dimmed to 50% so that you can easily draw on top of it.
Do not unlock the Template Layer.

Make sure the **Fill** and **Stroke** colors are set to **Default** (White fill and Black Stroke).

You can do this by using the "**D**" key on your keyboard or by clicking on the **Default Icon** near the bottom of the **Tool Bar**.

Default

Now that the **Template** is set we can start.

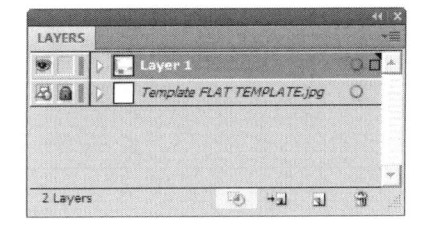

Select the **Pen Tool**
- Click on high point shoulder (**1**)
- Click on low point shoulder (**2**)
- Click inside the armhole (**3**)
- Click the bottom of the armhole (**4**)
- Click on the hip (**5**)

Now we can refine the shape.

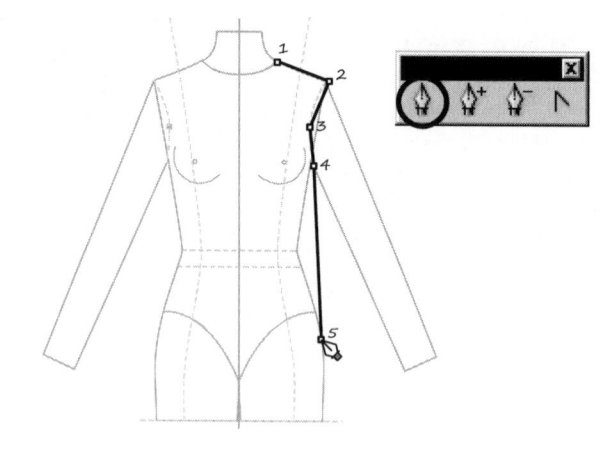

With the **Convert Anchor Point tool**
Click and drag straight down from Anchor Point **3** to create the armhole curve.

Now you have an open path that is 1/2 of the T-shirt bodice.

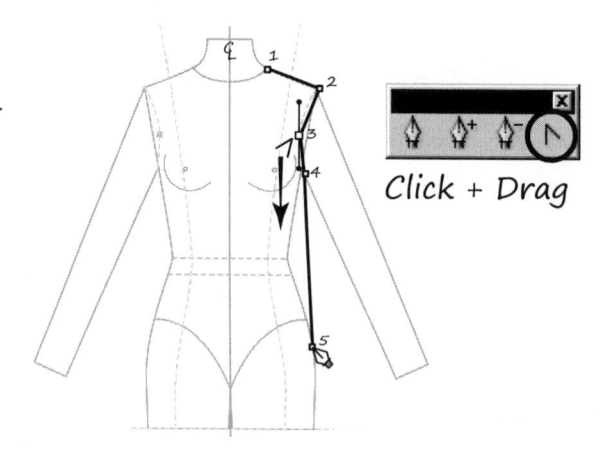

Click + Drag

Switch to the **Selection tool**

First we need to release anchor point **3** by clicking on an empty area of the page.

Marque Select the entire path.

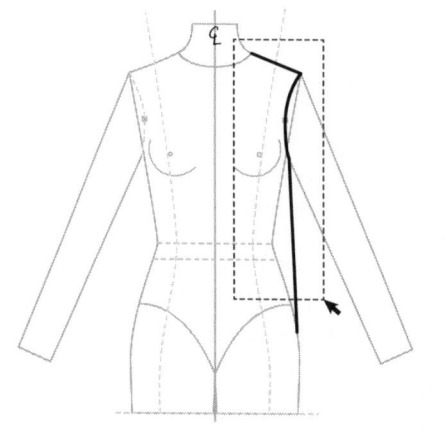

adobe® for fashion : illustrator CS5 | **41**

Click once on the **Reflect Tool**.

Alt+click (*Opt + Click*) anywhere along the **Center Line** to define the axis.
This will open the Reflect Options Box.

Select **Vertical** and click **Copy**
to create the other side of the bodice.

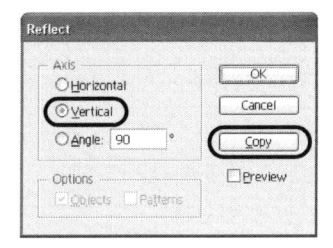

Use the **Selection Tool**
to Marquee select both sides of the bodice.

Right click and **Join**
to connect the top neckline.

While still selected **Right click** and **Join**
again to connect the bottom hemline.

Now you have a closed path that can be filled.

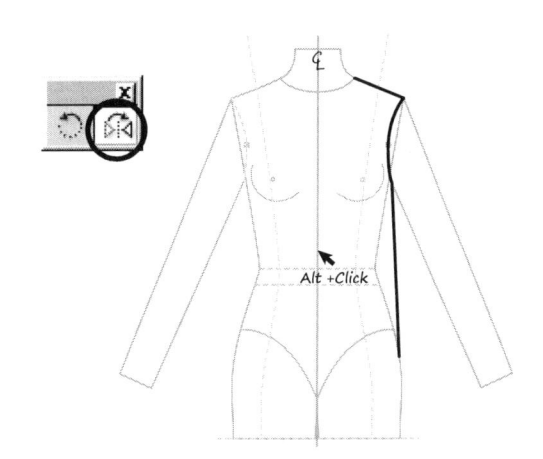

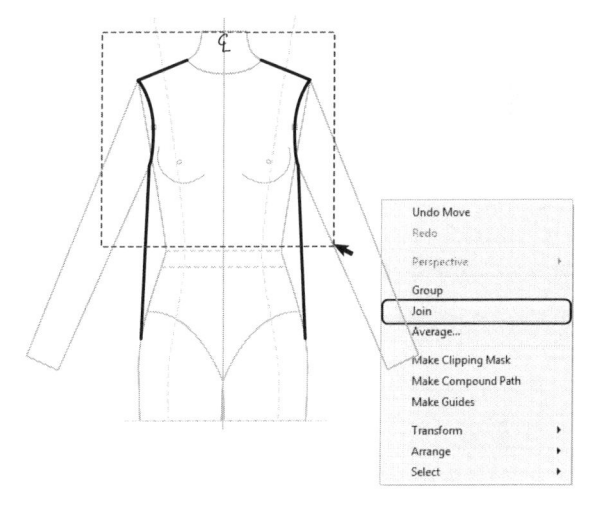

Lesson 2: The Basics

With the **Add Anchor Point tool**
Click once at the **center of the neckline** to add an anchor point and use the **down arrow** key on the keyboard to nudge it into place.

Add an anchor point at the center of the hemline.
Use the down arrow to lower it just a few clicks.

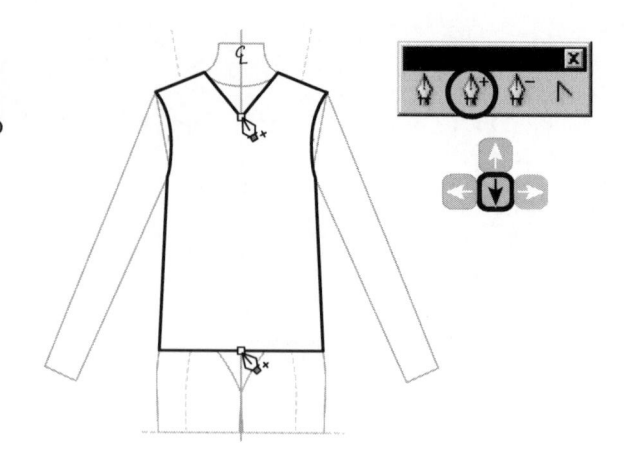

With the **Convert Anchor Point Tool**
Click on the neckline anchor point and **drag to the RIGHT** to create a smooth curve.

Holding the Shift key while you drag will help keep the handles constrained to 0 degrees (*you must click an the anchor point before you depress the Shift key and release the mouse before you release the Shift key*).

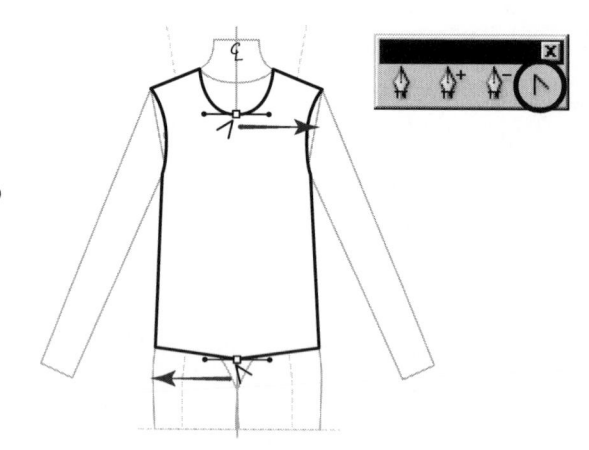

Click on the hemline anchor point and **drag to the LEFT** to create a **smooth curve**.

Congratulations on your first bodice!

adobe® for fashion : illustrator CS5 | **43**

Juan Sim
Art Institute of Ca-Hollywood
http://www.coroflot.com/juan_sim

lesson three

ADDING THE BACK NECKLINE

Using the **Direct Selection tool**
click on anchor point **2**.
Make sure to avoid selecting points **1** and **3**.

Copy (**Ctrl + C** /*Cmd + C*)

Paste in Front (**Ctrl + F** /*Cmd + F*)
This will paste a copy of the neckline directly
on top of the original.

While the neckline is still selected
Right click and **Join**
to close the back of the neckline.

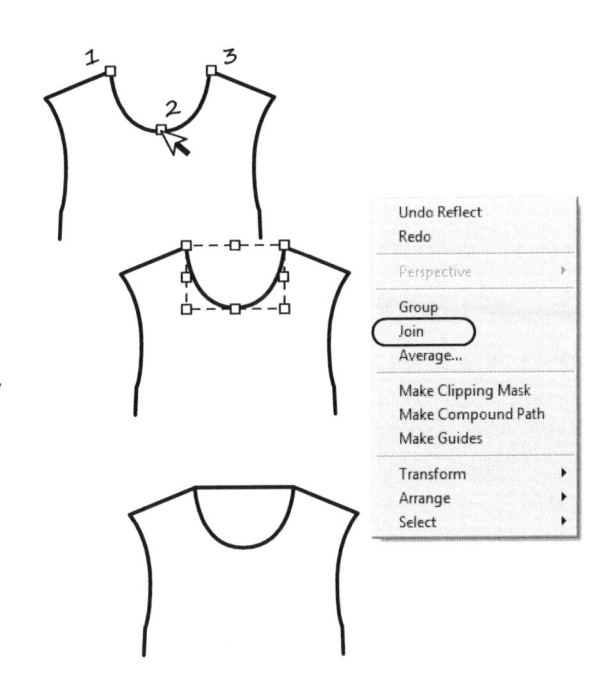

To shape the back neckline
Add a point at **Center Back** using the
Add an Anchor point tool.

Using the **Down Arrow Key** on
your keyboard nudge the point down.

With the **Convert Anchor point tool** click
and drag horizontally to curve.

Select and **Fill** with a light gray to indicate
the wrong side of the fabric.

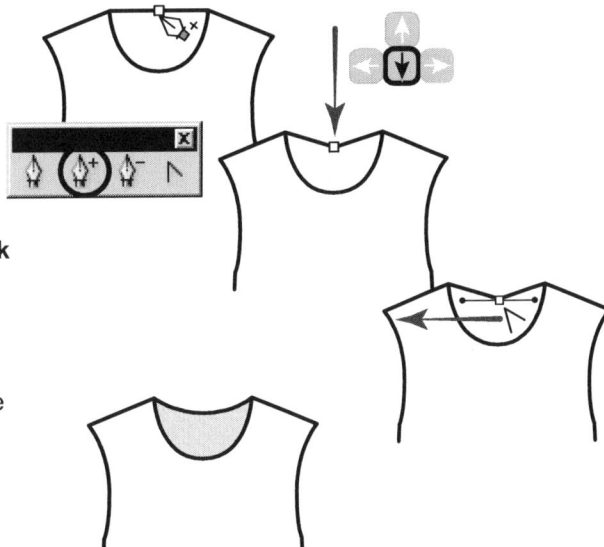

ADDING SLEEVES

To add sleeves we will repeat the same process as the back neck line.

With the **Direct Selection tool**
Select Anchor point **2**, making sure to avoid selecting points **1** and **3**.

Copy (**Ctrl + C** /*Cmd + C*)

Paste in Front (**Ctrl + F** /*Cmd + F*)
This will paste a copy of the armhole directly on top of the original.

Right Click and **Join**.

Using the **Add Anchor point tool** click to add two additional anchor points to the sleeve. (**4** and **5**).

With the **Direct Selection tool** click on the **line segment** between points **4** and **5**.
Drag it to where you want the sleeve to end.

You can further adjust the sleeve by moving points **4** and **5** individually with the **Direct Selection tool**.

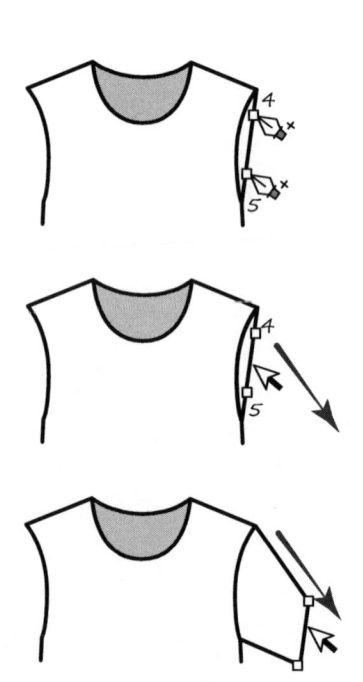

Now for the second sleeve. The good news is that we don't have to draw another one. All you need to do is reflect the one you've already created.

Start by selecting the first sleeve with the **Selection tool**.

Click once on the **Reflect tool** in the **tool Bar** and **Alt+click** (*Opt+click*) anywhere along the center line to open the Reflect options box.

Select **Vertical** and click **Copy** to create the other sleeve.

Note: If you didn't click directly on the center line to reflect, you can use the right and left arrow keys to nudge the sleeve into place.

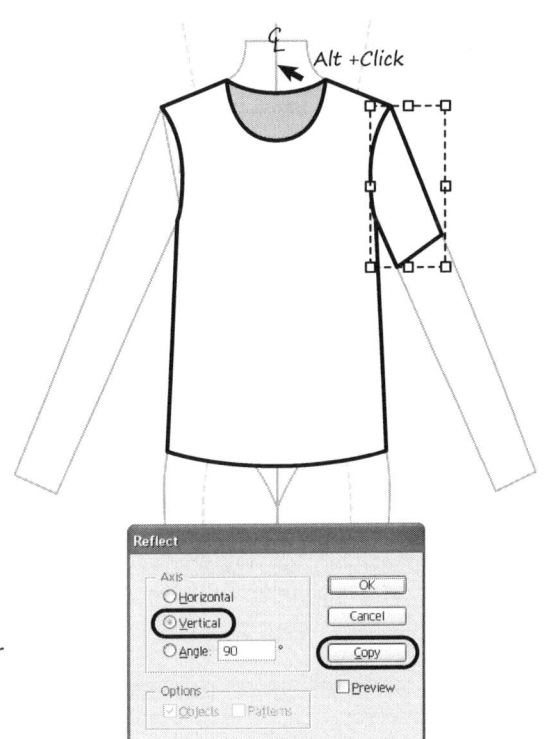

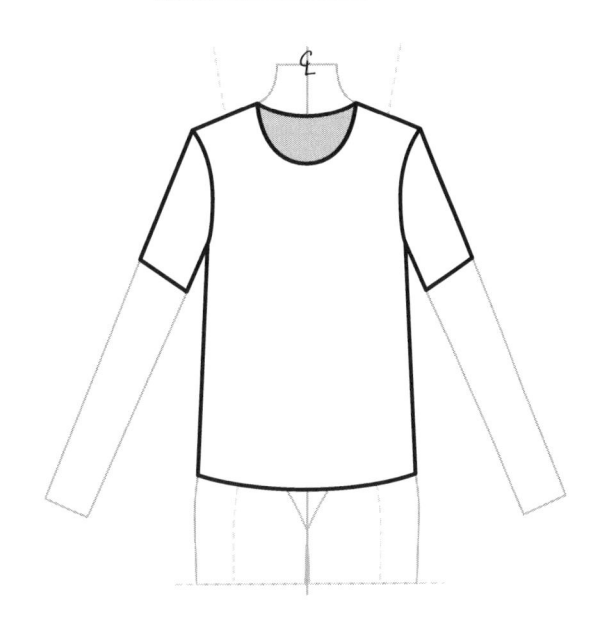

Lesson 3: Basic Flats

THE BACK VIEW

Marque Select the entire shirt.
Right click and **Group**.

Grouping lets you select and move multiple objects with only one click. It keeps your workspace less cluttered - like using paper clips to hold loose papers together. Just like with a paper clip **Groups** can always be **Ungrouped**.

Reflect by clicking once on **Reflect** and **Alt+click**(*Opt+click*) next to the shirt.

Select **Vertical** and click **Copy**.
Now you have two.
We are going to use the one still on the template for the back view.

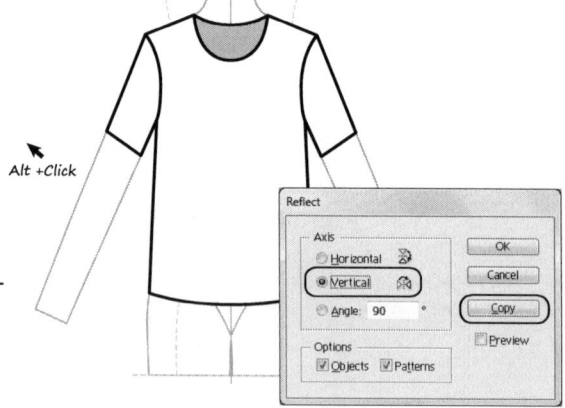

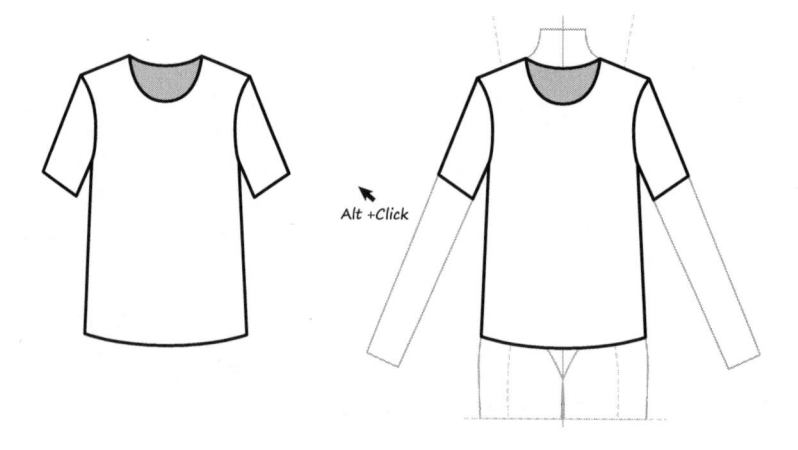

ORGANIZING LAYERS

This would be a good place to stop and organize and label the Layers.

Open the **Layers Panel** by clicking on the **Layers Icon** in the **Panel Dock** on the right side of your screen. (If you can't find it try the Window drop down menu)

Double click on "**Layer 1**" (the actual text) and change the name to T-shirt.

Click the arrow in the T-shirt layer in order to open it up and show the two sub layers labeled group.

Select the front view of your T-shirt and **double click** on the **word group**.
Change the name from "group" to "front".

Now select the other one and change the name to "back". This is going to make it much easier to navigate the **Layers Panel**.

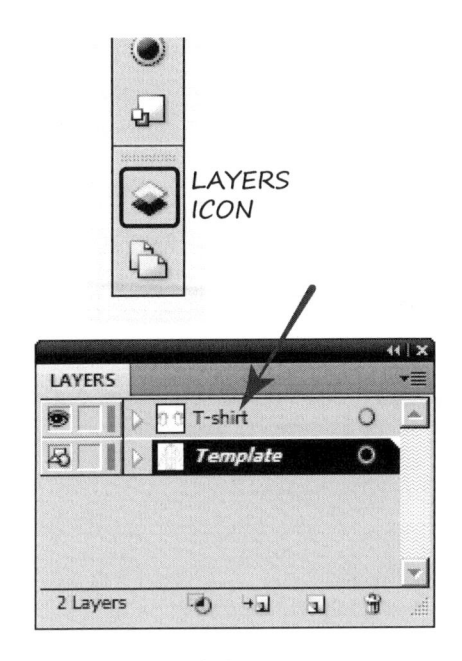

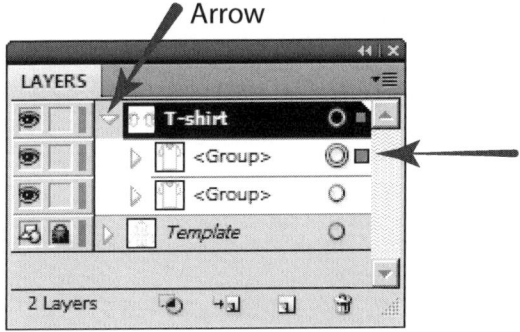

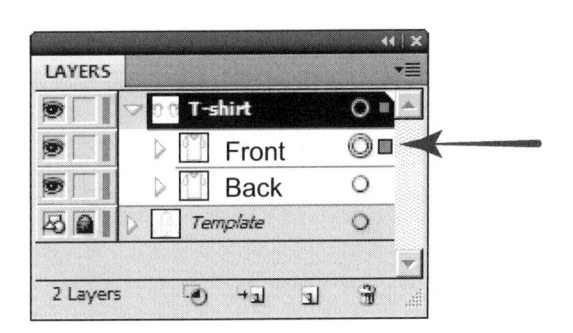

ISOLATION MODE

Isolation mode allows you to work within a group without ungrouping it. When you are in **Isolation Mode** the objects that are not part of the group will appear gray.

Double click on the **Grouped** shirt back to enter **Isolation Mode**. The layers panel will change to **Isolation Mode**.

With the **Selection tool** drag through the center of the shirt to select the bodice and the back neckline.
DO NOT SELECT THE SLEEVES.

Open the **Pathfinder panel** by clicking on **Window>Pathfinder**.
Click on **Unite** and the two shapes merge into one. Also, the fill changed to gray. This is because gray was the last fill color you chose.

Change the **Fill** back to white.

Double click anywhere on the **art board** to **exit Isolation Mode**. *(Notice all of the grayed areas are now black again and the layers panel is back to normal)*

You have just completed your first basic T-shirt flat. I recommend drawing at least 3 more t-shirts to cement the process in your head before moving on.

STROKES

Every combination of **anchor points** and **line segments** drawn in Illustrator® is called a path. A path will only be visible if you assign it a **Stroke**.

A **Stroke** can be assigned using the **Stroke Panel** located in the **panel dock** on the right side of your screen, or from the Window drop down in the **Menu Bar**. Here you can adjust the stroke weight, end caps, corners, create dashed lines, add arrowheads and change profiles.

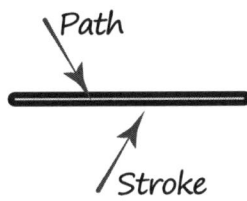

Path
Stroke

The **line weight** or thickness of the **Stroke** can be changed using the **Weight** drop down at the top of the **Stroke Panel**.

The appearance of the **Stroke** can be changed by selecting one of three different end caps.

A **Butt cap** ends where the path ends.
A **Round Cap** rounds off the end of the path.
A **Projecting Cap** extends beyond the end of the path.

The appearance of the corners can be changed as well.

A **Miter Join** forms a mitered corner like a picture frame.
A **Round Join** forms a rounded corner-this is great for fabric.
A **Bevel Join** forms a beveled corner.

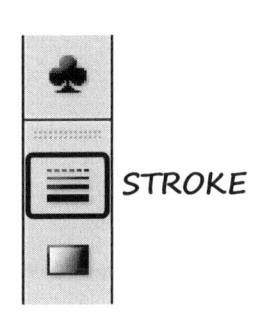

STROKE

STROKE PANEL

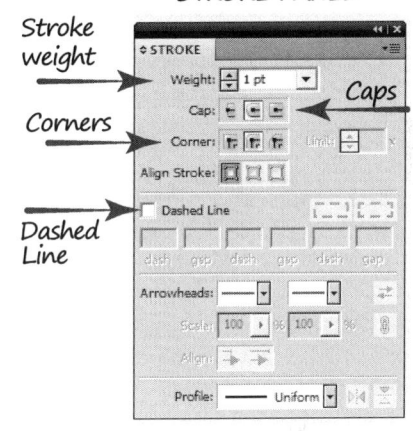

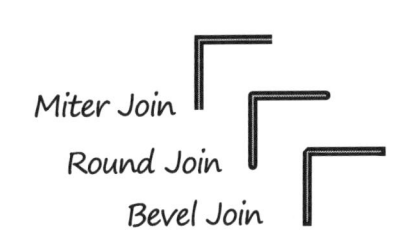

Stroke weight
Caps
Corners
Dashed Line

Butt Cap
Round Cap
Projecting Cap

Miter Join
Round Join
Bevel Join

Lesson 3: Basic Flats

When mitered corners meet they don't always line up neatly. Sometimes they form sharp pointy angles that don't look natural on a flat. We can avoid this by using **Round Joins** instead.

Just Select the entire shirt flat.
Open the **Stroke Panel** and select **Round Cap** and **Round Join**.
Problem solved!

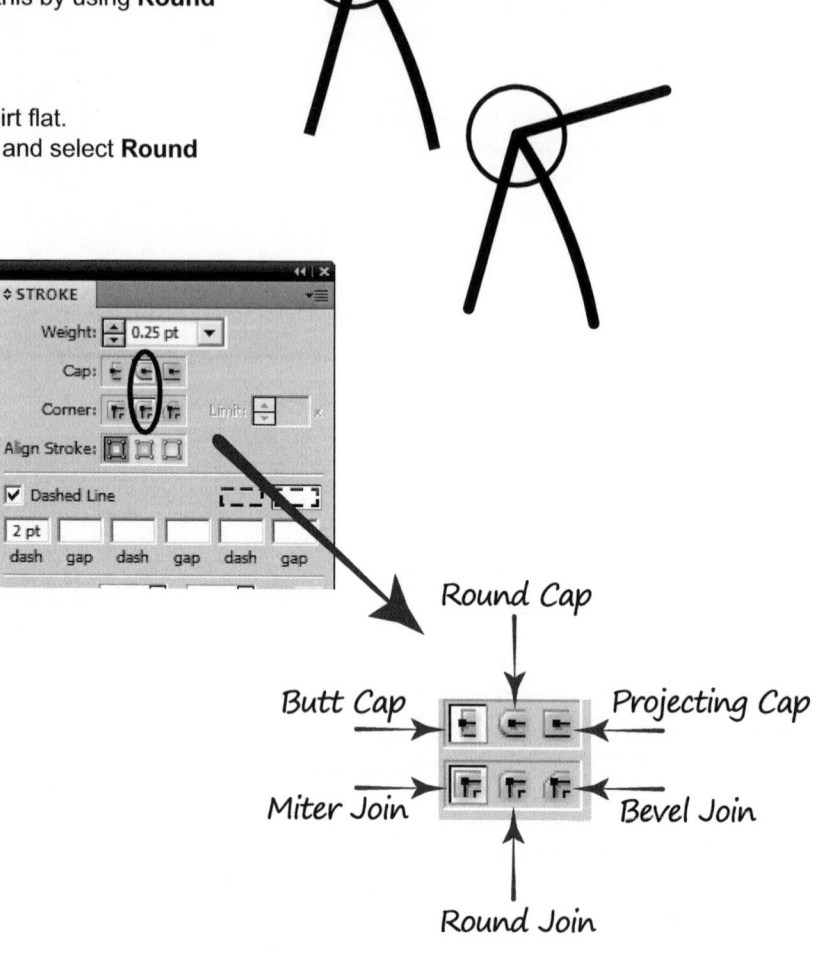

Round Cap

Butt Cap — Projecting Cap

Miter Join — Bevel Join

Round Join

CREATING STITCHES

To add the look of stitches to a path just change the appearance of the **Stroke**.

Select the Path
Open the **Stroke Panel**
Change the Weight to .25 pt.
Select **Round Caps** and **Round Corners**.
Check the **Dashed Line** box
Type in 2pt dash and enter.

Note: Don't be fooled into thinking the dash is already set to 2pts. The default setting is actually 12 pts, but since you can only see three characters in the dash box it will look like 2pt.

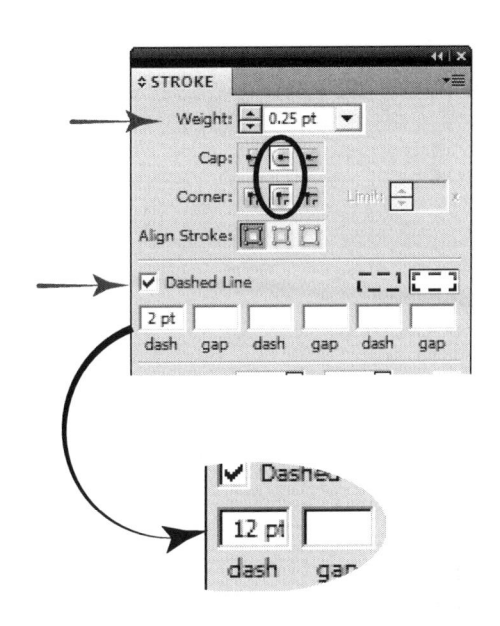

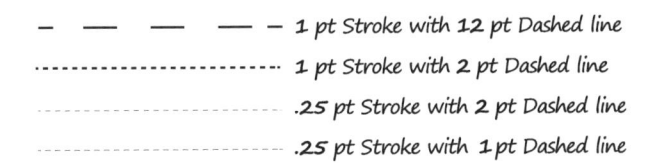

— — — — — 1 pt Stroke with 12 pt Dashed line
·························· 1 pt Stroke with 2 pt Dashed line
------------------------ .25 pt Stroke with 2 pt Dashed line
------------------------ .25 pt Stroke with 1 pt Dashed line

These are the settings I find work the best for indicating stitches. The .25pt weight is a nice balance to the 1pt weight of the rest of the flat.

A 1pt dash would be technically accurate but when it prints the dashes bleed together and look like a solid line so 2 points is much better for printing. I also prefer round caps and corners because we are representing thread and fabric, neither of which have sharp edges.

ADDING STITCHES

Lets add some stitching to the front of the T-shirt.

HEM LINE
Start by using the **Direct Selection tool** to select the anchor point at the center of the hem.
Copy (**Ctrl+ C** /*Cmd+C*)
Paste in Front (**Ctrl+F** /*Cmd+F*)
While it's still selected change the Fill to None. Use the **Forward Slash** (/) key.
Use the **Up arrow** key to nudge it up two or three points.

Now we can apply a dashed line.
Open the **Stroke Panel** and change the line weight to .25
Select **Round Caps**
Check Dashed Line and make sure the dash is **2pts** (not 12pts)

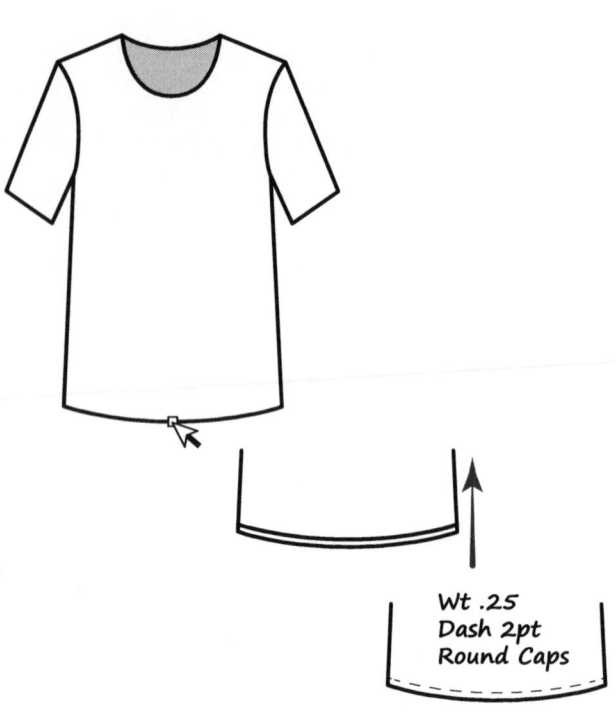

Wt .25
Dash 2pt
Round Caps

NECK LINE
Direct Select the anchor point at the center of the neck.
Copy (**Ctrl+ C** /*Cmd+C*)
Paste in Front (**Ctrl+F** /*Cmd+F*)
While it's still selected change the Fill to None. Use the **Forward Slash** (/) key.
Use the **Down arrow** key to move it Down two or three points.

To make the curves match
switch to the **Selection tool**
Click on the center right handle and
Alt+Drag (*Opt+Drag*) to the right to widen.
Release the mouse.
Release the **Alt**(*Opt*) key.

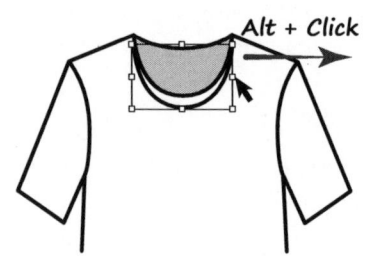

Alt + Click

Select the top handle and drag up until the path touches the shoulders.

Since we've already established the Stitches you can use the **Eye Dropper** to copy them from the hem.

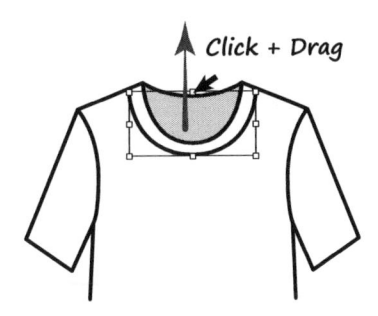

EYE DROPPER TOOL

Once you have the stitching adjusted you can use the **Eye Dropper tool** to duplicate it instead of typing in the settings every time.

Select a new path for stitches.
Select the **Eye Dropper tool** from the **Tool Bar.**

With the **Eye Dropper** click on the stitches at the hem.
This should have changed the neck path to a dashed line that matches the one at the hem.

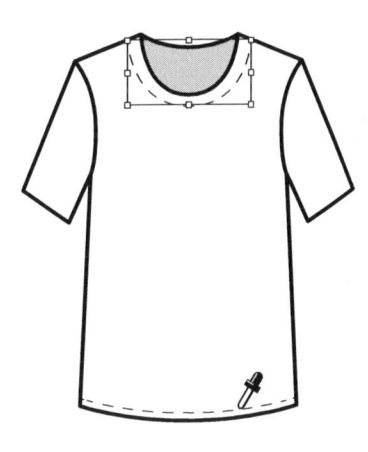

BACK NECK

Direct select the anchor point at the center back neck.
Copy (**Ctrl+ C** /*Cmd+C*)
Paste in Front (**Ctrl+F** /*Cmd+F*)
While it's still selected change the **Fill to None**.
Use the **Down arrow** key to nudge it down two or three points.
Use the **Eyedropper** to copy the stitches from the hem.

You can use the same technique to add stitching to the sleeves.

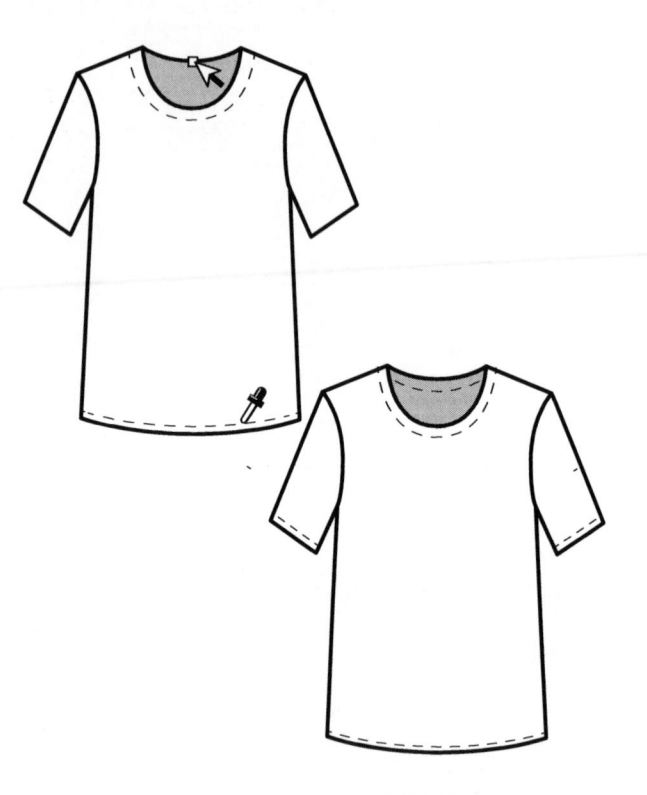

adobe® for fashion : illustrator CS5 | **57**

SOME KEY POINTS TO REMEMBER

So far we have covered three different ways to combine objects Join, Unite and Group.

JOIN
The Join command is used only when connecting two open end points on a path. It can not be used to join more than 2 anchor points together at a time. Join can NOT be used to combine two closed paths.

PATHFINDER UNITE
Pathfinder Unite is used to combine or merge 2 or more closed paths into one shape. It can NOT be used to combine open paths. Just like sewing two pattern pieces together. To separate them again you have to pull out the scissors and cut. (Pathfinder Divide)

GROUP
Grouping objects together is more like temporarily paper clipping them together. It allows you to select and move them as one object but you can always remove the paper clip and "Ungroup" them at any time.
For example: If a shirt has 12 buttons, it would be a good idea to group them together. This way you could select all 12 with one click rather than having to click on each one individually. It's a great time saver.

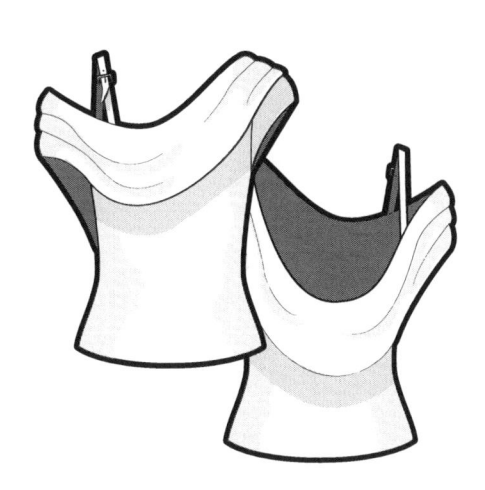

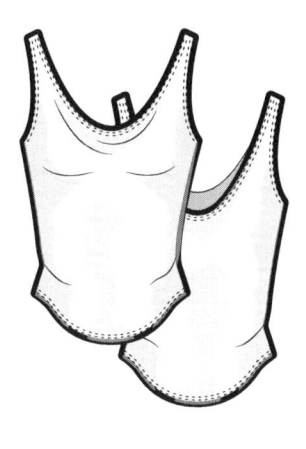

Brooke Belden
Art Institute of Ca-Hollywood
http://www.coroflot.com/brooke_e_belden

lesson four

Placing buttons is so much quicker and easier when you let Illustrator® do all the work.

ALIGN

Align is a great way to center buttons with just one click.

Draw a Circle and **Duplicate** by dragging while holding the **Alt**(*Opt*) key. Release the mouse, then release the **Alt**(*Opt*) Key. Make as many buttons as you need.

Marque Select all of the buttons with the **Selection tool**.
Open the **Align Panel** by going to **Window>Align** in the Menu drop down.

Click on **Align Center** and all of your buttons will jump into a straight line.

To control this command further, you can choose one of the objects as the **Key Object** to which all other objects will **Align**.

Marquee select the objects you want to Align with the **Selection tool**.
Now click on any of your selected objects to make it the **Key Object**. *Watch for the bounding box to change around the key object.*
Click on **Align center** and all of the other objects will **Align** to the Key **Object**.

This is a great way to align the buttons to a placket.

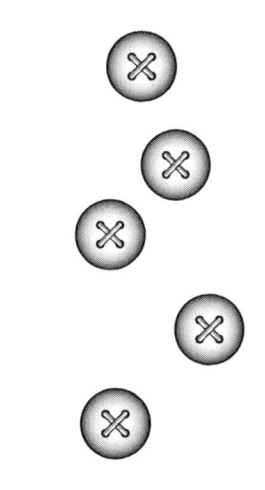

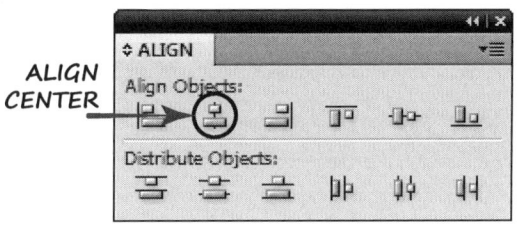

ALIGN CENTER

DISTRIBUTE

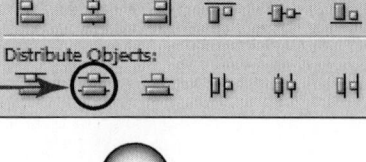

A great way of evenly spacing the buttons.

Distribute notes the placement of the top and bottom buttons and evenly distributes the rest in between.

Select all of the buttons
Click on **Distribute Center**
and the spacing will adjust so that all of the buttons will be evenly distributed.

So much faster than measuring!

DISTRIBUTE CENTER

DRAWING COLLARS

Collars may look complicated but worry not, I'm going to simplify them for you.

Open a New File: **File>New**.
Place the template: **File>Place**
Check the **template box** and **Un-Check** the **Link** box. Click **Place**.

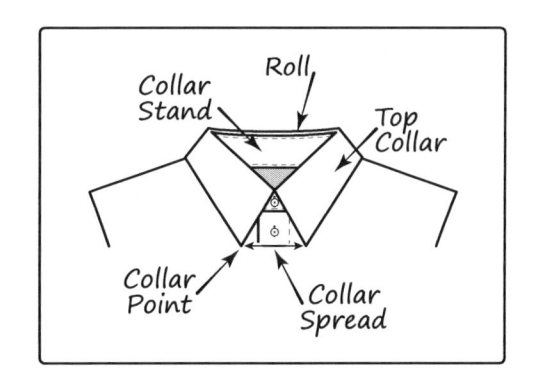

We're going to start by drawing the collar stand. It should be the height you want the collar and it should rest centered on the shoulders.

Select the **Rectangle tool**,
Starting from the center line **Alt+drag** *(Opt+drag)* until you have the size you need.
Don't worry about placement.
Use the **Up** or **Down arrow** key to nudge it into place.

Select the collar stand and **Copy**
Ctrl + C (*Cmd+ C*).
We are going to paste it back later, in the meantime it will be waiting safely in your clipboard.

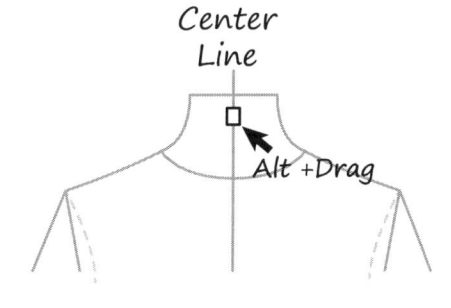

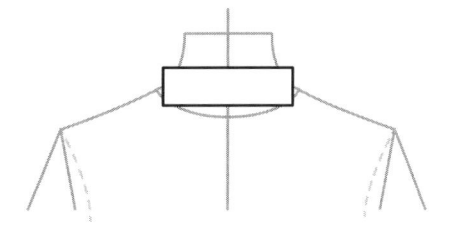

Lesson 4: Buttons, Collars & Cuffs

Use the **Pen Tool** to draw the collar.
- Click on the center front neckline (**1**)
- Click on the upper right corner of the collar stand (**2**)
- Click on the shoulder (**3**)
- Click to create the collar point (**4**)
- Click back on the center front to close the path (**1**)

Select the top collar piece only (***NOT THE STAND***)
Reflect (**Alt+click** /*Opt+click*) on the center line
Select **Vertical** and **Copy**.

Looks good but we are going to take it a bit further and create the collar roll.

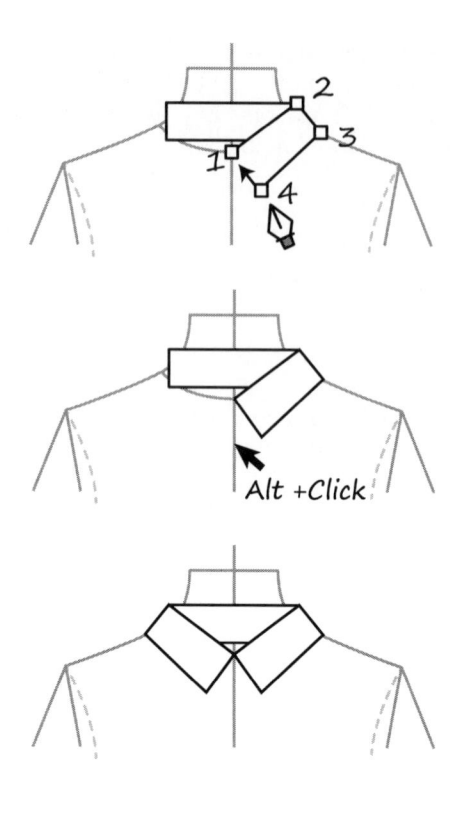

Marque Select all of the collar pieces.

Open the **Pathfinder Panel** by clicking on **Window > Pathfinder** in the Menu drop down.

Select Pathfinder **Unite** to merge the three pieces into one.

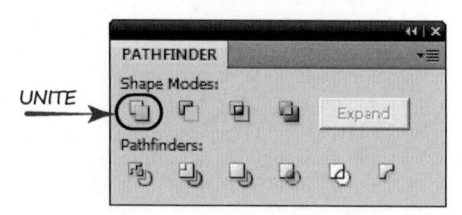

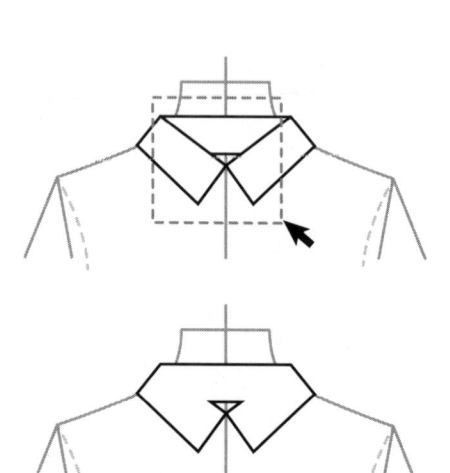

With the **Direct Selection tool double click** on point **1** and drag it toward the upper left corner.

Select point 2 and drag it to the upper right corner to form the roll.

Remember that collar stand we copied to save for later?

Paste in Back (**Ctrl+B** /*CMD+B*) to restore the collar stand.

Select the entire collar with the stand and **Group** them together. (**Ctrl+G** /*CMD+G*)

You have just drawn a collar!

Remember: If anything goes wrong along the way just **UNDO** (**Ctrl+Z** / *Cmd+Z*)

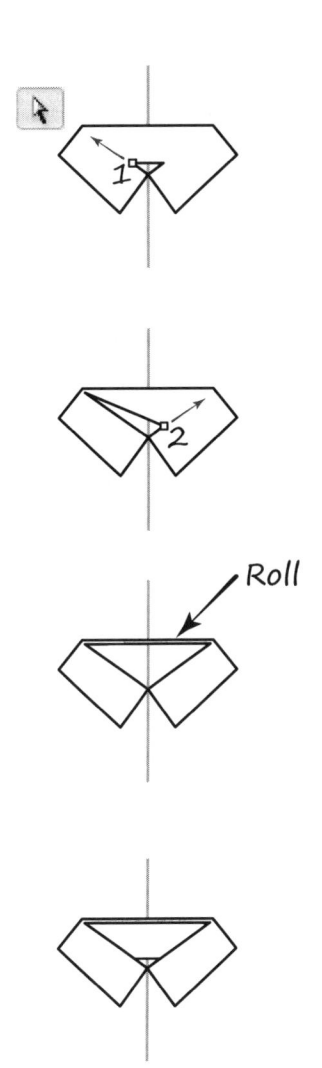

Lesson 4: Buttons, Collars & Cuffs

Lets draw the bodice, it's just like the t-shirt. Click on the **New Layer icon** to make a new Layer and **drag it below the collar layer**. Click on the **Eye** to hide the collar so we can see the entire template.

Select the **Pen Tool**
- Click on high point shoulder (**1**)
- Click on low point shoulder (**2**)
- Click inside the armhole (**3**)
- Click the bottom of the armhole (**4**)
- Click on the hip (**5**)

With the **Convert Anchor Point tool drag straight down** to create the armhole curve.

Marque Select the entire path,
Reflect: **Alt** (*Opt*) **+ click** on the Center line. Select **Vertical** and **Copy** to create the other side of the bodice.

Marquee select both sides of the bodice.

Right click and **Join**
to connect the top neckline.

Right click and **Join** again to connect the bottom hemline.

Now you can make the collar layer visible again.

Notice that the collar covers the neckline so there is no need to curve it.

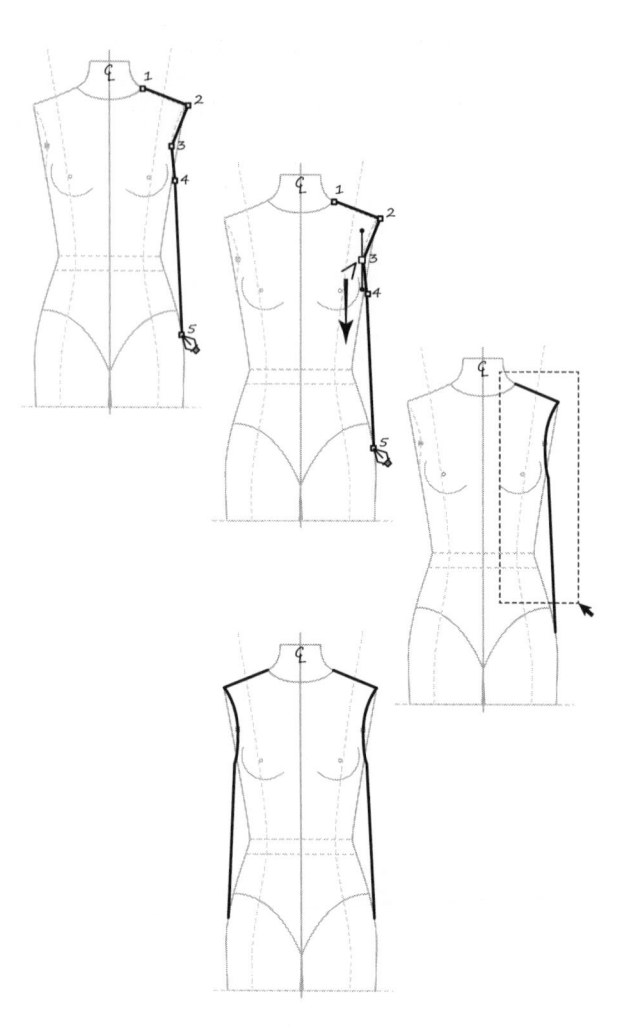

adobe® for fashion : illustrator CS5 | 65

Add an anchor point at the center of the hemline.
Use the down arrow to nudge it down a bit.

With the **Convert Anchor Point Tool** click on the center hemline anchor point and **drag to the LEFT** to create a smooth curve.

With the **Direct Selection tool**
Select the center of the armhole

Copy (**Ctrl + C** /*Cmd + C*)

Paste in Front (**Ctrl + F** /*Cmd + F*)

Right click and **Join**.

Using the **Add Anchor point tool** add two additional anchor points to the sleeve.

With the **Direct Selection tool** click on the line segment between the points .Drag it to the wrist finish the sleeve.

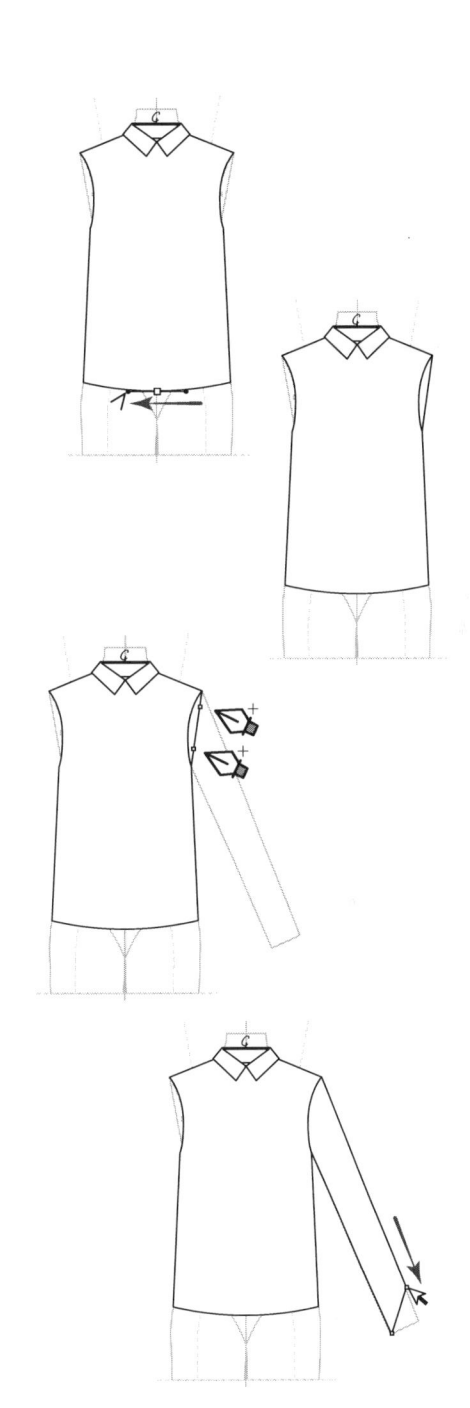

FRONT PLACKET

The Placket is really just a rectangle drawn on top of the shirt bodice but beneath the collar. You can draw it with the Rectangle tool and then align it to the collar.

Draw a rectangle starting at the neck and ending at the hemline. Make it as wide as you want the placket. *Don't worry about centering it yet.*

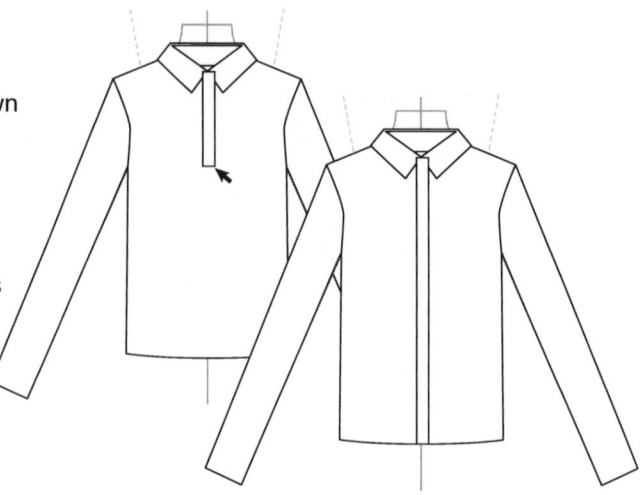

With the **Selection tool**, Select the collar(**1**), hold down the **Shift key** and click on the placket(**2**) to add it to the selection.

Release the Shift Key and Click once more on the collar(**3**) to define it as the **Key object.**
Open **Align** and click on **Align Center** to align the placket to the collar. *It should jump right into place.*

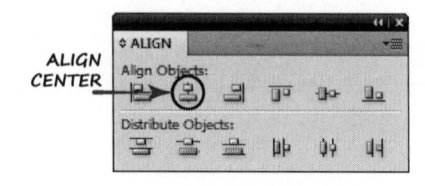

To move the placket behind the collar release your current selection by clicking on an empty spot on your art board.

Select the placket
Right Click > Arrange> Send to Back

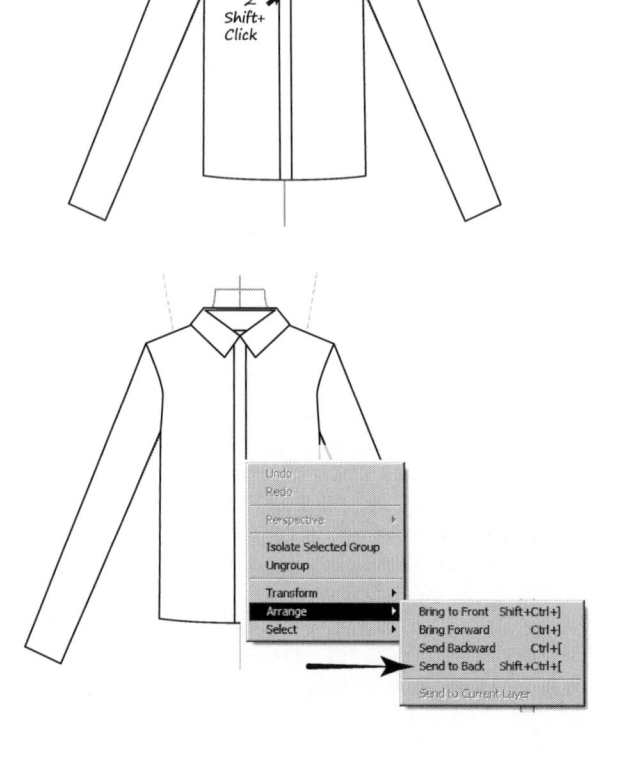

CREATING CUFFS

Using the **Pen Tool**, draw a line parallel to the bottom of the sleeve to divide the cuff from the sleeve. Make sure it extends beyond the sleeve on both sides and has a fill of None.

Marque select the sleeve and the dividing line with the **Selection tool**.

Click on **Pathfinder Divide** (*Remember you can find Pathfinder in the Windows drop down on the Menu bar at the top of your screen*).

Right click and **Ungroup**.

Now you have a cuff you can fill with a contrast color.

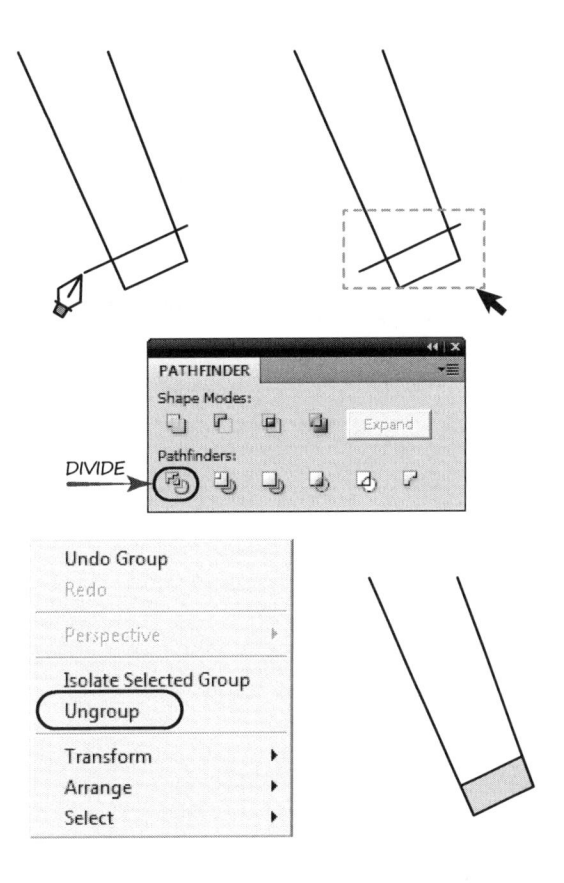

Use the **Add Anchor Point tool** to add a point to the bottom left of the sleeve just above the cuff.
Use the **Left Arrow** Key on your keyboard to nudge it one or two clicks to the left.

Add a point to the bottom right sleeve and use the **Right Arrow** Key to nudge it one or two clicks to the right.

Instead of repeating the process for the other sleeve just Select this one and **Reflect** it to the other side.

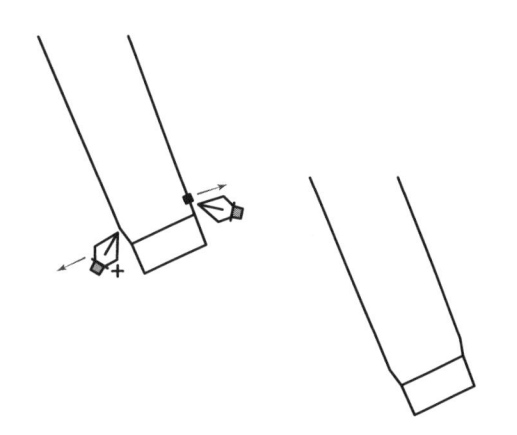

Lesson 4: Buttons, Collars & Cuffs

This would be a really good time to stop and save the file you are working in - just in case.
File>Save as
Name the File and click OK.

GROUPS

Before we move on let's **Marque Select** the entire shirt and **Group** it together.

TO GROUP OBJECTS

Select the entire shirt.
Right click and **Group**.

or if you prefer
Ctrl+G (*CMD+G*) to **Group**.

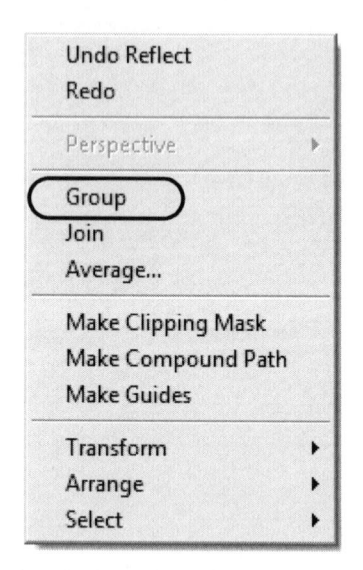

GROUP SELECTION TOOL

To select one or more objects within a group with out ungrouping use the **Group Selection tool**.

In the **Tool Bar** hiding behind the **Direct Selection tool** (White Arrow) you will find the **Group Selection tool**. *It looks like the Direct Selection tool with a plus sign.*

Click once on an object to select it.

Double click on the object to select it along with its entire group.

BUTTONS

Use the **Selection tool** to **Double click** on the shirt and enter **Isolation Mode**.

Use the **Ellipse tool** to draw one button (*remember to hold Shift for a perfect circle*)

Select the button and place it in its spot at the top of the placket.

Copy (**Ctrl + C** /*Cmd + C*)
Paste in Front (**Ctrl + F** /*Cmd + F*)
as many buttons as you need.
Move one of the buttons into its spot at the bottom.

Select all of the buttons
Open the **Align Panel** and **Align Center**

While they are still selected **Distribute Center**.

Once all of the buttons have been **Aligned** and **Distributed** it is a good idea to **Group** them all together. This way you will be able to select them all with one click and they can't easily be moved out of alignment.

Right click and **Group** them together so they stay in order.

Select the group of buttons, **hold Shift** and select the placket.
Release Shift and click on the placket one more time to define it as the **Key object**.

Now you can **Align Center** and the buttons will jump to the center of the placket.

Double click on the **Artboard** to **exit Isolation Mode**.

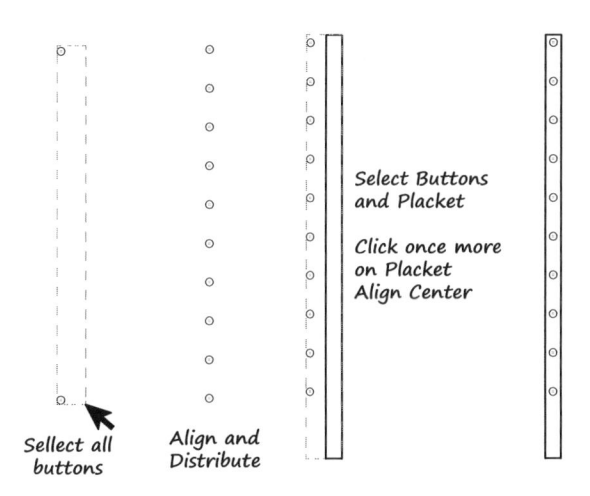

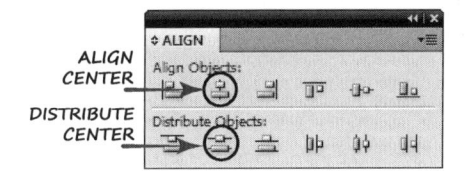

Sellect all buttons

Align and Distribute

Select Buttons and Placket

Click once more on Placket Align Center

ALIGN CENTER

DISTRIBUTE CENTER

Lesson 4: Buttons, Collars & Cuffs

SHIRT BACK
Now you can **Reflect** the shirt-just like we did with the T-shirt so we can work on the back. Select the Shirt and click on **Reflect**. **Alt+click** (*Opt+click*) next to the shirt to make a copy.

You might want to take a moment to label your layers as well. Oh and maybe SAVE?

Double click on the shirt back to enter **Isolation Mode**.

First step is to delete any elements we don't need on the back. This would include the front placket and any stitching.

Drag the group of buttons over near the sleeve cuff. **Double click** on the group of buttons and **select and delete** all but one for the cuff.

With the **Selection tool** drag through the center of the shirt to select the bodice and the collar. *DO NOT SELECT THE SLEEVES.*

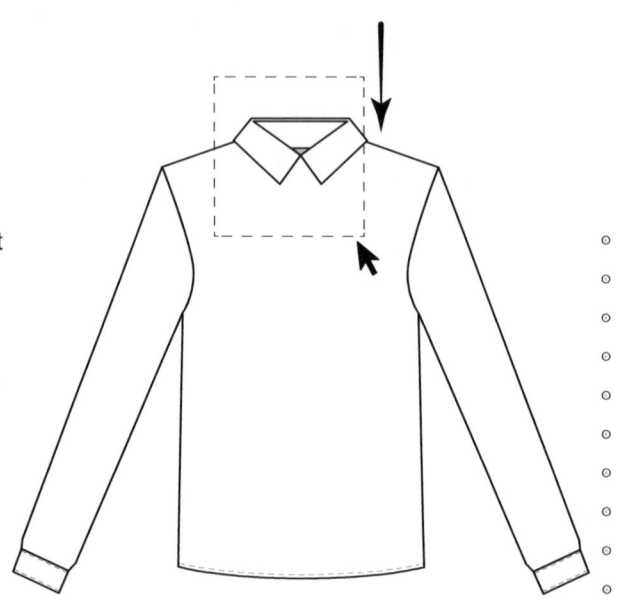

Open **Pathfinder** and click on **Unite** and all the shapes merge into one silhouette.

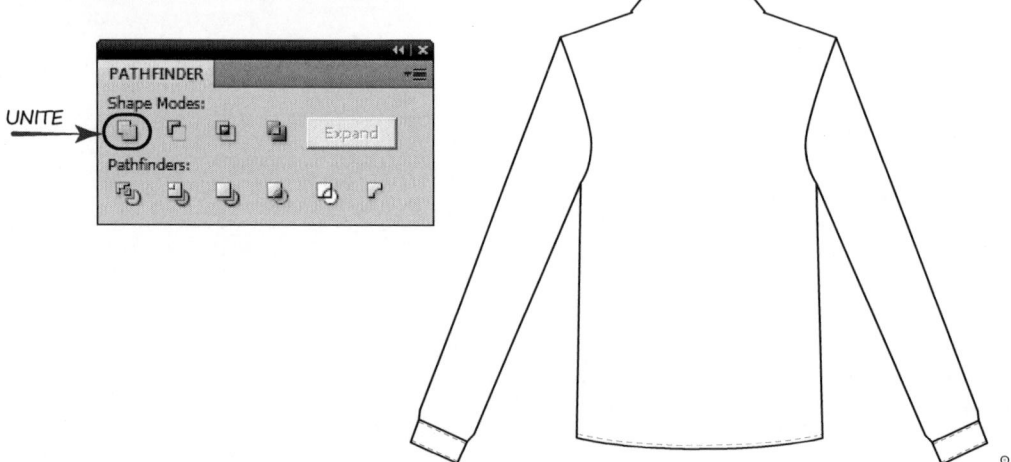

UNITE

adobe® for fashion : illustrator CS5 | 71

If you Unite the shirt bodice and collar together and end up with artifacts you must remove them before you move on.

Select the shirt bodice
Right click > Release Compound path
Now you can click on the unwanted artifacts and delete them.

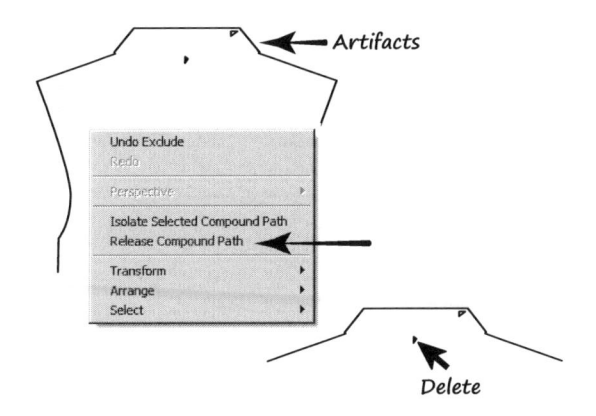

← Artifacts

Delete

To redefine the collar draw a path with the **Pen tool** across the back where the collar meets the shoulder. It should overlap on both sides and have no fill.

With the **Selection tool** drag through the center of the shirt to select the bodice and the dividing line.

Pathfinder> Divide

Right click and **Ungroup**.

If your stitches disappeared don't worry they are actually just hiding behind the bodice.

Right Click > Arrange> Send to back

Easy right?

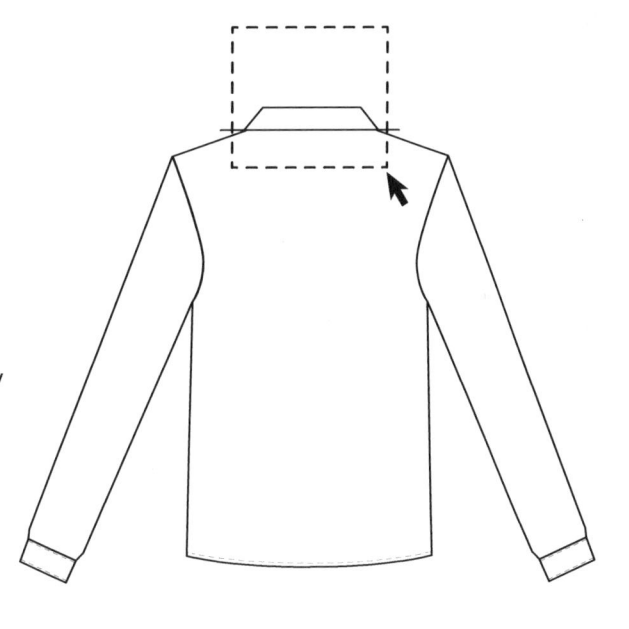

Lesson 4: Buttons, Collars & Cuffs

YOKE
Add a yoke the same way we did the collar.
Draw a path for the yoke making sure to intersect the armholes.
Set the **fill to None**.
Select the Bodice and the Yoke line
Pathfinder Divide
Right click and **Ungroup**.

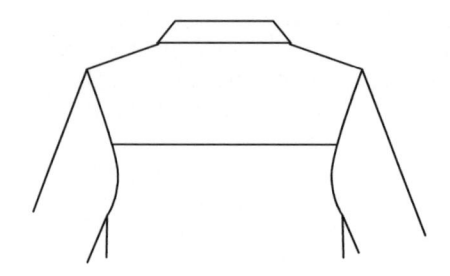

SLEEVE PLACKET

Use the **Rectangle tool** to draw a rectangle for the sleeve placket. Draw it near the sleeve so you can visually gauge the correct size.

With the **Add Anchor Point Tool**, add a point to the top center of the rectangle.

Move it up one or two clicks using the **Up Arrow** on your keyboard.

Select the bottom segment with the **Direct Selection tool** (white arrow) and **Delete** to complete the placket shape.

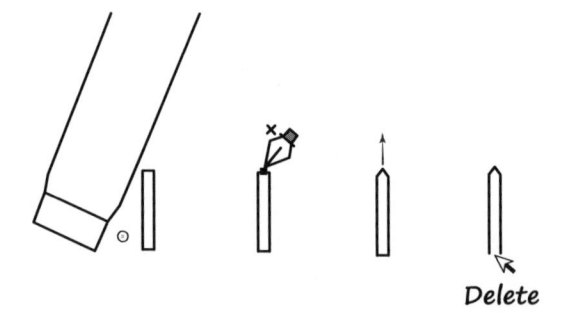

Switch to the **Selection tool** (black arrow) and drag the placket over to where the cuff meets the sleeve. Make sure the bottom left point is correctly positioned on the cuff.

Click once on the **Rotate tool**,
Click on the **bottom left point** of the placket where it touches the cuff(*this defines the pivot point for rotation*).

Click and drag any where near the placket to rotate it until it is parallel to the sleeve.

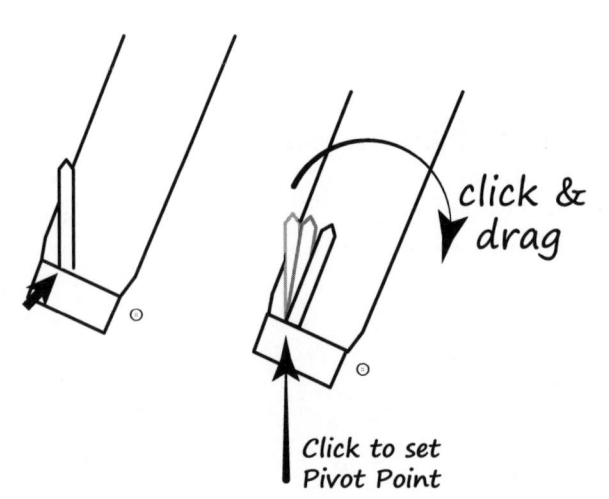

Delete

click & drag

Click to set Pivot Point

Use the **Direct Selection tool** to **double click** on the bottom left anchor point of the placket and drag it down to the edge of the cuff making sure to stay perpendicular to the cuff.

*If the entire placket moves **UNDO (Ctrl+Z/Cmd+Z)**.Click once on a blank area of your page to release the selection. Now reselect the anchor point by clicking directly on it.*

Move the button into place to complete the sleeve.

Delete the other sleeve and **Reflect** this one to the other side.

Double click on the page to **exit Isolation Mode**.

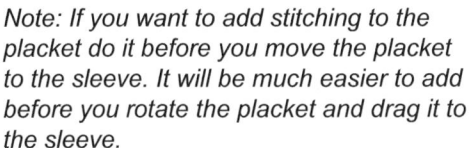

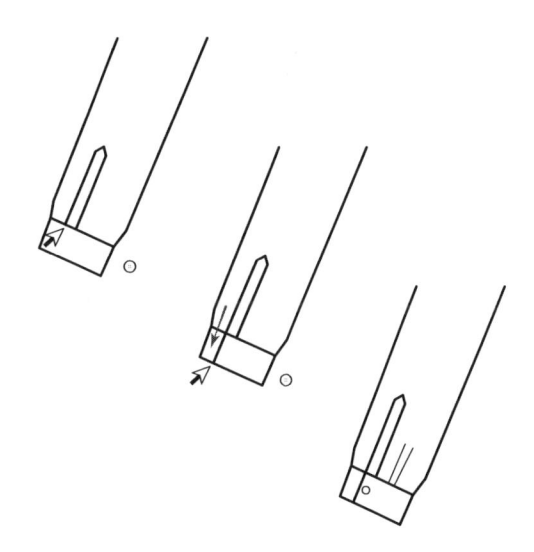

Note: If you want to add stitching to the placket do it before you move the placket to the sleeve. It will be much easier to add before you rotate the placket and drag it to the sleeve.

74 | Lesson 4: Buttons, Collars & Cuffs

adobe® for fashion : illustrator CS5 | 75

Juan Sim
Art Institute of Ca-Hollywood
http://www.coroflot.com/juan_sim

lesson five

SKIRTS & BLAZERS

FLARED SKIRTS

Getting a soft look can be difficult on the computer, but if you follow these steps you will be drawing fluid draping with ease.

The following steps should give you great results. The key to remember is that we are going for a shallow curve. Save those scallops for the beach.

Lesson 5: Skirts and Blazers

DRAWING SKIRTS

Open a new file **File>New**
Place the template **File>Place**
Locate the template, **Check Template**, **Un-Check Link** and click **Place**.

With the **Pen tool** draw a curve for the hem line of the skirt so you will have a path to follow. It should be smiling. We will need two so **Copy** the path **Ctrl+C** (*Cmd+C*) and **Paste in Front** (**Ctrl+F** /*Cmd+F*).
Down arrow two or three clicks. Don't put too much space between the two guidelines.

Select both guidelines and change the stroke to **.25 wt. Red. Lock the layer.**

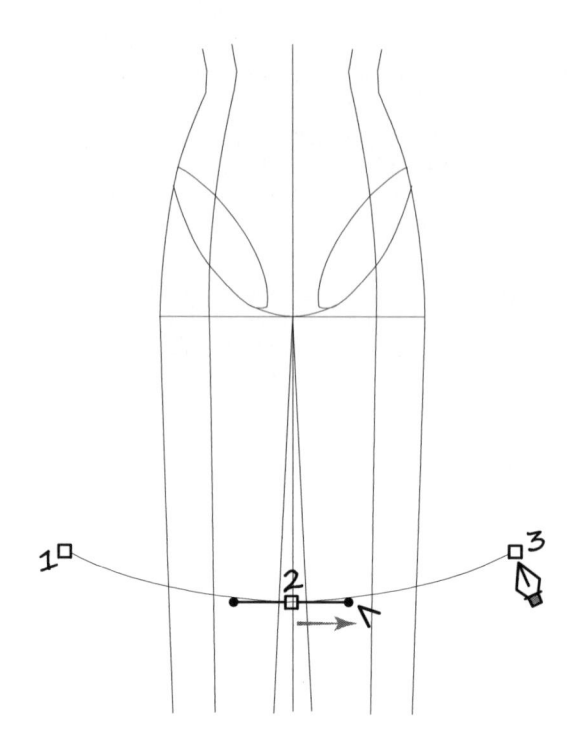

Make a **New Layer**.
Select the **Pen tool.**
- Cick on the waist to place the first anchor point (**1**).
- Click on the hip (**2**).
- Click on the outer hem (**3**).
    Use the upper guideline.

To create fullness at the bottom of the skirt we need to add additional points in a zig zag pattern following the curve of the hem. points **4**, **5**, **6**, **7** and **8**.
You will get a better result if you keep the zig zag shallow.

With the **Convert Anchor point tool** click on anchor point **2** and drag straight down to curve the hip.

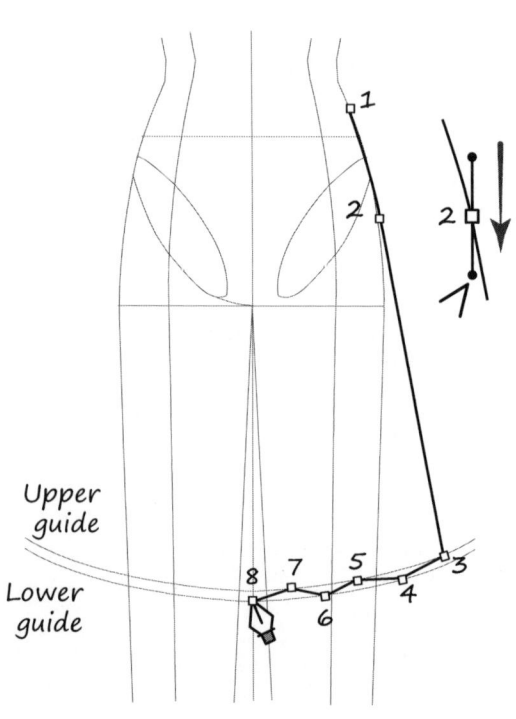

With the **Selection tool** reselect the entire path.
Click once on the **Reflect tool**.
Alt (*Opt*) **click** on the center line.
Select **vertical** and click **Copy**.

Select both sides of the skirt
Right click and **Join** to join the bottom.
Right click again and **Join** to join the top

Use the **Delete Anchor point tool** to **delete** point **8**. There are currently two, one on top of the other and we only want one.

With the **Convert Anchor point tool** click and drag horizontally on point **11** to curve.

Pull the handle until it reaches the nearest anchor point on either side.

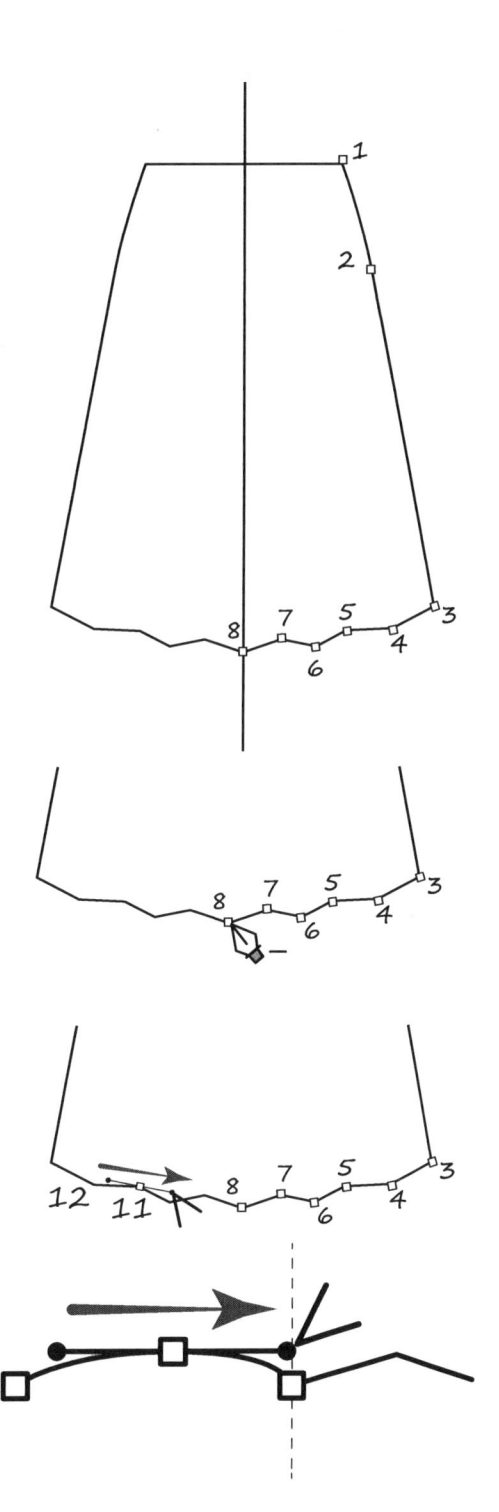

Lesson 5: Skirts and Blazers

Do the same for all of the upper points **5,7,9**. This should create something that looks like upside down scallops.

Now repeat the process with all of the lower anchor points, pulling out handles as far as the next anchor point.

Drag the handles until the curve starts to square off for a more natural flair.

Squared off

Scalloped

If it looks like scallops you did not drag the handles out far enough.

NOT like this

To create the appearance of fullness we need to draw cone shapes. Think of the curves you just made as a series of smiles and frowns. All of the smiles should now be made into cone shapes.

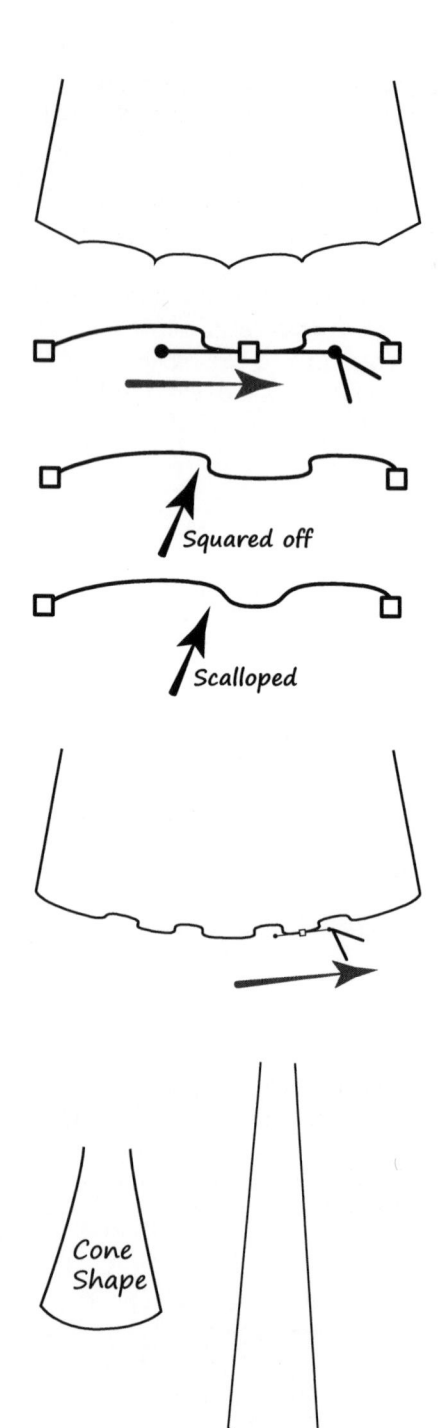

Cone Shape

In the **Layers Panel lock the skirt layer** so it won't move around during the next step.

Make a **New Layer**.
With the **Pen tool** click once at point **2**.
Move the **Pen tool** up and slightly to the right **2A**.
Click and drag straight up from this point toward the top of the skirt.

To **release** the **Pen tool** press **Enter** or *Return* on the keyboard.

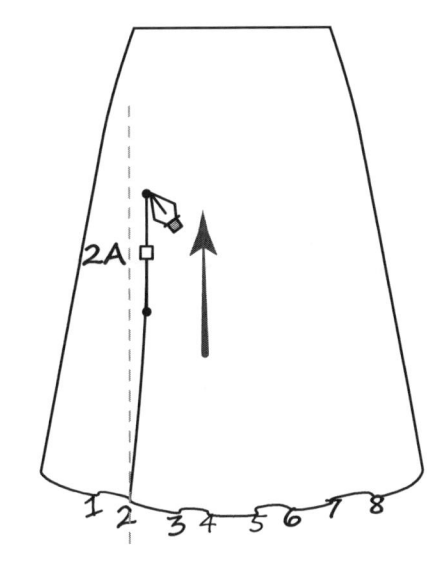

Now click at point **3**.
Move the **Pen tool** up and slightly to the left **3A**.
Click and drag straight up from this point toward the top of the skirt.
The goal is to create an elongated cone shape.

Continue the process with points **1**, **4**, **5**. **7** and **8**.
Since there is no defined drape at **6** we do not need to draw a line.

Marque Select all of the fullness lines and **Group** them **Ctrl+G** (*Cmd+G*).

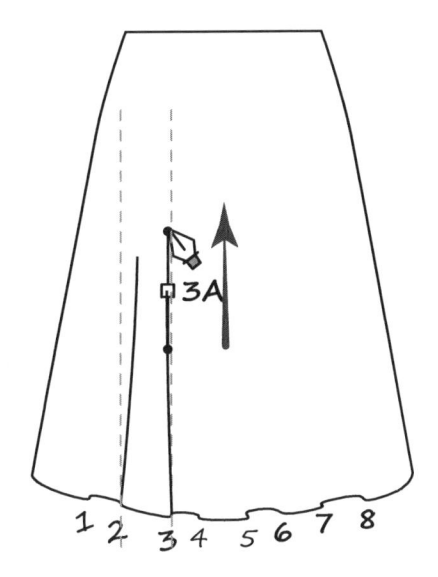

Open the **Stroke Panel**.

Change the **stroke weight to .5pts**.

Change the **Profile** to ▶

This will make the details look more delicate and taper off at the top for a more hand drawn appearance.

PROFILES

Profiles are a great addition to Adobe® CS5. By applying a **Profile** you can change the look of a stroke from a consistent line to a more finessed stroke that tapers or flairs. You can find them at the bottom of the **Stroke Panel**.

Select a path and click on a **Profile** to apply.

This would be a good time to save.
I can't stress this enough-
Save, Save, Save.

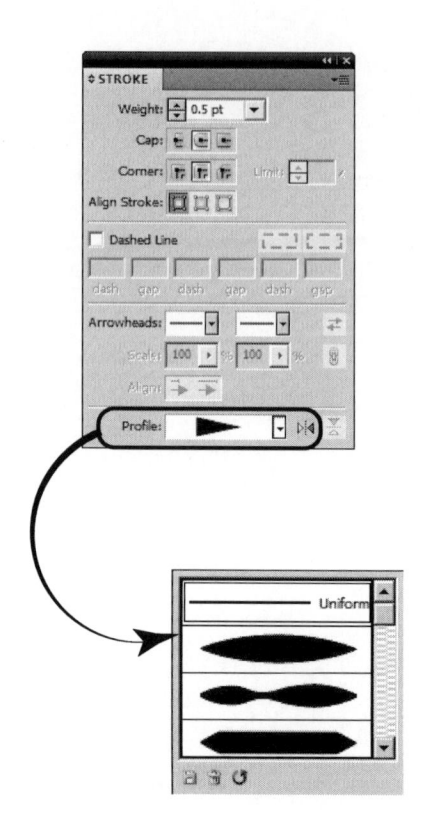

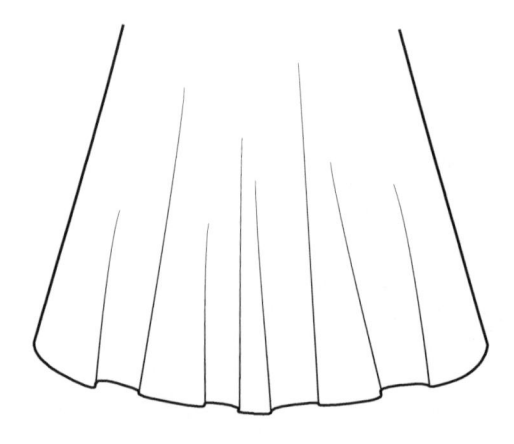

BASIC BLAZER

SETTING THE GUIDELINES

Before we start the blazer we need to draw some guide lines that will be specific to this garment.

You need to decide on the placement of the **Roll line**, the **Notch** and the **Break point**.

Open a **new file** and **place the template**.

In a new layer above the template use the **Pen tool** to draw two horizontal lines, one for the **notch** and one for the **break point**.

Now for the **Roll line** and the **Extension** click once at the High Point Shoulder(**1**).

Move across the center line to the break line and click once for the **Break Point** (**2**)

Hold the **Shift key** and click at the hem(**3**).

Select the line and **Reflect**.

Select both guide lines
Change the **Stroke weight to .25**
Set the **Stroke color to red**.
Set the **Fill to none**.

Lock the layer so it won't move.
This will make the template easier to work with.

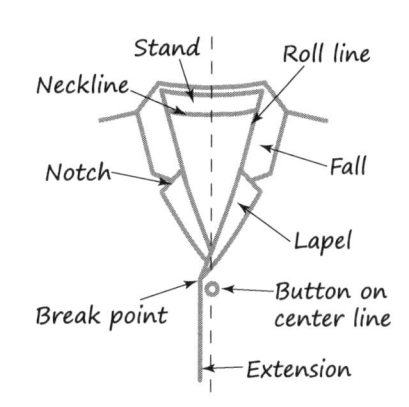

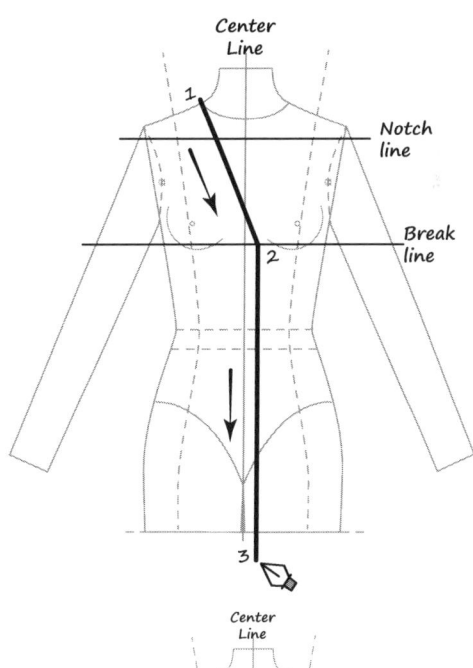

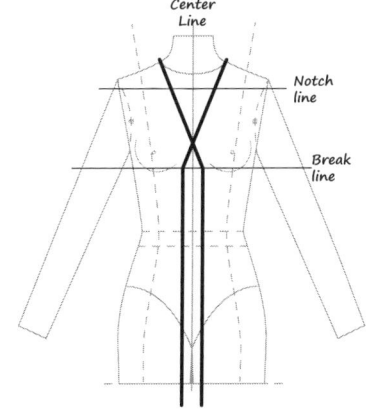

Lesson 5: Skirts and Blazers

LAPEL

Make a **New layer**.
Using the **Pen tool**
- Click on the **break point (1)**
- Click on the **notch point (2)**
- Click on the **tip of the lapel (3)**
- Click back at the **break point (1)** to close the path

Select the lapel and **Reflect**.
Click once on the **Reflect tool**
Alt +click (*Opt+click*) on the center line
Select **Vertical** and **Copy**.

Select both the lapel pieces and
Pathfinder Divide.
Right click and **Ungroup**.

Select the piece that would be hidden when the blazer is closed (lower left for a woman). Press the **Delete** key.

Select pieces **1**, **2**, and **3**.
Hold the **Shift key** to **select multiple objects**.

Use **Pathfinder Unite** to unite them back together.

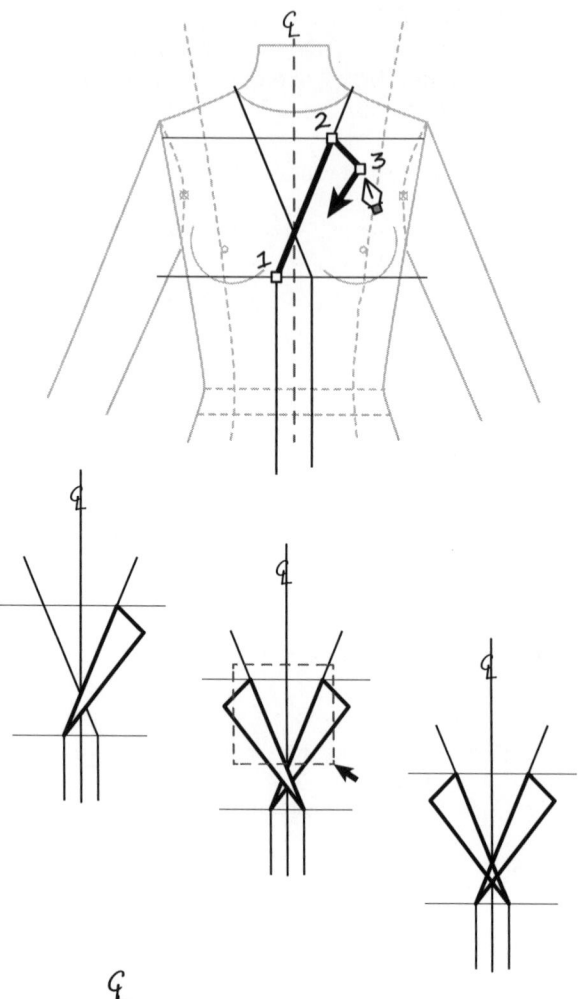

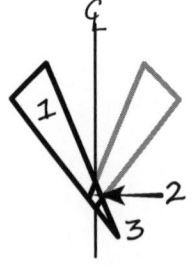

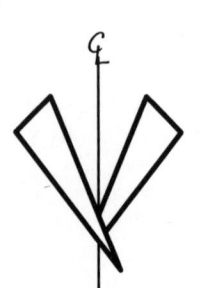

Using the **Rectangle tool** draw the collar stand starting at the center line while holding the **Alt** (*Opt*)key. Move it up or down with the arrow keys as needed.

Select the rectangle and
Copy (**Ctrl+C** /*Cmd+C*)
We are going to paste it back later, just like we did with the shirt collar.

Determine where you want the **collar fall** to end and click on that point along the guide-line with the pen tool (**1**).
- Click the **upper outer corner** of the collar stand (**2**)
- Click on the **shoulder** (**3**)
- Click on the last point of the fall (**4**)
- Click back at point (**1**) to close the path.

Select and **Reflect** the collar fall.
Select both collar falls and the collar stand (*not the lapels*) and use **Pathfinder Unite**.

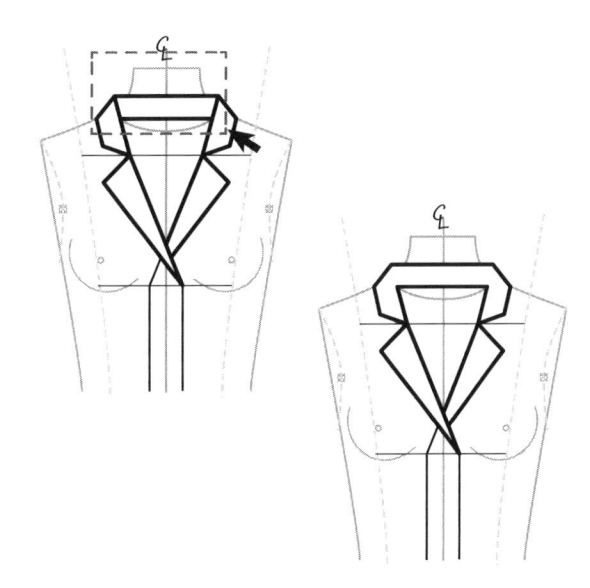

Lesson 5: Skirts and Blazers

With the **Direct Selection tool**,
Select point **1** and drag it into the upper left corner.

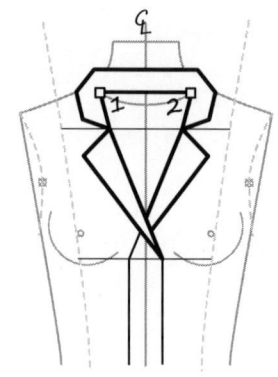

Select point **2** and drag it into the upper right corner. This creates the collar roll just like we did with the shirt.

Now all we need to do is paste the collar stand back in place.

Ctrl+B (*Cmd+B*) to **Paste in Back**.

Select the entire collar with lapel and **Group** (**Ctrl+G** /*Cmd+G*)

Lock the Lapel Layer.

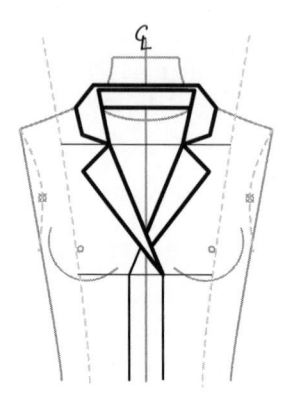

BLAZER FRONT

Make a **New layer**.
Using the **Pen tool**

- click on the break point (**1**)
- click at high point shoulder (**2**)
- click at low shoulder (**3**)
- click inside the armhole (**4**)
- click under the arm (**5**)
- click at the waist (**6**)
- click at the hem (**7**)

Move back across the center line to the break line and **shift+click** (**8**) to insure a constrained line.
Click back where we started (**1**) to close the path.

Notice we are building the blazer with two closed paths instead of one the way the t-shirt was built.

With the **Convert Anchor point tool** drag straight down at the armhole (**4**) and the waist (**6**) to curve.

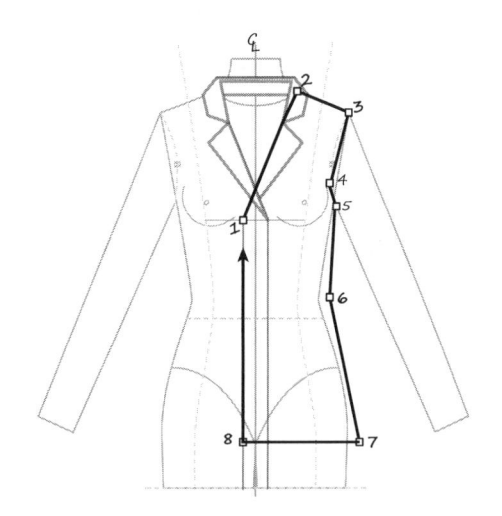

Direct Select the armhole
Copy (**Ctrl+C** /*Cmd+C*)
Paste in Front (**Ctrl+F** /*Cmd+F*)

Right click and **Join**

Add two anchor points
Drag the line segment with the **Direct Selection tool** to form the sleeve.

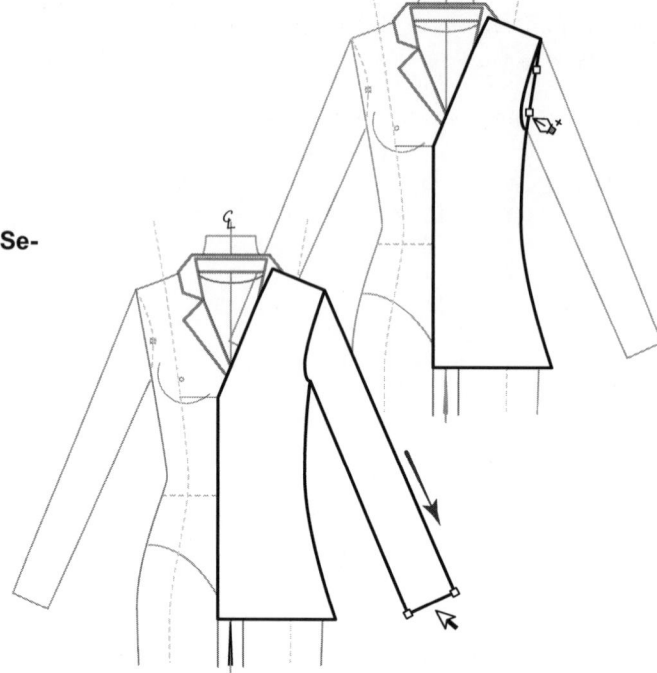

For a two piece sleeve
draw a path with the **Pen tool**
Make sure to extend it beyond the armhole and the hem.

Change the **fill to None**.

Select the path and the sleeve (***DO NOT SELECT THE BLAZER FRONT***)
use **Pathfinder Divide**.
Right click and **Ungroup**.

TO ADD A PRINCESS LINE

- Use the **Pen tool** to click just outside of the armhole (**1**)
- at the apex (**2**)
- **Shift +click** just below the hemline.

To curve the apex drag straight down (**2**) with the **Convert Anchor point tool**.

Select the Princess line and the blazer front (***DO NOT SELECT THE SLEEVES***) and **Pathfinder Divide**.
Right click and **Ungroup**.

Select the sleeve and blazer front **Reflect** (**Alt+Click** /*Opt+Click*) on the center line. Select **Vertical** and **Copy**.

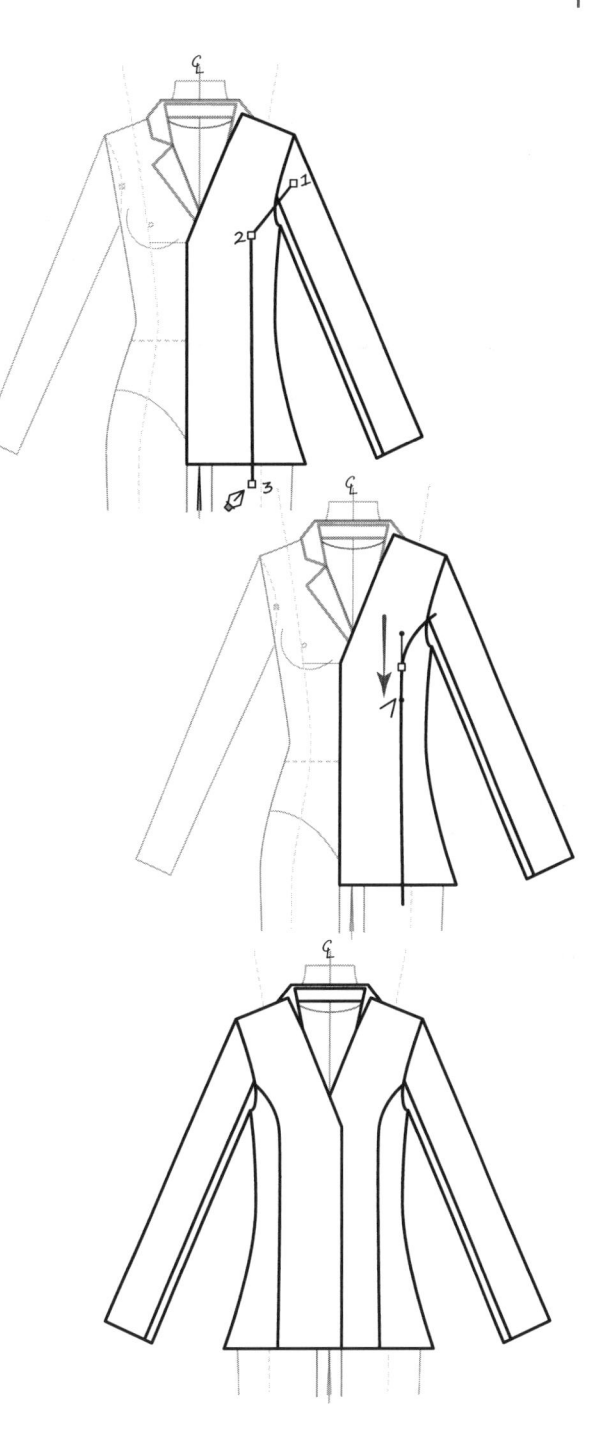

Lesson 5: Skirts and Blazers

In the Layers Panel, drag the layer with the Lapels on top of the Blazer front layer.

Unlock the Lapel layer.
Use the **Rectangle tool** to draw a rectangle that covers the open neck line. Fill with gray.

Right click >Arrange>Send to back.

Now you can add details like pockets and buttons. But if you can wait until we cover Symbols in lesson Six, it will be much faster and easier.

Approach the back view of the Blazer the same way we did the shirt back.
Remove any unneeded details. Unite the back with the collar and add back details.

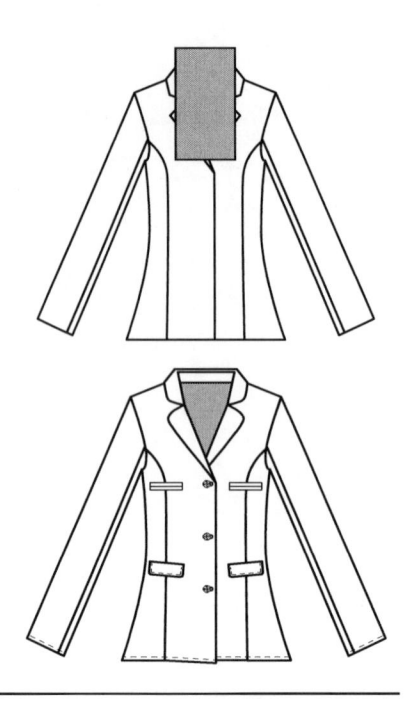

adobe® for fashion : illustrator CS5 | 91

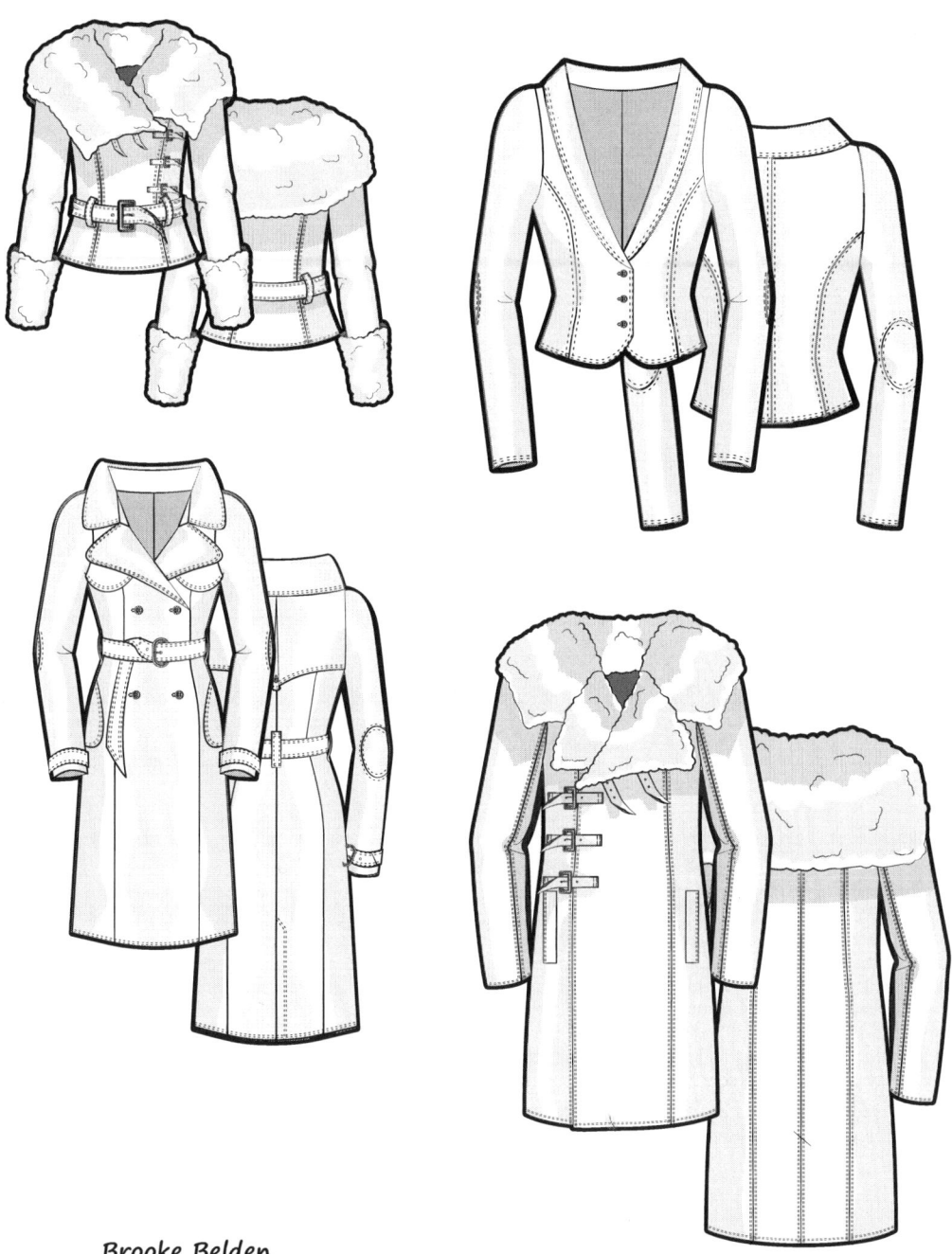

Brooke Belden
Art Institute of Ca-Hollywood
http://www.coroflot.com/brooke_e_belden

lesson six

BRUSHES

There are 5 different types of brushes available in Illustrator:
- Pattern Brush
- Art Brush
- Scatter Brush
- Caligraphic Brush
- Bristle Brush

BRUSH TIP SHAPE

PATTERN BRUSH

A **Pattern Brush** is made up of a brush tip shape that is repeated in a linear pattern. The shape can be as simple as a circle or as elaborate as a piece of lace.

An **Art Brush** uses the brush tip shape and stretches it along the entire length of the path.

ART BRUSH

A **Scatter Brush** allows you to scatter the brush tip shape by adjusting the size, rotation, spacing and distance from the original path.

SCATTER BRUSH

A **Caligraphic Brush** is the equivalent to using a traditional calligraphy pen.

CALIGRAPHIC BRUSH

A **Bristle Brush** is the newest addition to Illustrator and is used to mimic the look of and actual paint brush.

BRISTLE BRUSH

Let's focus on the **Pattern Brush** since it is the one we will be using most often. We will be using Pattern brushes to create all types of stitching, gathers, ruffles, trims, cording and zippers.

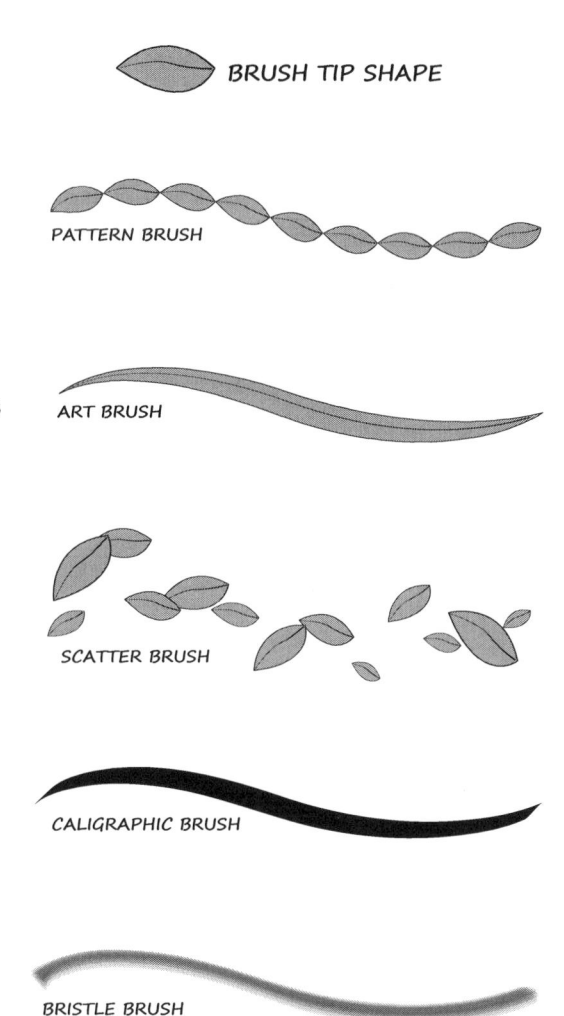

Lesson 6: Brushes and Symbols and Jeans

You can find the **Brush Panel** in the panel dock.

Illustrator® comes with an assortment of brushes that can be accessed through the **Brush Libraries menu** in the **Brushes Panel**. Many of them are useful but not fashion specific.

Luckily the people at Adobe® realized we may not want to be limited to their selection of brushes and have included the option of letting us design our own.

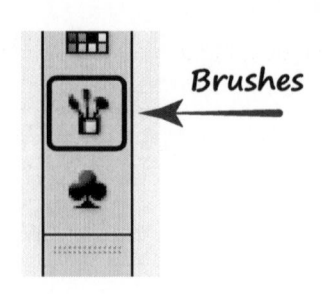

Brushes

Brushes Panel

APPLYING BRUSHES
Just Select the path and click on a Brush from the **Brushes Panel** to apply.

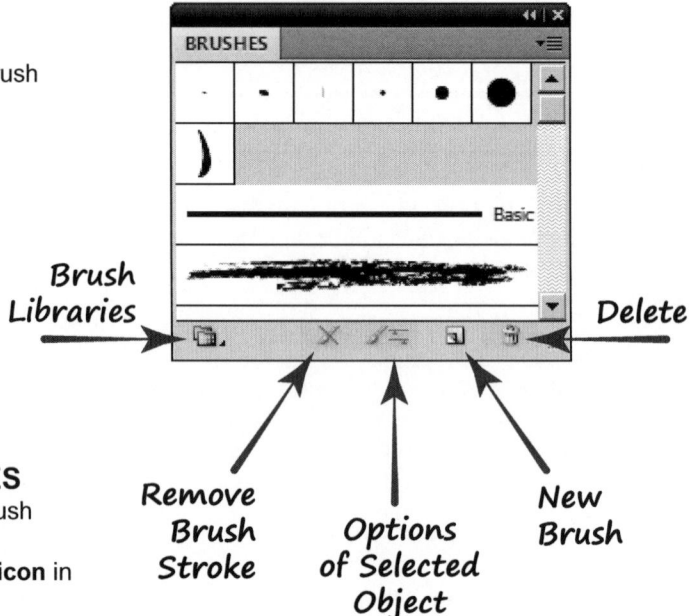

Brush Libraries

Delete

Remove Brush Stroke

Options of Selected Object

New Brush

REMOVING BRUSH STROKES
Select the Path or Object with the Brush Stroke.
Click on the **Remove Brush Stroke icon** in the **Brushes Panel**.

CREATING BRUSHES
Creating brushes is very straight forward.
Just draw the brush tip shape,
Select it and click on the **New Brush icon**.
Select type of brush click OK.
Give it a name and click OK.

DOUBLE NEEDLE TOP STITCH

Let's make a double needle top stitch brush. Start by using the **Line Segment tool** so we can control the size of the stitch. You can find it in the **Tool Bar**.

Double click on the **Line Segment Tool** to open the options box.
Set the LENGTH to 2pt
Set the ANGLE to 0
Click OK

Use the **Stroke Panel**
to change the **Weight to .25pt**
and use **Round Caps**
(*This is so they will match the stitches we made for the t-shirt using Dashed line*)

Copy (**Ctrl+C** /*Cmd+C*)
Paste in Front (**Ctrl+F** /*Cmd+F*)
Use the **Down Arrow** to nudge it down 2 clicks.

Select both line segments and click on the **New Brush** in the **Brushes Panel**.

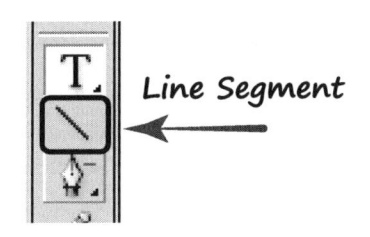

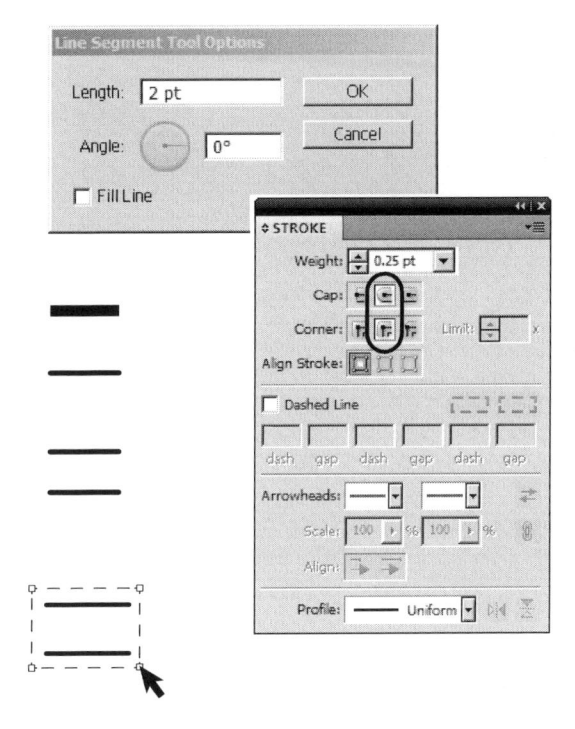

Lesson 6: Brushes and Symbols and Jeans

The **New Brush window** will open, select **Pattern Brush** and click OK.

The **Pattern Brush Options** box will open. Type in a brush name.

Click OK.

Now we can try out our new brush. Draw a path with the **Pen tool**

Click on your brush in the **Brushes Panel** to apply.

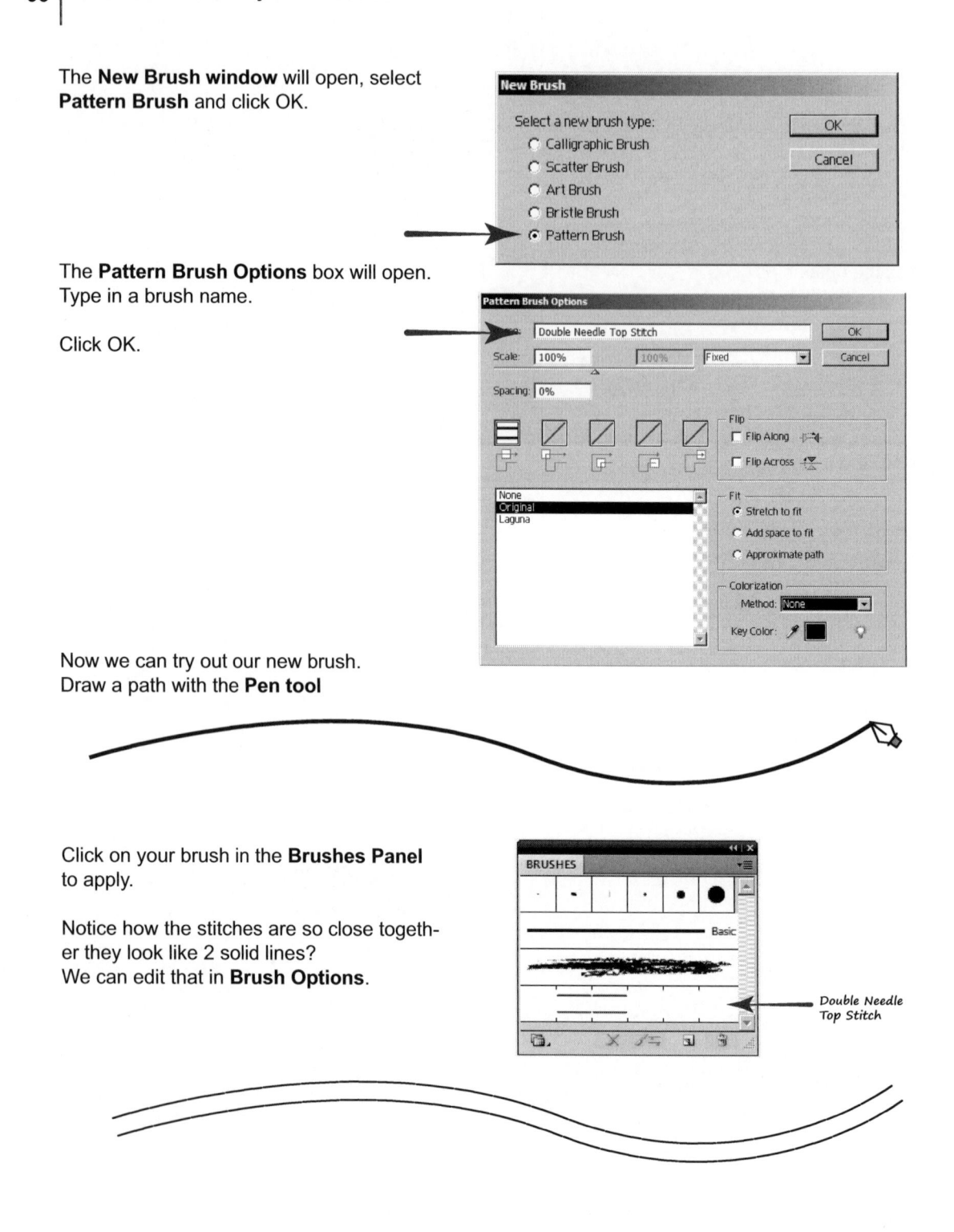

Notice how the stitches are so close together they look like 2 solid lines?
We can edit that in **Brush Options**.

Double Needle Top Stitch

EDITING BRUSHES

Select the path with the brush stroke.
Double click on the **Brush** in the **Brush panel** to open the **Pattern Brush Options**.

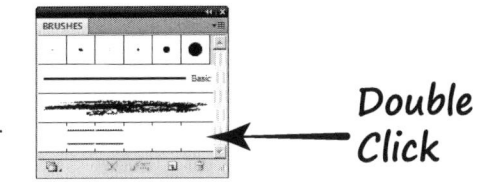

Double Click

Change the **Spacing to 50%**
to add space between the stitches.

Click OK.

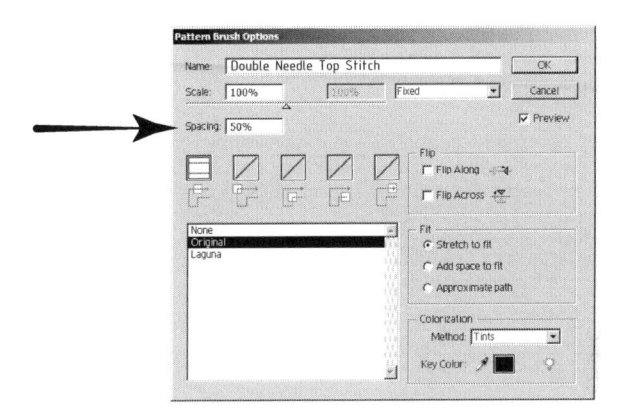

A **Brush Change Alert** will open
Select **Apply to Strokes.**

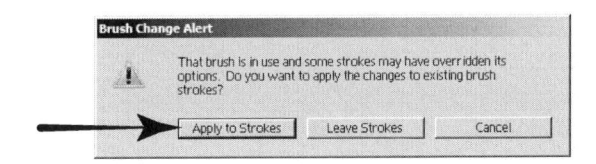

Now the bush should look like this.

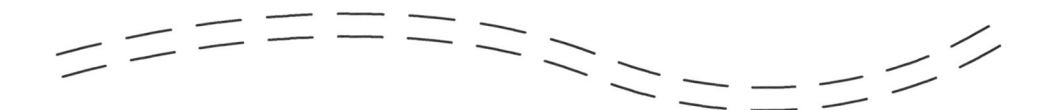

The editing we just did was a **universal edit**. That means it will be applied every time that brush is used.

But what if you only want to make changes to a single instance of that brush?

EDITING A SINGLE BRUSH INSTANCE

Select the path with the brush stroke you would like to edit.

Click on **Options of Selected Object** at the bottom of the **Brushes Panel**.

Options of Selected Object

It will open **Stroke Options**.
Make changes and click OK.

This time it will only change the features of the brush instance you have selected.

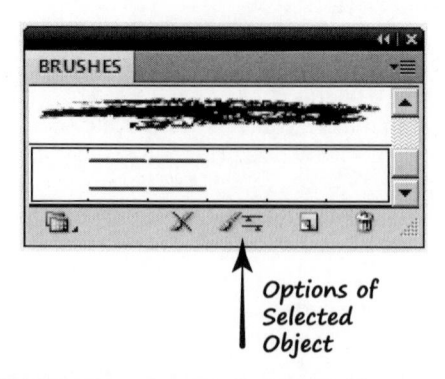

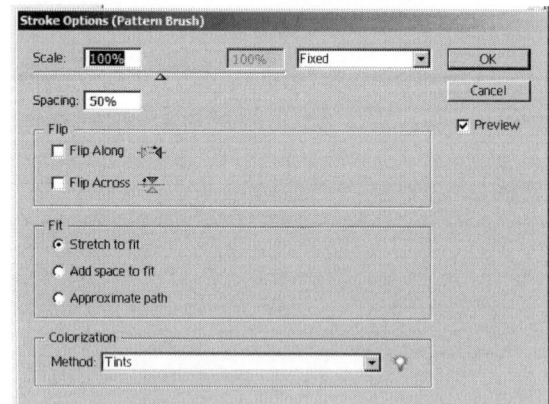

CHANGING BRUSH COLOR

Since Brushes are applied to strokes, you must change the **Stroke color** to change the brush color. But first you need to set the **Brush Options** correctly.

Double click on the Brush in the **Brush panel** to open the **Brush Options**.

Change the **Colorization Method to Tints**. Click OK.

Now the **brush color** will change to match the selected stroke color.

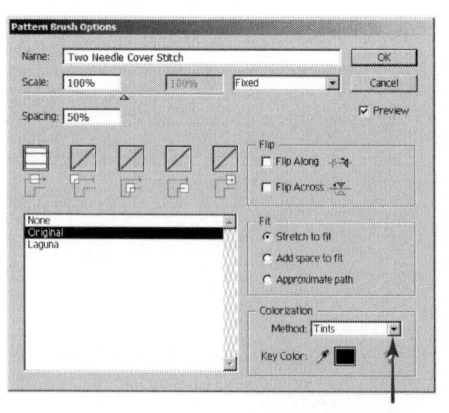

Colorization

SAVING BRUSHES

Another great feature of Illustrator® is that the brushes save along with the file they are being used in. Just save the file and the brushes save with it. I recommend making a folder called "Brushes and Symbols" where you save all your brush files. That way you can always locate them when you need them.

LOADING BRUSHES

You can load brushes from one file into another through the **Brush Panel**.

Click on **Brush Libraries** and select **Other Library**.

Navigate to your "Brushes and Symbols" folder and select the brush file you saved. Click OK.

A new **Brush Panel** will open with the brushes from that file. Click on any brushes you want and they will appear in the **Brush Panel** of the current document.

You can also **Copy** and **Paste** an object with a Brush applied to it from one file to another.

Select the object with the Brush
Copy it (**Ctrl+C**/*Cmd+C*)
Open a new file
Paste (**Ctrl+V**/*Cmd+V*)

The **Brush** will appear in the **Brush panel** of the file you pasted it into.

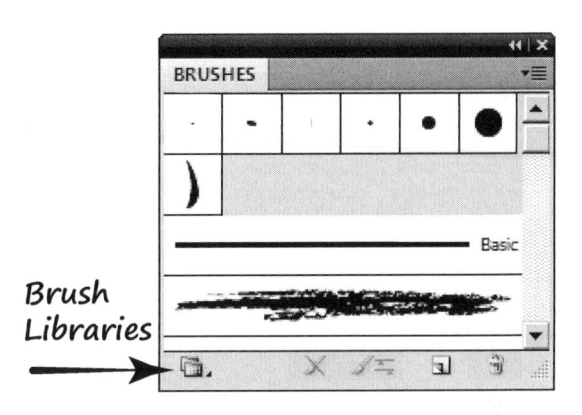

Brush Libraries

Lesson 6: Brushes and Symbols and Jeans

ZIG ZAG
Double click on the **Line Segment tool**
and draw a line that is **2pts** and **90°**
Set the **Stroke to .25**
Select **Round Caps** and **Round Joins**
Copy (**Ctrl+C** /*Cmd+C*)
Paste in Front (**Ctrl+F** /*Cmd+F*)
Arrow right a couple of clicks
Direct Select the **2 top Anchor points**
Right Click> Average> Both
Select the stitch and Click on **New Brush**
in the **Brushes Panel**.
Select **Pattern Brush** and Click OK.
In the second window Click OK.
Draw a path and apply the brush.

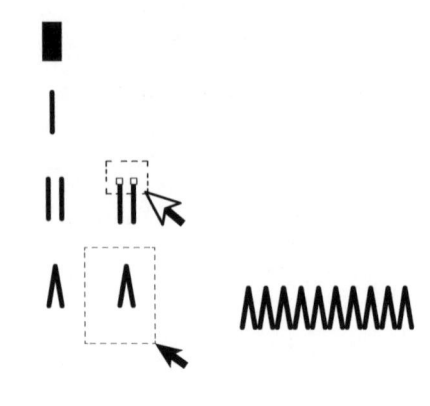

OVERLOCK
Double click on the **Line Segment tool**
and draw a line that is **2pts** and **0°**
Set the **Stroke to .25**
Select **Round Caps** and **Round Joins**
Copy (**Ctrl+C** /*Cmd+C*)
Paste in Front (**Ctrl+F** /*Cmd+F*)
Arrow down a couple of clicks.

To draw the loop Click once on the page to deselect the bottom stitch.

With the **Pen tool**
Click the left end of the stitch (**1**)
Click and drag to the right (**2**)
Click to close (**1**)

Select the entire stitch and make a **New Brush**.
Select **Pattern** and click OK.
In the second window click OK.
Draw a path and apply the brush.

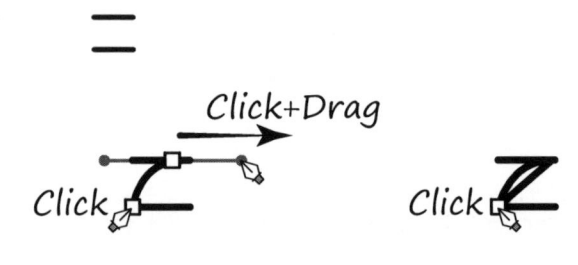

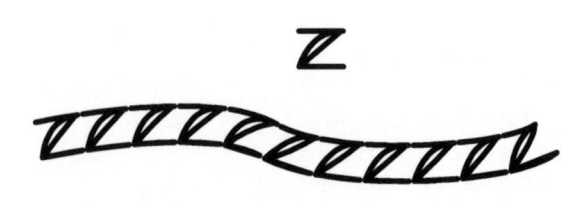

OPEN ZIPPER
Double click on the **Rectangle tool**.
Width **.75pt**
Height **3pt**
Set the **Fill to white and the stroke to .25**
with **Round Caps** and **Joins**.

Select it and make a new **Pattern Brush**.
Name it **Open Zipper**
Set the **spacing to 100%**
click OK.
Draw a path and apply the brush.

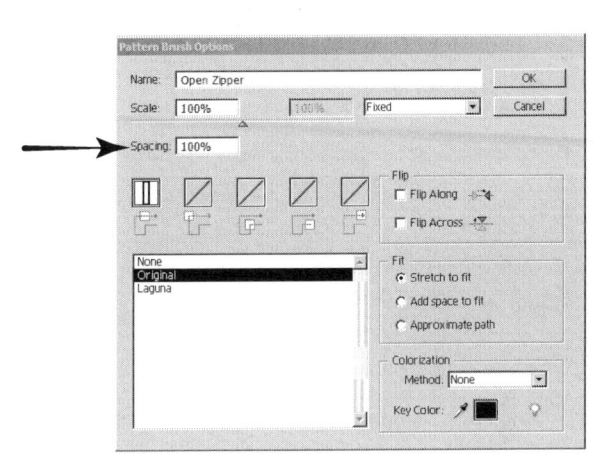

CLOSED ZIPPER
Draw a **Rectangle**
Width **.75pt**
Height **3pt**
Set the **Fill to White and the stroke to .25**
with **Round Caps** and **Joins**.

Copy (**Ctrl+C** /*Cmd+C*)
Paste in Front (**Ctrl+F** /*Cmd+F*)
Nudge it over and down.
Select both rectangles and
make a **New Pattern Brush**.
Click OK.
Draw a path and apply the brush.

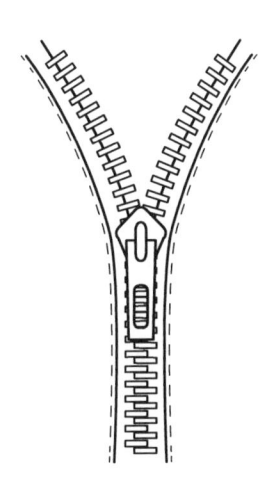

Lesson 6: Brushes and Symbols and Jeans

SYMBOLS

Symbols are libraries of objects that can be saved and accessed when needed. They can be moved, scaled, rotated, reflected and even edited. A big benefit of using symbols is the ability to replace symbol instances in just a few clicks.

For example: You have a line sheet with 80 buttons scattered throughout. The buttons are no longer available and need to be replaced with a new style. Instead of selecting each individual button one at a time you can select one symbol instance and let Illustrator find and replace the rest. It's a big time saver.

You can find **Symbols** in the Panel dock or the Window drop down menu.

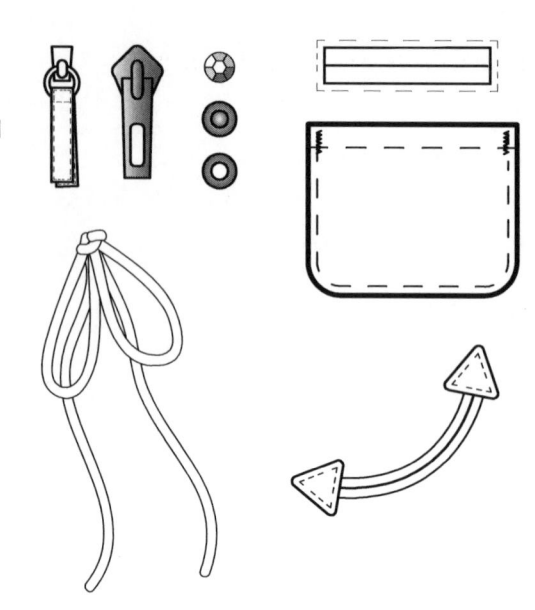

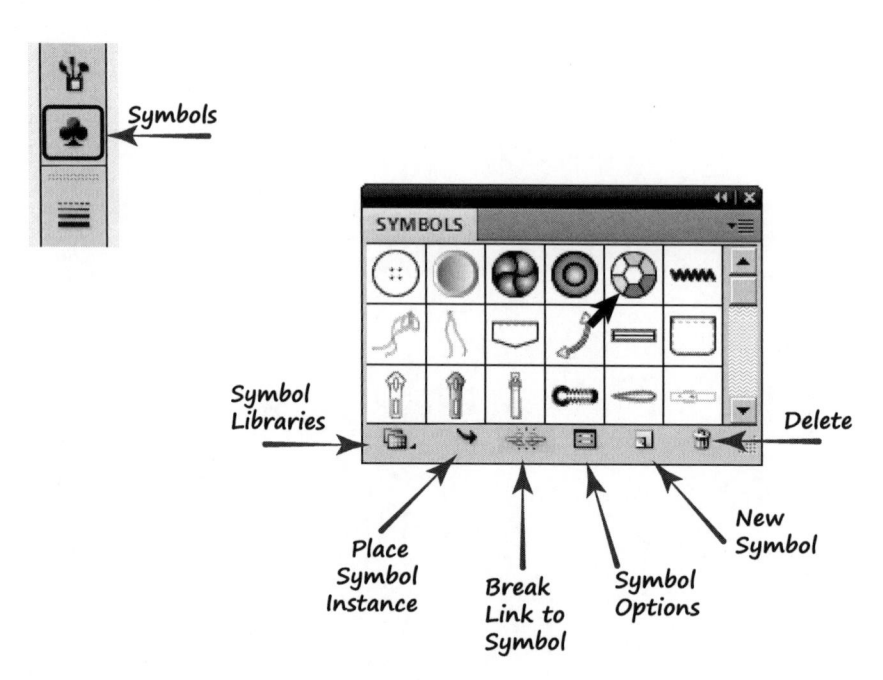

Symbols

Symbol Libraries

Delete

Place Symbol Instance

Break Link to Symbol

Symbol Options

New Symbol

USING SYMBOLS

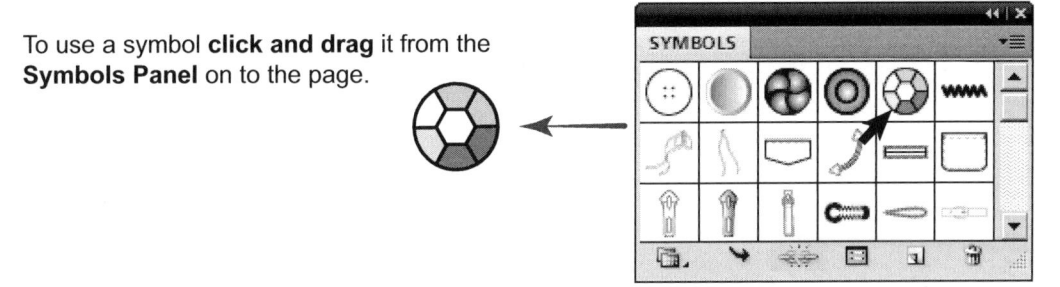

To use a symbol **click and drag** it from the **Symbols Panel** on to the page.

CREATING SYMBOLS

Select the object you would like to turn into a symbol. Click on the **New Symbol Icon** in the **Symbols Panel**.

New Symbol

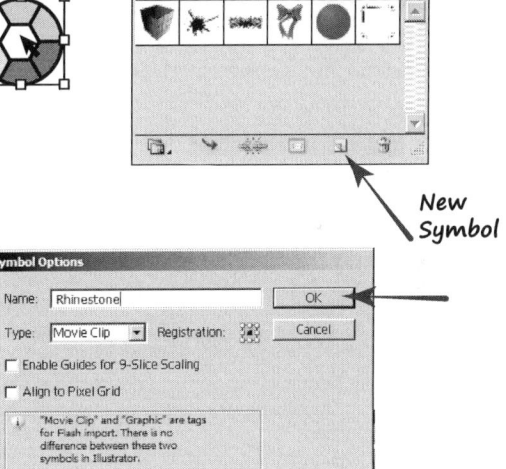

When the **Symbols Options** window opens name the symbol and Click OK.
Now your symbol is in the **Symbols panel**.

EDITING SYMBOLS

UNIVERSAL EDITS
To universally edit the symbol **double click** on the symbol in the **Symbols panel**. Make any changes you want and then **double click** on the page to return it to the **Symbols panel**.

Now all existing instances of that symbol will have been edited and any instance from now on will be the new version of the symbol.

EDITING A SINGLE INSTANCE
Select the **Symbol**.
Right click and **Break Link to Symbol**.

Now you can make changes without effecting any other instance of that symbol. But the object is no longer a symbol.
To make it a symbol again click on the **New Symbol Icon**, Name it and click OK.

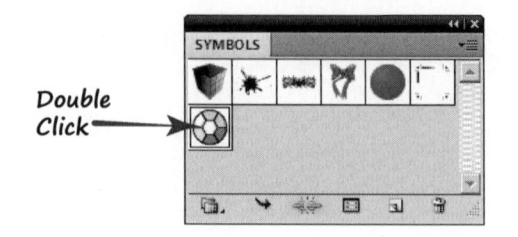

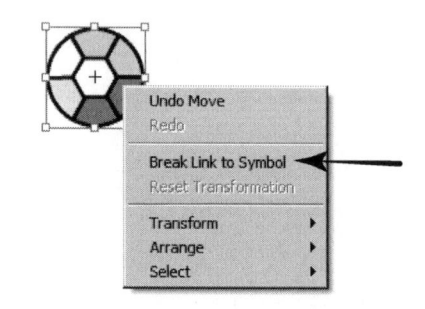

REPLACING SYMBOLS

Select one of the symbol instances of the symbol you would like to replace.

From the **Menu bar**
Select >Same >Symbol Instance
This will select every one of these symbol instances on your page.

In the **Control Panel** you will see a drop down called **Replace**.

Select a new symbol from the drop down and all of the selected symbols will be replaced with the new symbol.

Yep, it's that easy.

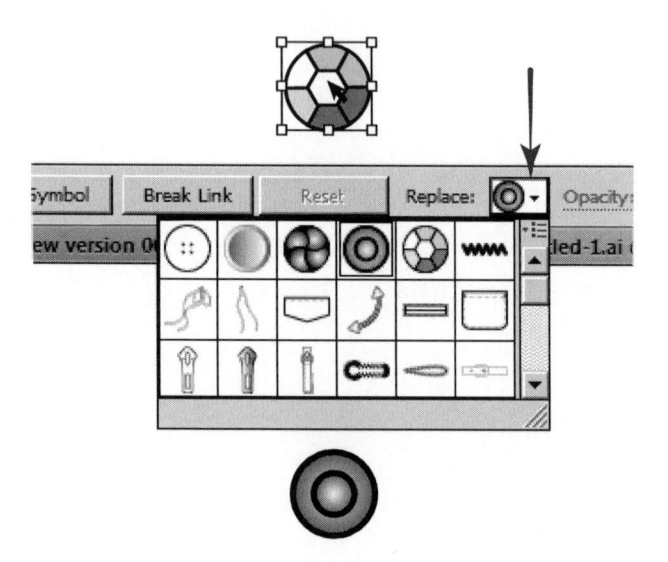

RIVET

- Draw a **4pt** diameter **circle**.
- Change the **Stroke to .25 wt**.
- **Double click** on the **Scale tool** type in **50%** and **Copy.**
- Select both circles and Fill with a **Radial Gradient**
- Make new Symbol

EYELET

- Draw a **4pt** diameter **circle**.
- Change the **Stroke to .25 wt**.
- **Double click** on the **Scale tool** type in **50%** and **Copy.**
- Select both circles and
- **Pathfinder >Exclude.**
- Fill with a **Radial Gradient.**
- Make new Symbol

BUTTON

- Draw a circle.
- Change the **Stroke to .5**
- Draw a tiny circle for the hole with a **black Fill and no Stroke**.
- **Copy**
- **Paste in Font**
- **Arrow down**
- Select both holes and **Group**
- **Copy**
- **Paste in Front**
- **Arrow right**
- Select all four holes and **Group**
- Select the grouped holes and the button.
- **Align Horizontal Center**
- **Align Vertical Center**
- Make new Symbol

You can make additional versions by adding smaller circles for detail.

FANCY BUTTON

- Draw a circle.
- Fill with a **Linear Gradient**
- Change the **Stroke to None**.
- **Double click** on the **Scale tool** type in **80%** and **Copy.**
- **Double click** on **Reflect** select **Vertical** and OK.

Make new Symbol

This fancy button comes from my friend Chris Schiotis. Thanks Chris!

ZIPPER PULL

A zipper pull is really much easier then it looks. It is made up of three basic shapes that you already know how to draw.

With the **Rounded Rectangle tool**
Click once on the page
Width 16pt
Height 16pt
Corner Radius 3pt. Click OK

Direct Select the bottom **Anchor Points**.
Nudge the with the **Down Arrow**.

Draw a **12pt x 39pt Rectangle**.
Direct Select the **bottom right anchor point** and **nudge Left**.
Direct Select the **bottom left anchor point** and **nudge Right** to taper the bottom.

Nudge Left   *Nudge Right*

Draw a **5pt x 15pt Rounded Rectangle**.
Place it on top of the big rectangle.
Select both and **Align** center.
Pathfinder>Exclude
to punch out the hole.

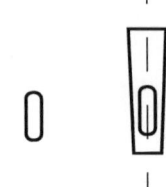

Draw a **3.5pt x 12pt Rounded Rectangle**.

Assemble as shown
Select all and **Align** Center.

Scale to 25%

Make a Symbol.

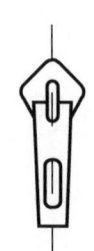

POCKET FLAP
Draw a **Rectangle**.
Add an **Anchor Point** at center bottom.
Nudge it with the **Down Arrow**.
Add a row of stitching.
Save as a **Symbol**.

POCKET
Draw a **Rounded Rectangle**.
Draw a **Path** with the **Pen tool**.
Select both, **Pathfinder>Divide**
Delete top.
Object>Path>Offset Path
Offset -1.5 or -2pts.
Direct Select the top segment and **Delete**.
Draw top stitching path and apply stitches.
Add **Bar Tacks** (page111).
Save as Symbol.

WELT POCKET
Draw a **Rectangle**.
Object>Path>Offset path.
Offset 1 or 2 pts.
Apply Stitches.
Draw the center line.
Save as Symbol.

Lesson 6: Brushes and Symbols and Jeans

DRAWSTRINGS

EXPAND

Click on the **Pencil tool**
Set the Stroke to Black
and the Fill to NONE

The stroke weight will determine the width of the drawstring so try a 2 or 3 pt. stroke and use round caps for rounded ends.

Go ahead and freehand the elements of the bow. Two loops and two strings

Select all of the bow elements.
In the Menu Bar select **Object>Expand**
Make sure that **Stroke is checked**
and **Fill is NOT checked**.
Click OK.

*By using **Expand** you have just turned a Stroke into an object.*

Select all the pieces and change the Fill to white and the Stroke to .5 black.

Move the bow pieces so they meet at the knot point.

With the **Pencil Tool** draw a small knot shape.

Hold the **Alt** (*Opt*) key while drawing to close the path.

Give the knot a white Fill and .5 black Stroke.
Drag it on top of the bow.
Select entire bow and **Right click Group**.

Make it a Symbol.

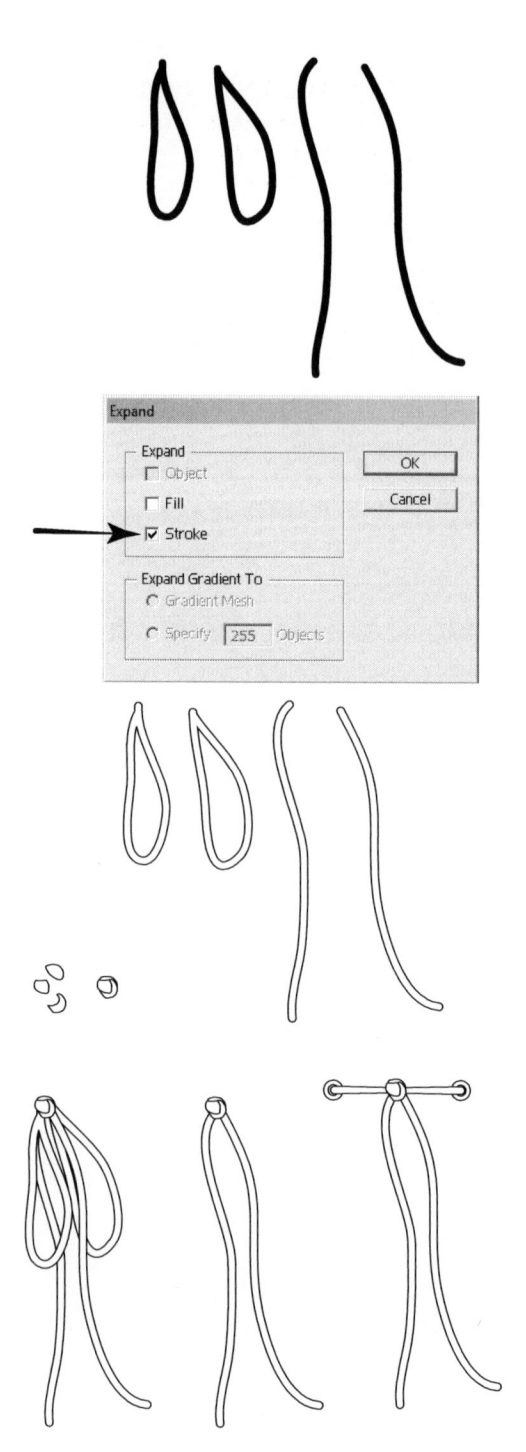

RIBBONS

CALLIGRAPHIC BRUSH
To make a ribbon you can use a **Calligraphic brush**. You can find them in the top section of the **Brushes Panel**.

Draw a path with the **Pencil tool** and apply one of the **Calligraphic brushes**.

Object> Expand Appearance

Change the **Fill to white**
Change the **Stroke to black** and the line **weight to .5** for a more delicate bow.

Assemble the pieces and you're done.

Now save it as a Symbol.

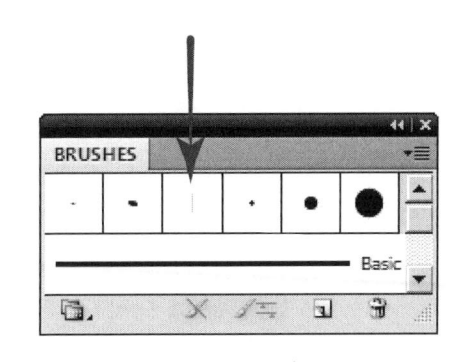

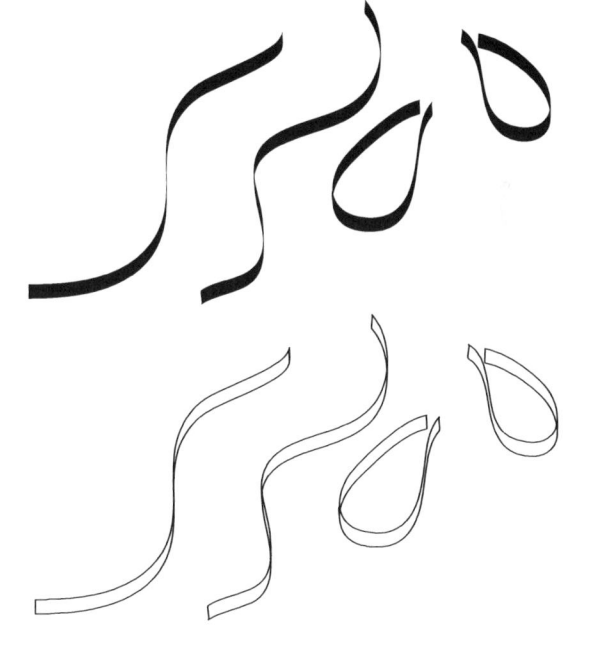

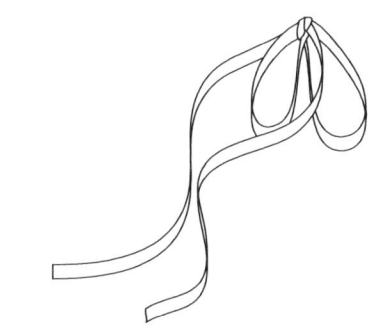

Lesson 6: Brushes and Symbols and Jeans

THE BLOB BRUSH

Now that you understand how to use **Expand** I want to show you an even faster way...using the **Blob Brush**.

The **Blob Brush** isn't actually a brush - It's a tool and it's located in the Tool Bar.

Select the **Blob Brush**.
You can make the brush larger or smaller by using the **bracket** keys **[ ]** .
Set the Stroke to Black
and the Fill to NONE
Adjust the size of the brush to your flat.
*The color of of the **Blob Brush** is determined by the **Stroke** Color.*

Now draw the same two loops and strings as before. *The **Blob brush** automatically draws shapes not paths. This saves you the step of **Expanding**.*

Select all the pieces and give them a white Fill and black Stroke
Change the line weight of .5

Assemble them and you're done.

Now save it as a **Symbol**.

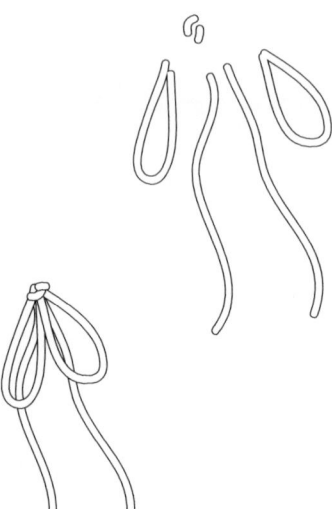

BAR TACKS

Bar tacks are short sections of Zig Zag stitches used to reinforce stress areas on a garment like belt loops and pockets.

They can be created using the **ZIG ZAG Effect**.

Draw a 5 pt line segment with the **Line Segment tool**.
Set the wt. to .25, Round Caps
black Stroke and a Fill of None.

In the **Menu Bar** click on
Effect>Distort and Transform>Zig Zag
Check the Preview box
Check **Relative** and set the **size to 2 or 3%**.
Adjust the **Ridges per Segment**
Click OK.
Save as a Symbol.

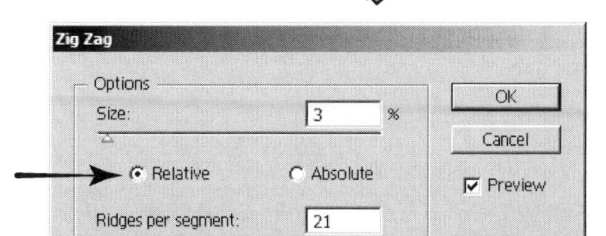

RIPS AND TEARS

Draw a shape for the rip using the **Pen tool**.
Select it and give it a weight of .25, black Stroke and a Fill of None.

Effect>Distort and Transform>Roughen
Check the Preview box
Check **Relative** and drag the slider until the height looks appropriate.
Adjust the **Detail slider**.
Click OK.

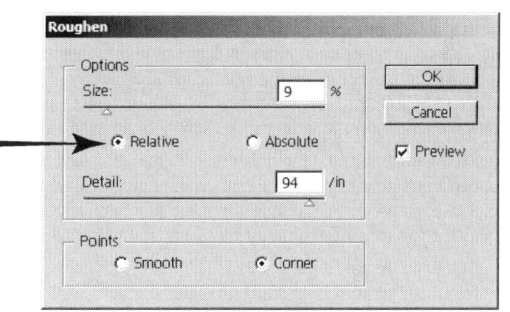

BUTTONHOLES

Using the **Rectangle Tool**, draw a rectangle that is slightly longer than your button. Give it a black **Stroke and a Fill of None**. Stroke weight should be .25 with Round Caps and Round Joins.

Select the rectangle.
In the **Menu Bar** click on
Effect>Distort and Transform>Zig Zag
to open the options box.
Check Preview so you can watch the effect as you create it.

Check Relative and drag the slider until the stitch height looks appropriate. (**4%** or **5%**)

Adjust the **Ridges Per Segment** slider to taste. Click OK

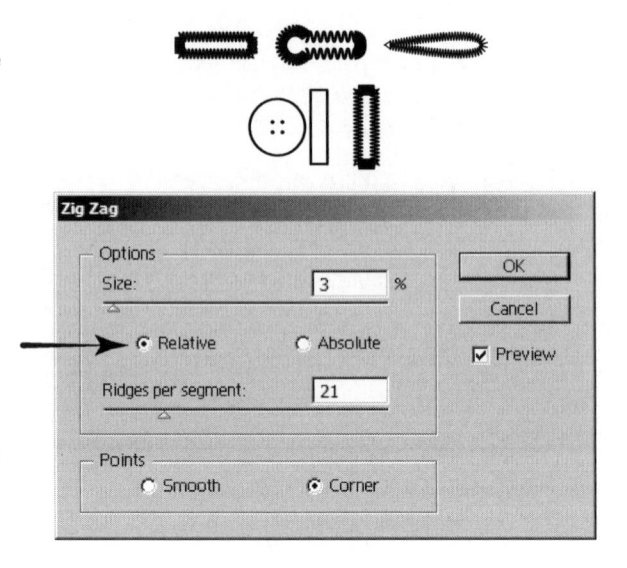

KEYHOLE BUTTONHOLES
There are two different styles of keyhole buttonholes we can make.

With the **Pen tool** click at **1**.
- **Click and drag straight down** at **2**.
- Click back at **1** to close.
- Change the Stroke weight to .5 Round Caps and Round Joins.
- Apply **Zig Zag Effect**.
- Save as Symbol.

Using the **Rounded rectangle tool** draw a rounded rectangle.
Draw a circle with the **Ellipse tool**.
- Select both objects and **Pathfinder>Unite**
- Change the Stroke weight to .5 Round Caps and Round Joins.
- Apply **Zig Zag Effect**.
- Save as Symbol.

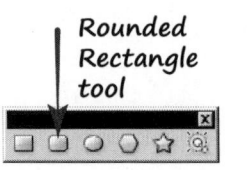

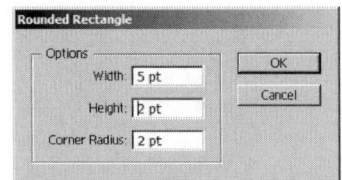

DRAWING JEANS

Using the **Pen tool**
- Start at the outer waist (**1**)
- Click at the hip (**2**)
- Click at the outer hem (**3**)
- Click at the inner hem (**4**)
- Click at the crotch (**5**)
- Click at the center front waist (**6**)
- and back at (**1**) to close the path.

Use the **Convert Anchor Point tool** to curve the point at the hip (**2**).

Select the leg and **Reflect** it.

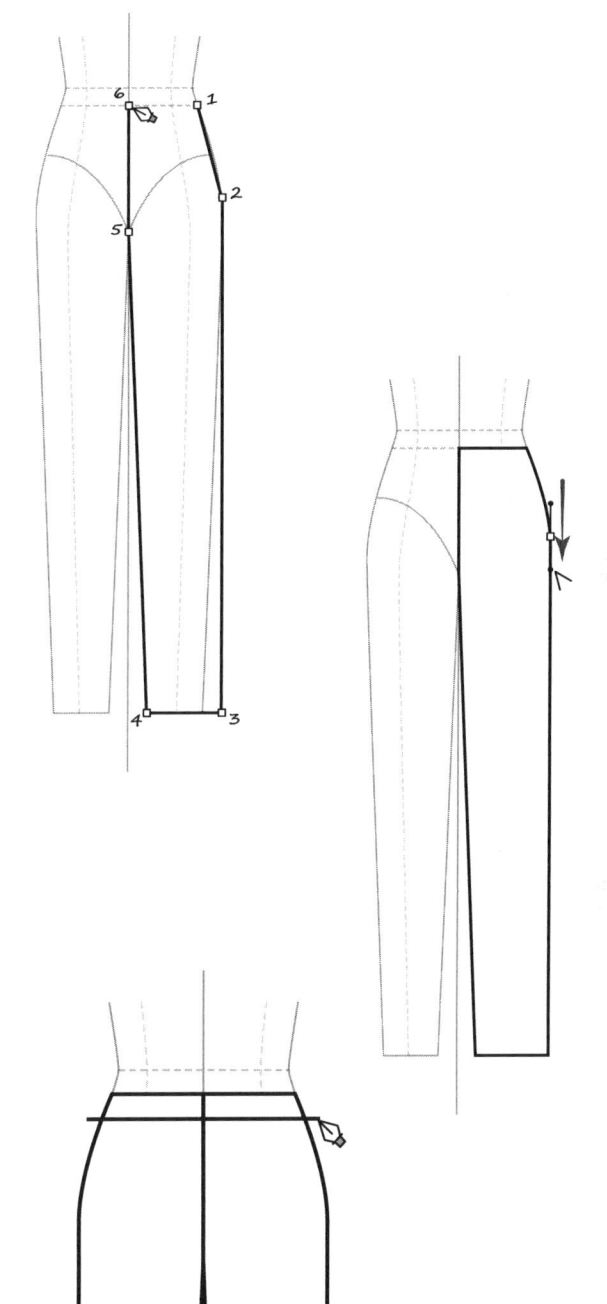

WAISTBAND
Draw a path to separate the waistband from the rest of the jean.
Marque select the path along with both legs and use **Pathfinder Divide**
Right click and **Ungroup**.

Lesson 6: Brushes and Symbols and Jeans

Draw the front pocket on one side
Select it and **reflect**.

Add the **crotch break** (a short diagonal line that indicates the location of the crotch)
Do not draw a "V" shape.

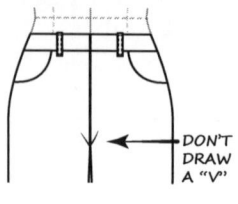

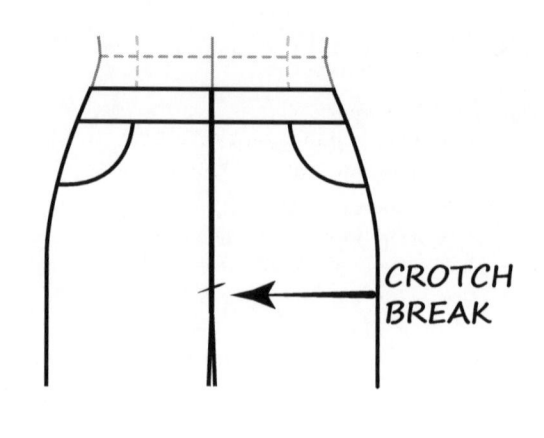

Add stitching using the **double needle top stitch brush**.

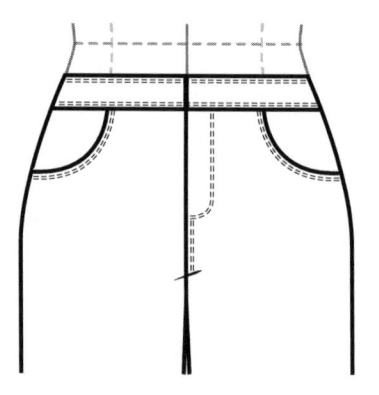

BELT LOOPS
Draw a rectangle
Add stitching to each side
Add a bar tack at top and bottom
Select it and make a **new symbol**

Place belt loops and rivets.
Add any other details you need.

Select all and **Group**.

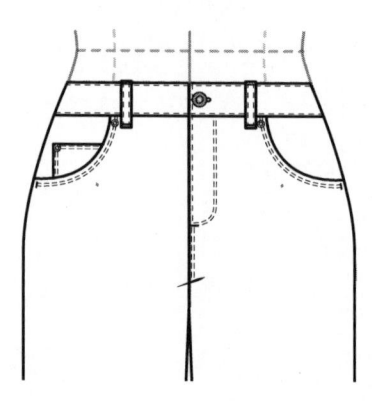

THE BACK VIEW

Reflect the Front View
Double click to enter **Isolation Mode**.
Select and **Delete** any details not needed on the back.
Draw a slightly larger crotch break for the back view.
Do not draw cheeks.

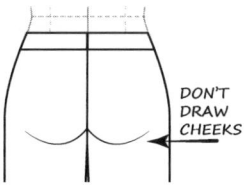

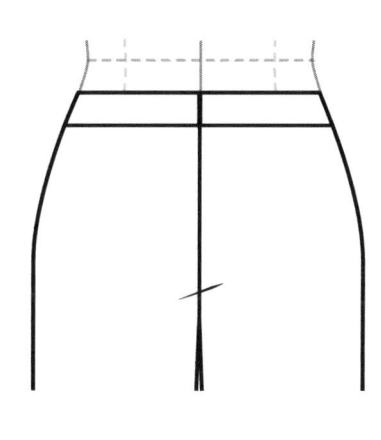

Select the two sides of the waistband and use **Pathfinder** to **Unite** them together.

Add yoke using the **Pen tool**.
Use **Pathfinder Divide** to separate.

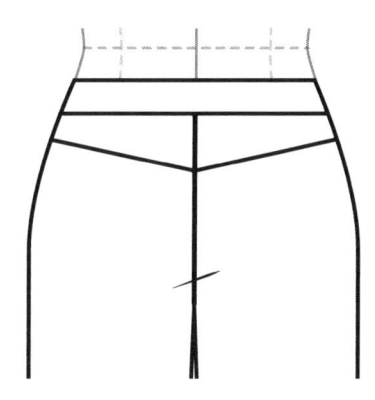

POCKETS
Draw a rectangle.
Direct Select the bottom right corner and nudge it toward the center.
Do the same for the bottom left corner.
Add a point at bottom center and nudge it down to create a point.

To add stitching
Select the Pocket.
Object> Path>Offset Path
Try an Offset of -3 and adjust if needed.
Click OK.
Apply the **double needle top stitch brush**.
Add **Rivets** or **Bar Tacks** and **Group**.

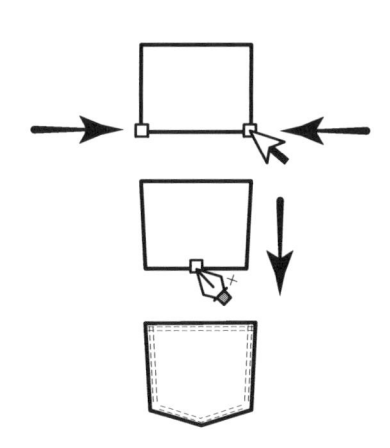

Lesson 6: Brushes and Symbols and Jeans

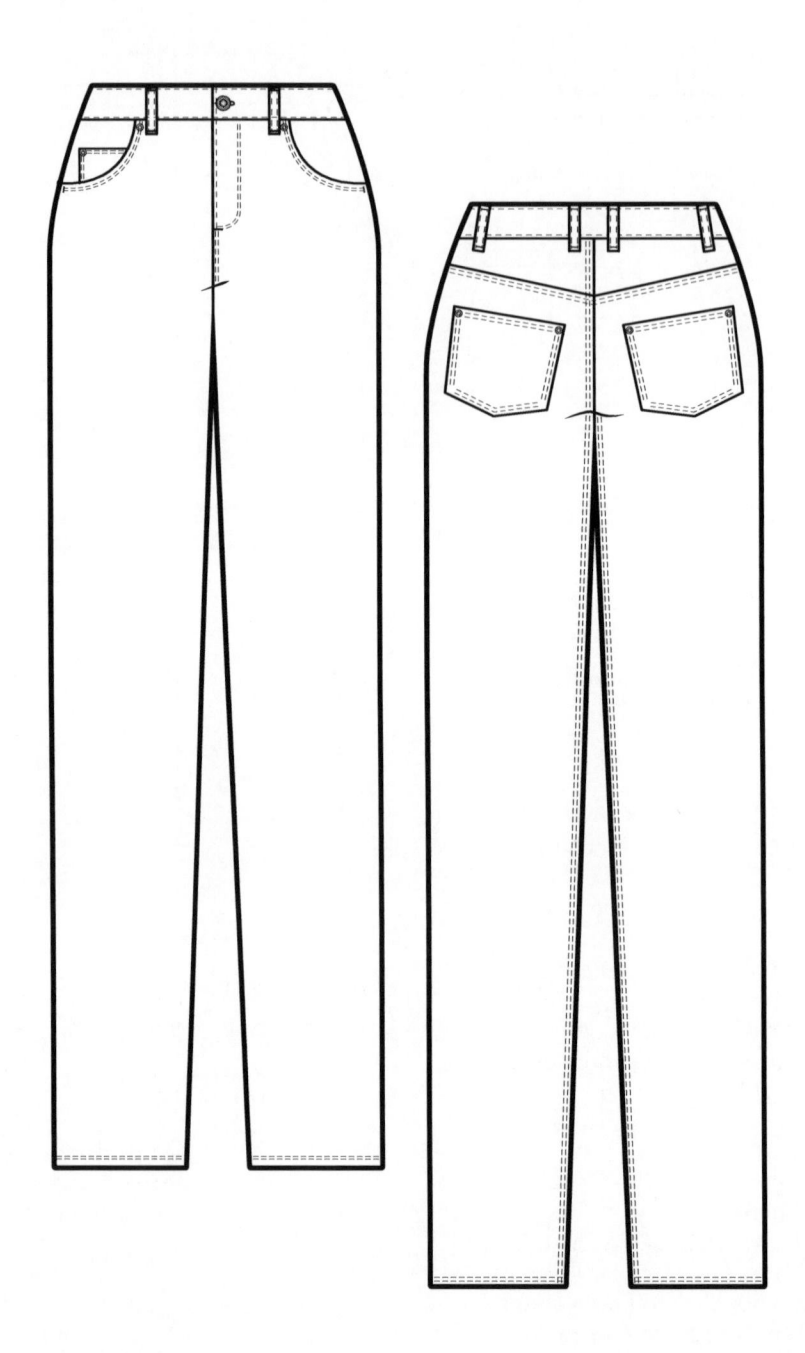

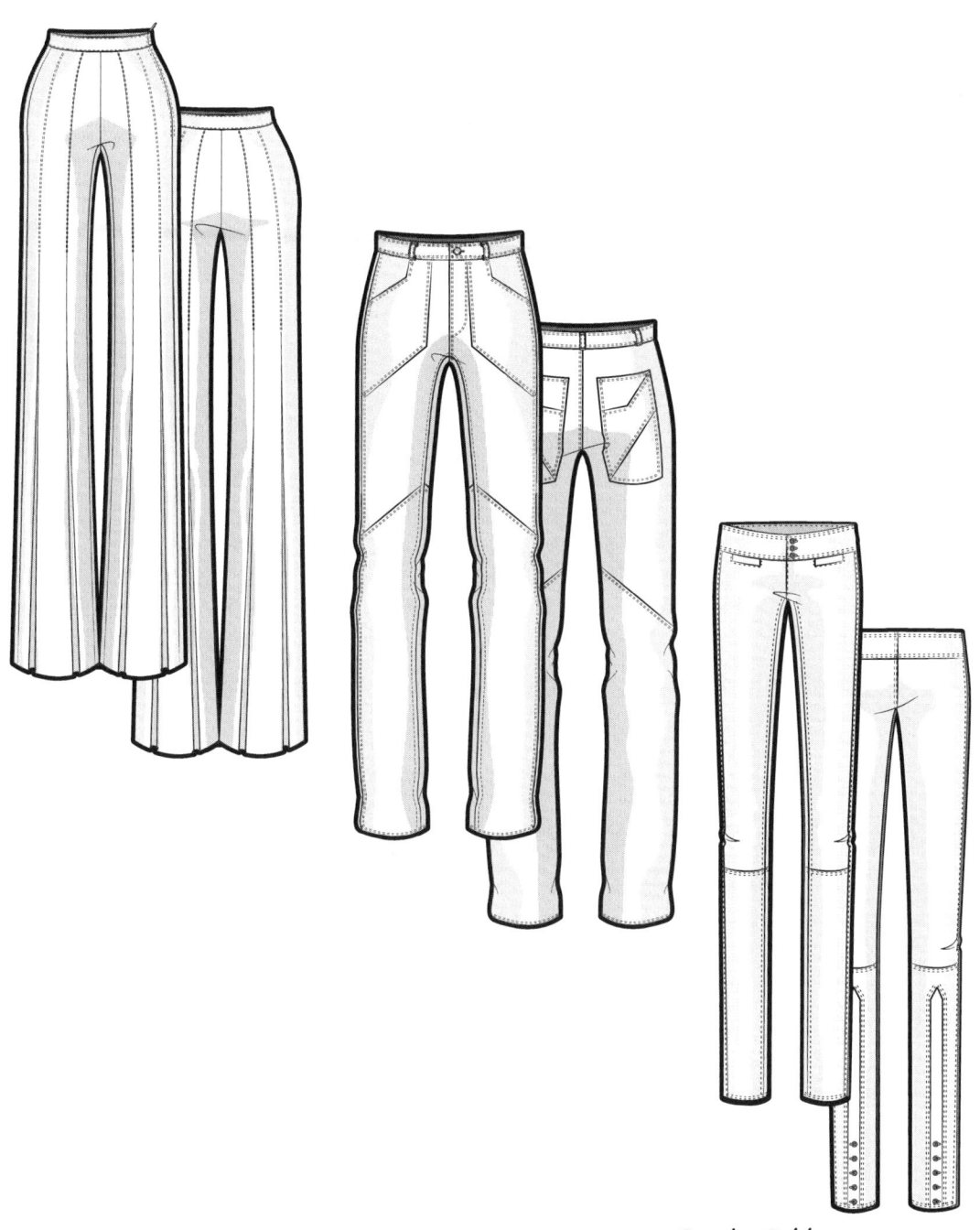

Brooke Belden
Art Institute of Ca-Hollywood
http://www.coroflot.com/brooke_e_belden

lesson seven

NOTATIONS FOR TECH PACKS

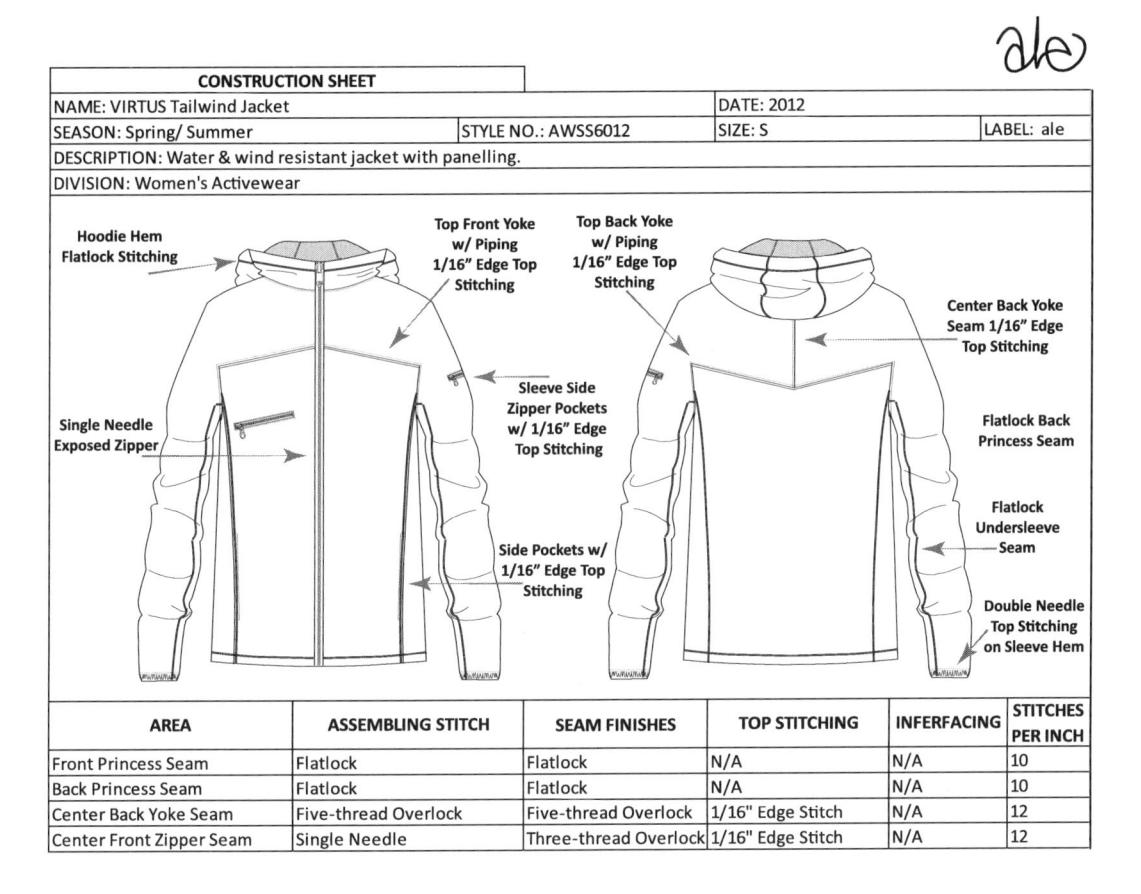

CONSTRUCTION SHEET

NAME: VIRTUS Tailwind Jacket DATE: 2012
SEASON: Spring/ Summer STYLE NO.: AWSS6012 SIZE: S LABEL: ale
DESCRIPTION: Water & wind resistant jacket with panelling.
DIVISION: Women's Activewear

Callouts:
- Hoodie Hem Flatlock Stitching
- Top Front Yoke w/ Piping 1/16" Edge Top Stitching
- Top Back Yoke w/ Piping 1/16" Edge Top Stitching
- Center Back Yoke Seam 1/16" Edge Top Stitching
- Sleeve Side Zipper Pockets w/ 1/16" Edge Top Stitching
- Single Needle Exposed Zipper
- Flatlock Back Princess Seam
- Flatlock Undersleeve Seam
- Side Pockets w/ 1/16" Edge Top Stitching
- Double Needle Top Stitching on Sleeve Hem

AREA	ASSEMBLING STITCH	SEAM FINISHES	TOP STITCHING	INFERFACING	STITCHES PER INCH
Front Princess Seam	Flatlock	Flatlock	N/A	N/A	10
Back Princess Seam	Flatlock	Flatlock	N/A	N/A	10
Center Back Yoke Seam	Five-thread Overlock	Five-thread Overlock	1/16" Edge Stitch	N/A	12
Center Front Zipper Seam	Single Needle	Three-thread Overlock	1/16" Edge Stitch	N/A	12

Amber Esparza
Art Institute of Ca-Hollywood
http://www.coroflot.com/ale_esparza

Lesson 7: Tech packs and Time savers

DRAWING ARROWS

Draw a path with the **Pen Tool**

Open the **Stroke Panel** and set the line weight to .5pt.

Click on the **Arrowheads** drop down and select one of the available arrowheads.
(I like arrow #2)

Repeat for the other side.

To make sure the **Arrowhead** doesn't extend beyond the length of the path select **Align : Place arrow tip at end of path**.

Change the Stroke to red and the Fill to None. Your arrow is complete.

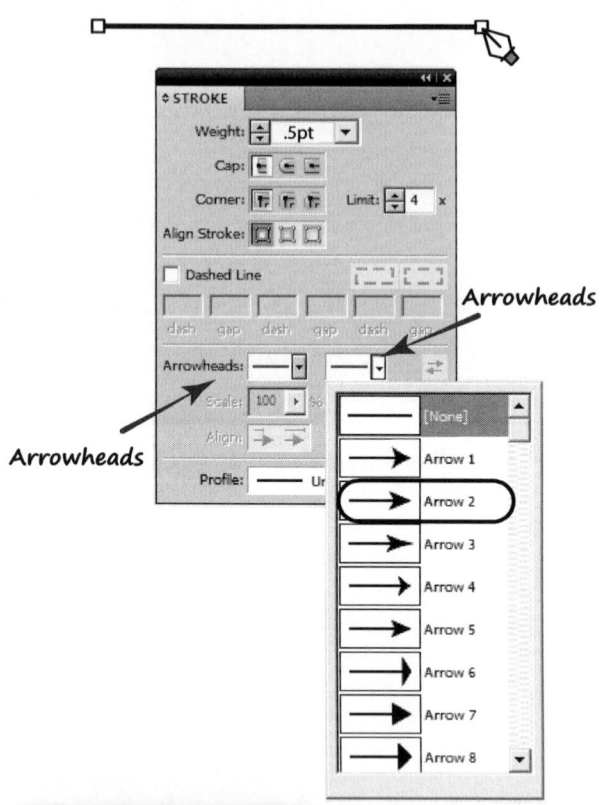

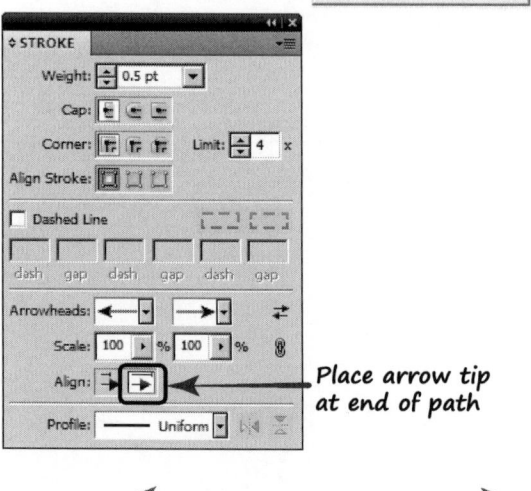

CURVED ARROWS

Draw an **Ellipse**.

Select one **anchor point** with the **Direct Selection Tool**.

Press **Delete** on the keyboard

Add **Arrowheads** from the **Stroke Panel** as before.

Change the **Stroke color to red** and the **Fill color to None**.

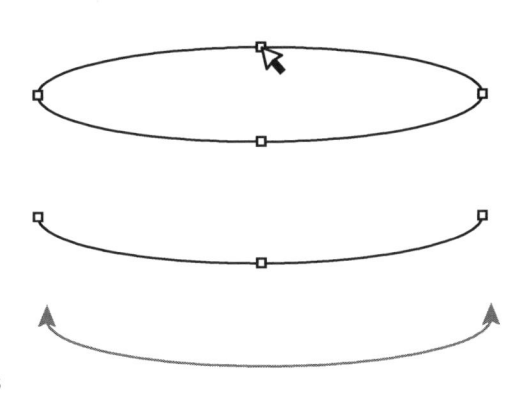

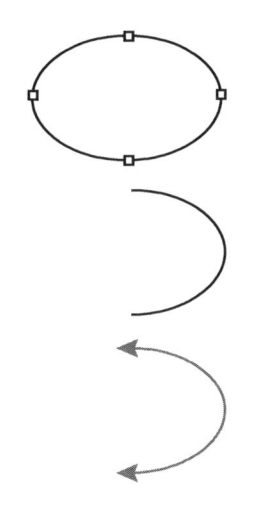

IMPORTANT:
When adding arrows and notations for tech packs always **Lock All Layers** and make a **New Layer** for the **Arrows**. This way nothing will move out of place and the Arrow layer can be made visible or invisible as needed.

Once the arrows are complete the file needs to be saved in a format that will be easy to import into **Microsoft Excel**.

SAVING FOR EXCEL

Make sure the image you want to use is the only image on the artboard. If not, **Copy** it and **Paste** it in a **new file**.

FILE>SAVE FOR MICROSOFT OFFICE
(*Wasn't that nice of Adobe®?*)

Now you can open Excel and insert the image.

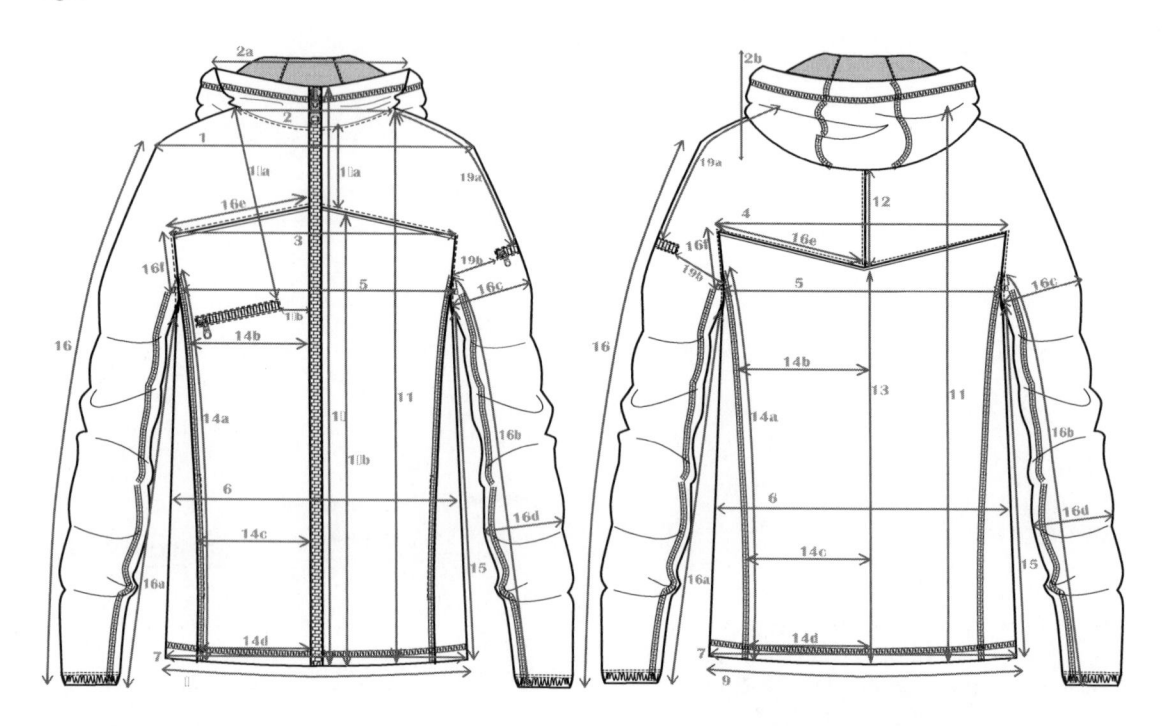

Amber Esparza
Art Institute of Ca-Hollywood
http://www.coroflot.com/ale_esparza

GRAPHIC STYLES

Once you have created an arrow it can be saved as a **Graphic Style**. The next time you need an arrow it will only be one click away.

Select one of your Arrows.
Make sure the **Fill is set to None**.
Open **Graphic Styles** from the **Panel dock** or from the Window Drop Down.

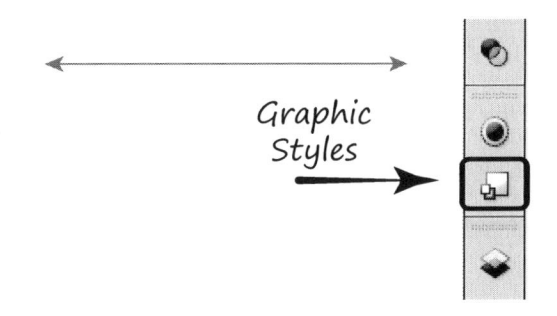

Click on **New Graphic Style** and your arrow style will be added to the **Graphic Styles Panel**.

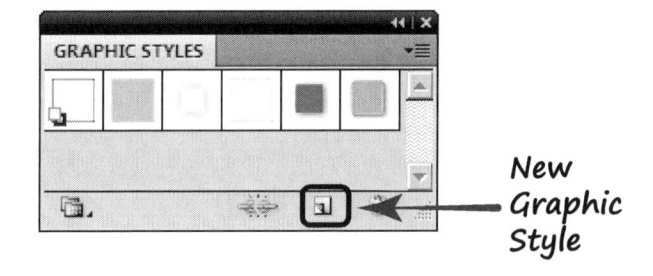

Double Click on your new arrow thumbnail Type in a name and click OK.

*Just like symbols and brushes Graphic Styles will save with the file and can be loaded through the **Graphic Styles Panel** when needed.*

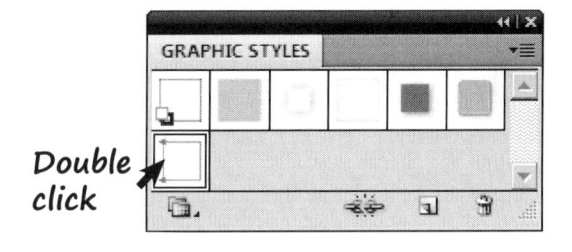

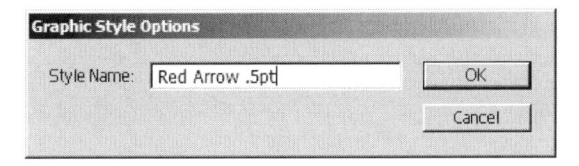

Lesson 7: Tech packs and Time savers

TO APPLY A GRAPHIC STYLE

Draw or Select a path.

Open the **Graphic Styles Panel**.

Click on the **Arrow Style** you just created.

It's that easy!

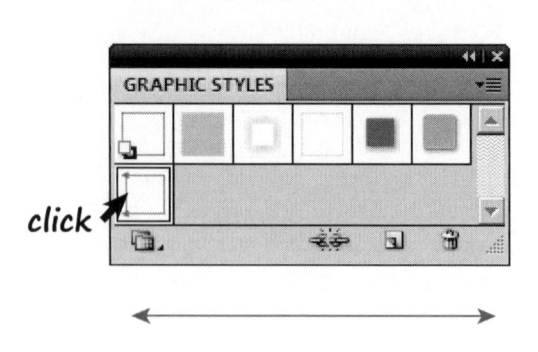

click

WORKFLOW

To save time and make life easier **lock all layers** before drawing arrows.

Make a **new layer** and name it Arrows. Use it to draw all of the paths needed for arrows. This allows you to turn the arrows on or off as needed.

Click on the **Radial button** for the **Arrows** layer in the **Layers panel** to select all of the paths.

Open the **Graphic Styles Panel**.

Click once on the **Arrow Style** and done.

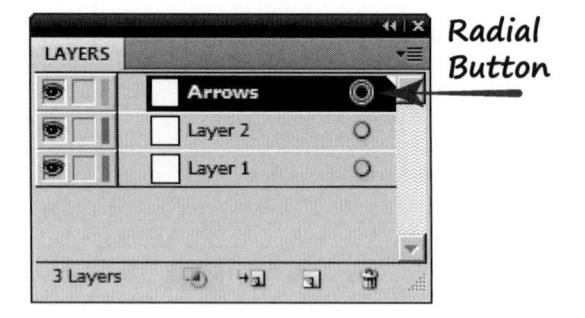

Radial Button

Sometimes it can be difficult to differentiate between different **Graphic Styles** in the **Thumbnail view**. To solve this problem I prefer to use the **Small List view**.

TO SWITCH VIEWS

Click on the **Drop down menu** in the upper right corner of the **Graphic Styles panel**.

Select **Small List view**

and your panel view will change from icons only to icons with names.

Now you can choose the **Graphic Style** by name.

Note: You can delete unused styles by dragging them to the trash.

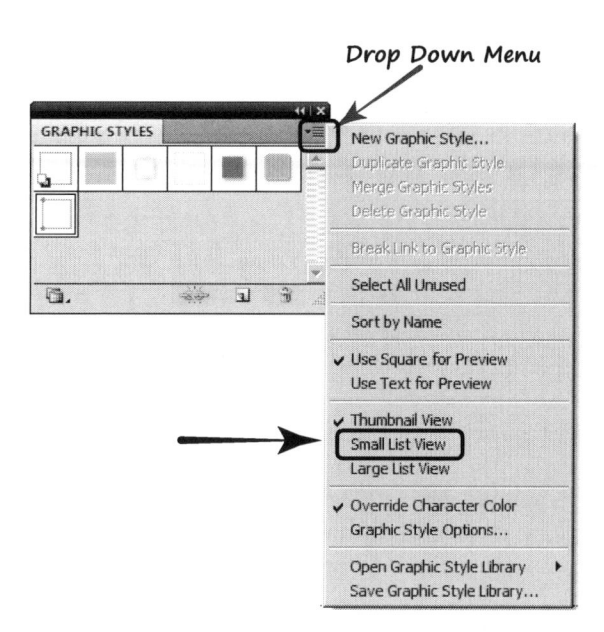

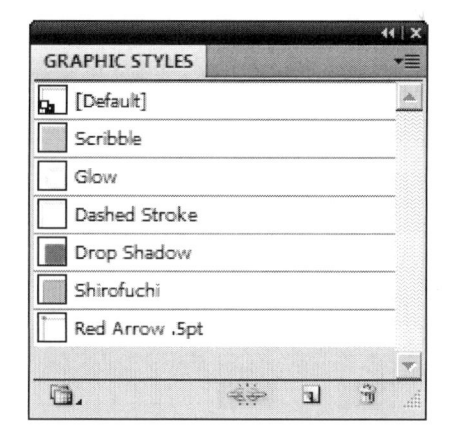

CHANGING DEFAULT SETTINGS

Another great use for **Graphic Styles** is to change the default settings.

Currently Illustrator's Default settings are:
White Fill
Black Stroke
1 pt Stroke Weight
Butt Caps and Miter Joins

A much more useful default setting for drawing flats would be **Round Caps** and **Round Joins**.

Here is how to change it.
Draw a path with the settings we need.
White fill
Black stroke
1 pt weight
Round Caps and Round Joins.

Select it and make a new **Graphic Style**.

Now hold the **Alt** (*Opt*) key while you drag this new style on top of the default icon.

Now the default will have round caps and joins.

This is a great timesaver. From now on when you use the "**D**" key or click the **Default icon** it will apply this new default setting.

Note: This will only work for the file you are currently working in. It will not change the Default universally. As far as I know Adobe® has not given us a way to do that yet. Maybe version CS6?

Default Setting

Preferred Setting

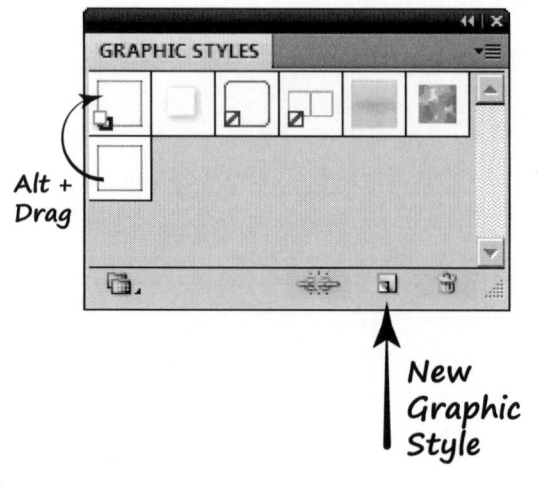

Alt + Drag

New Graphic Style

ZOOM IN FOR A CLOSE UP

CLIPPING MASKS

Select the flat you want to zoom in on.

Double click on the **Scale tool**

Type in 200% (or more) and select **Copy**.

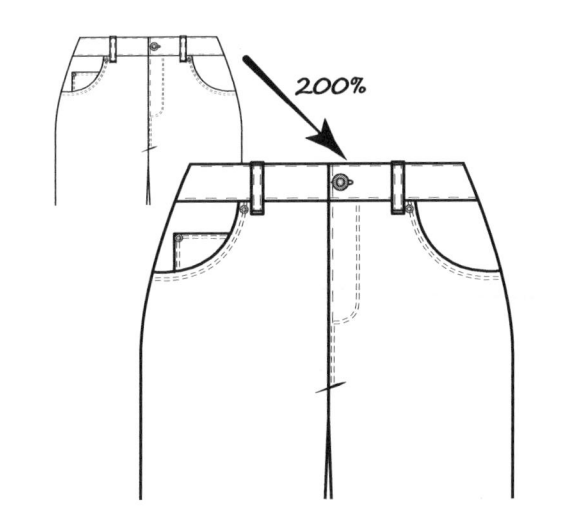

Draw a circle over the area you want to focus on.

Select the Circle and the flat.
Object > Clipping Mask > Make

This will allow only the part of the flat covered by the circle to be visible.

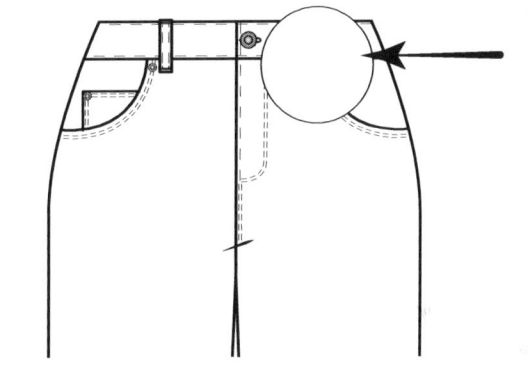

To restore the outline of the circle **Direct select** the edge of the circle.

Open the **Stroke Panel** and change the Stroke weight back to 1pt.

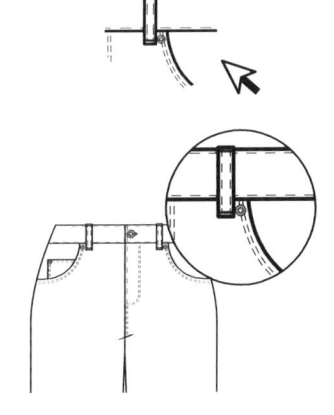

Front Zipper & Reflective Detail

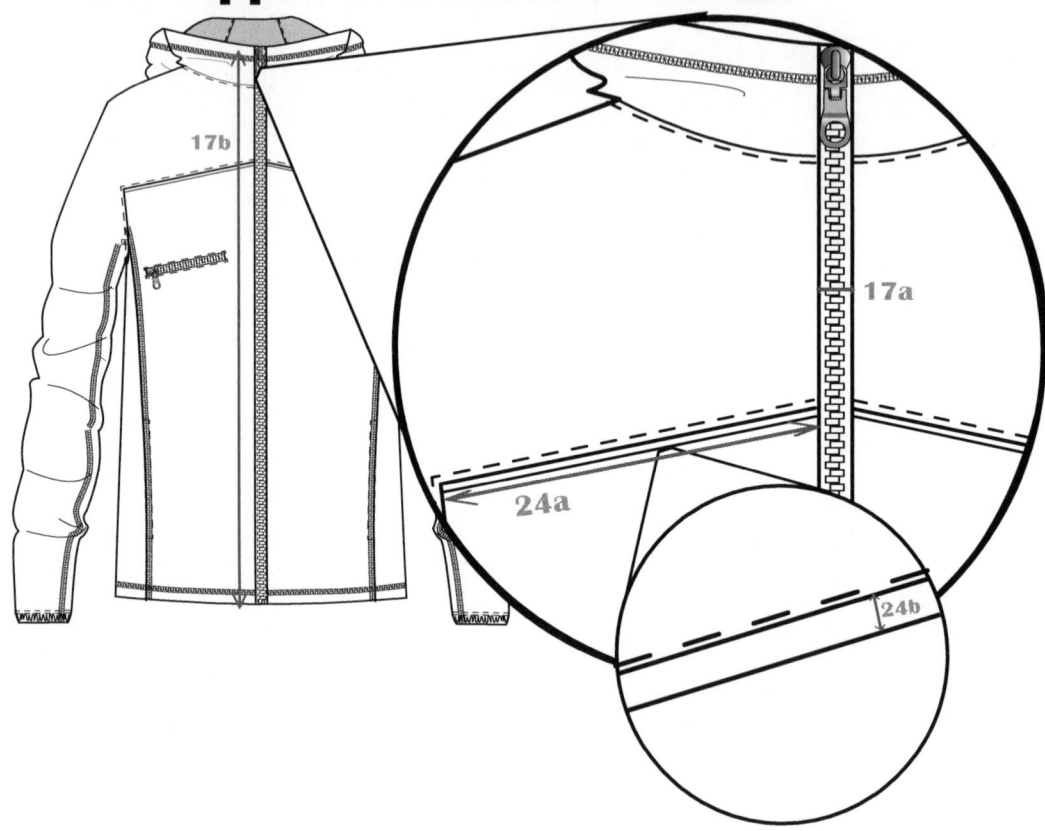

adobe® for fashion : illustrator CS5 | 129

Amber Esparza
Art Institute of Ca-Hollywood
http://www.coroflot.com/ale_esparza

lesson eight

PATTERNS

An Illustrator® pattern is made up of a tile and a motif. They will be repeated horizontally and vertically to generate a pattern. The goal is to create a seamless repeat.

The good news is that Illustrator® does all the work. We only need to design one tile and define it as a pattern.

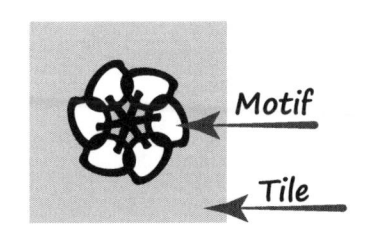

Tile Repeat

APPLYING PATTERNS

Applying a pattern to an object is as easy as adding a fill.

Select the object and make sure the **Fill** is active in the **Tool bar**.

Click on a **pattern** from the **Swatches Panel** and it will fill the selected object.

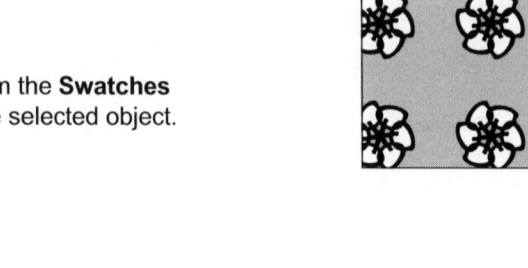

Note: If you are having trouble locating a swatch in the Swatches panel, never fear we can change the view and select it by name just like we did with Graphic Styles.

Click on the upper right corner of the **Swatch Panel** to access the Drop Down menu.

Select Small List View to change the appearance of the swatch panel.

Now you can choose the swatch by name.

You can always change the view back by selecting Small Thumbnail view from the same menu.

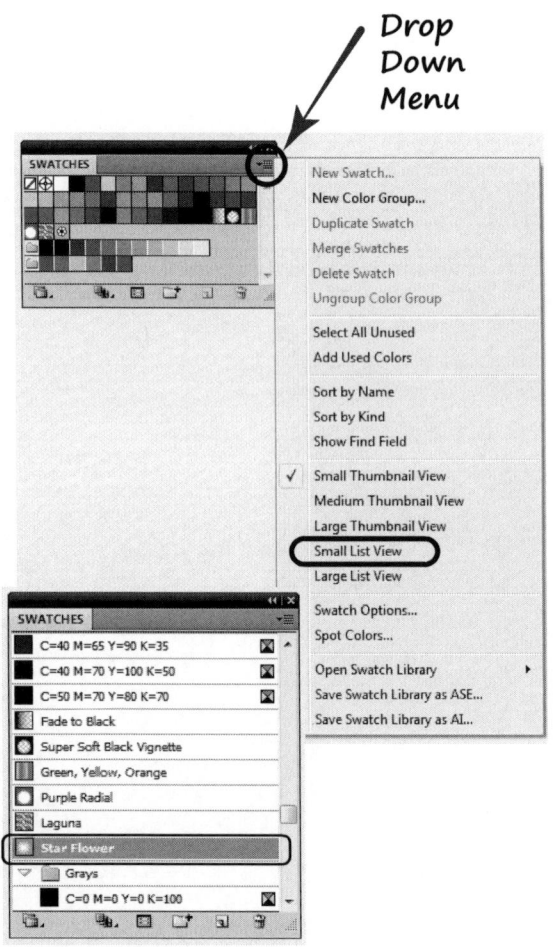

Drop Down Menu

CREATING PATTERNS

Creating patterns is a lot like creating brushes. First we will create a tile, then select it and define it as a pattern.

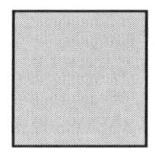

With the **Rectangle tool** draw a square.
(hold the **Shift** key)
This will determine the size of the Tile.
Fill it with a color for the background.

Make sure the **Stroke is set to None** or you will end up with an unwanted grid.

Create your Motif and center it on top of the Tile. **Align Vertical Center** and **Align Horizontal Center**.

Marque select the tile with the motif and **Edit > Define Pattern**

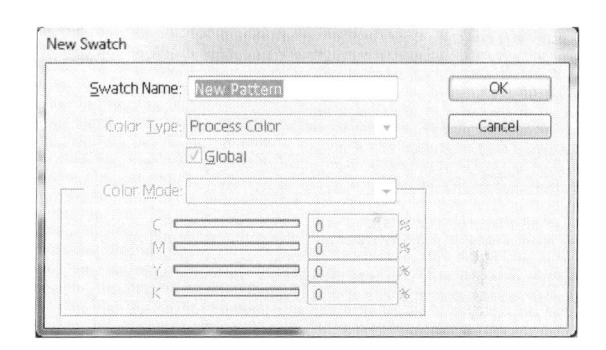

Name the swatch and click OK.

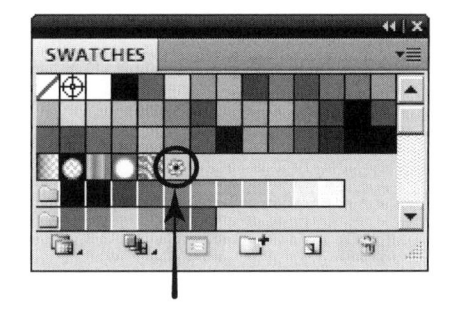

Open the **Swatches Panel** to find your pattern swatch.

SAVING PATTERNS

Just like Brushes and Symbols, any **Patterns** you create will save with the file. The next time you open this file you will find all of your **patterns** in the **Swatches panel**.

But what if you are in a different file and want to access the patterns you created in this one?

Swatch Libraries Menu

Open a **New File**.

In the lower left corner of the **Swatches Panel** you will find the **Swatch Libraries Menu**.

Click on **Other Library** and navigate to where you saved the Illustrator® file with the pattern.
Select the file and click OK.

A new panel will open with all of the swatches associated with the file you selected.
Click on the individual swatches to add them to the **Swatches panel** in the current file.
Close the panel.

EDITING A PATTERN

Click and drag the pattern out of the **Swatches panel** and on to the **Art Board**.

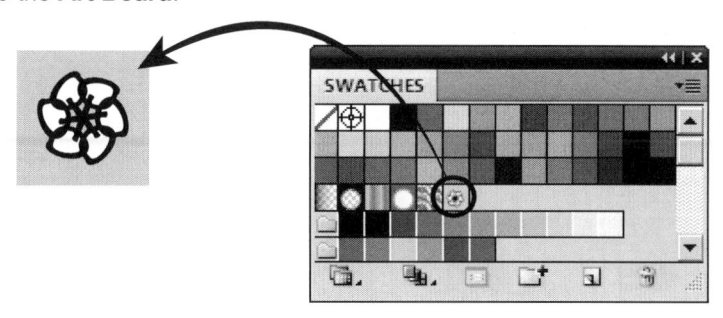

Select it and **Right Click >Ungroup**

Now you can edit the pattern any way you like. Change the color or add additional motifs. When you are happy with the changes marque select the entire swatch and

Edit>Define Pattern to create a new version of the pattern.

Lesson 8: Patterns

SCALING PATTERNS

SCALE TOOL

Pattern size can be easily adjusted by using the **Scale tool**.

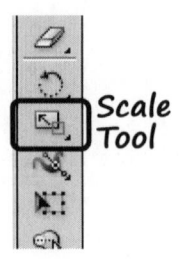

Select the object with the pattern fill.
Double click on the **Scale tool**.

When the **Scale Options Box** opens type in the scale percentage.

Since we only want to scale the pattern and not the object-
Check Patterns and
Un-Check Objects

Click OK.

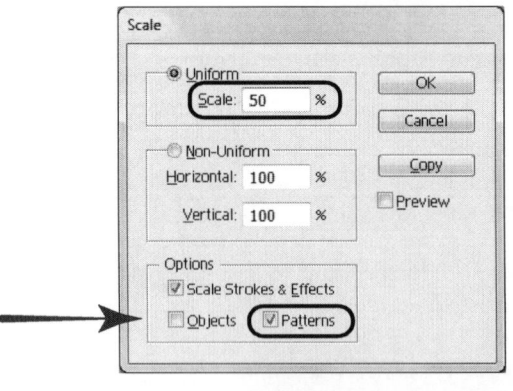

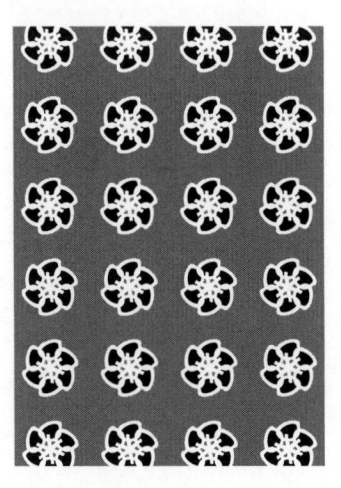

ROTATING PATTERNS

ROTATE TOOL

You can use the **Rotate tool** to adjust the angle of your pattern within an object.

Select the object and **double click** on the **Rotate Tool**.

Type in the rotation angle.
(45 degrees for Bias)

IMPORTANT- make sure to check Patterns, NOT Objects *so that only the pattern will rotate.*

Click OK.

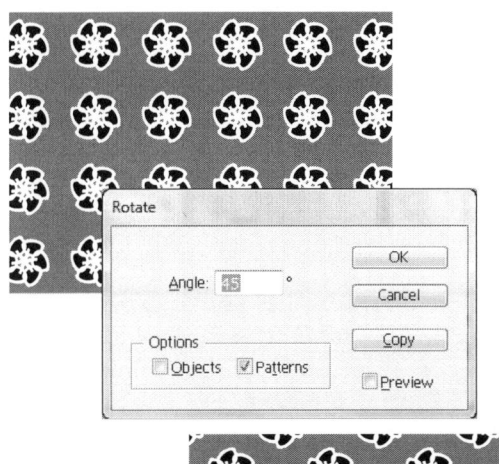

ROTATE VISUALLY

If you don't know the exact angle the pattern needs to be rotated you can rotate it visually using the **Tilde Key** (~). *The tilde key is in the upper left corner of the keyboard, next to the #1 key.*

Select the object and
Click once on the **Rotate tool**
Hold down the **Tilde key** while you
click and drag on the pattern to Rotate it within the selected object.

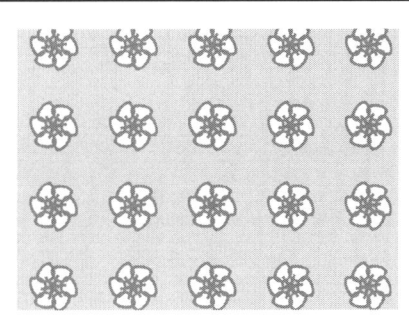

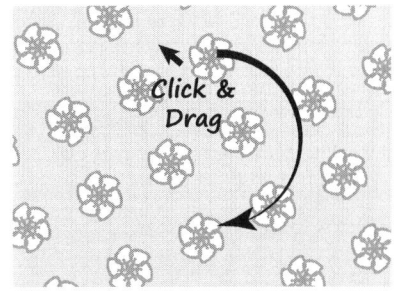

PATTERN PLACEMENT

You can move a pattern within an object to control the placement.

MOVING PATTERNS

Select the object filled with your pattern. With the **Selection tool** still active hold down the **Tilde Key (~) click and drag** inside the selected object to move the pattern around.

If you need a more exact movement of the pattern double click on the **Selection Tool**. When the **Move Options box** opens type in the Horizontal and/or Vertical movements you need.

IMPORTANT- make sure to check Patterns, NOT Objects so that only the pattern will move.

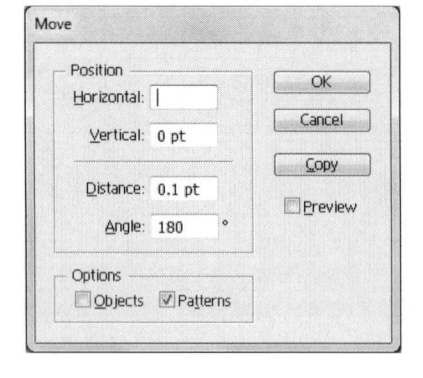

CREATING STRIPES

Using the **Rectangle tool** draw the tile. Select a **FILL** color and set the **Stroke to None**(/).

With the **Rectangle tool** draw a series of rectangles making sure they all start and end outside of the Tile.

Change all the **Strokes to None** or else it's the dreaded grid pattern.

Select only the **Tile (*NOT the Stripes*)**and
Copy (**Ctrl +C** /*Cmd + C*)
Paste in Back (**Ctrl +B**/*Cmd + B*)

Select only this
Copy
Paste in Back

While the **tile** is still selected change it's **Fill and Stroke to None**.
You can double check this in the **Layers Panel**. *(This is how Illustrator knows what size to make your pattern tile)*.

With the **Selection tool**, **marque select** the entire swatch with the stripes.

Select **Edit >Define Pattern** from the Menu bar. Name the swatch and click OK.

TO USE YOUR NEW STRIPE PATTERN

Select an object to fill, open the **Swatches Panel** and click on your New Stripe swatch.

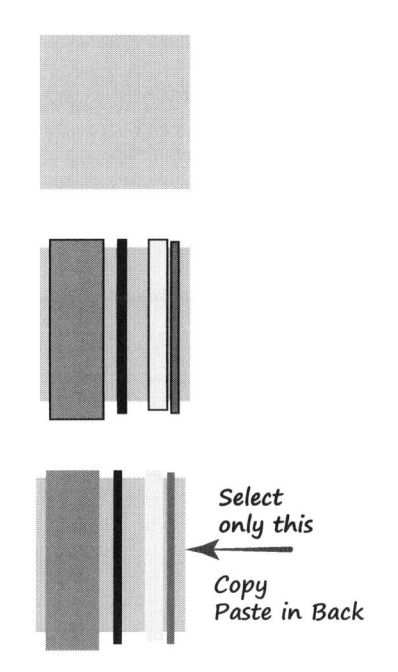

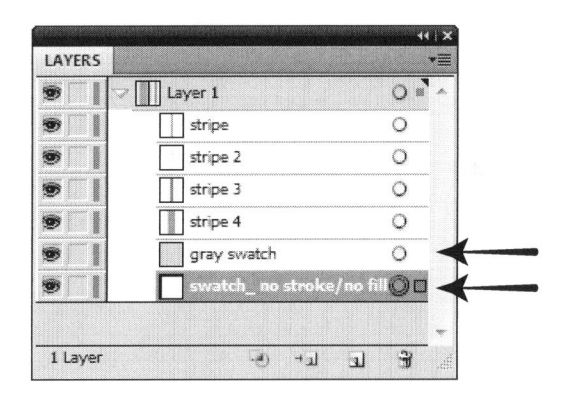

Lesson 8: Patterns

TROUBLESHOOTING:

1. If your pattern looks like this you didn't **Copy, Paste in Back** and change the **Fill and Stroke to NONE**. So a swatch was made from your entire selection and there are unwanted gaps in the repeat.

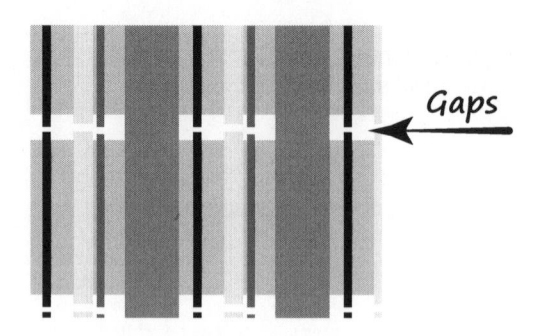

← Gaps

2. If your pattern looks like this you didn't have your **Stroke set to None** and as a result you have created the dreaded grid pattern.

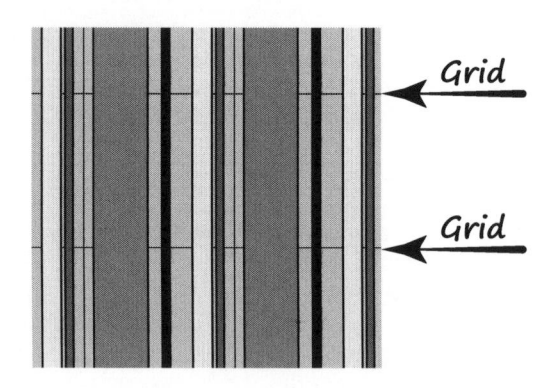

← Grid

← Grid

The important thing to understand is that we want to let Illustrator do all the work.
Always create your tile using the fewest possible elements.
For example a two color stripe tile would look like this.

CREATING PLAIDS

Using the **Rectangle tool**, hold down the **Shift Key** and draw a **perfect square**.
Fill the tile and create stripes as before.

Marque Select the entire tile including stripes.
Open **Pathfinder** and **Divide**.

Right click and **Ungroup**.

Select and **Delete** the pieces of stripe outside the boundary of the tile.

Select and **Group** the tile with the stripes.
Ctrl+G (*Cmd+G*)

Double Click on the **Rotate tool**
Type in 90 degrees
Check both Objects and Patterns in the Options box and click **Copy**.

While it is still selected lower the **Opacity** of the top group to **50%**. *You will find the Opacity box at the top of you screen in the Control Panel.*

Marque Select the entire swatch and
Edit>Define Pattern

And we have plaid!

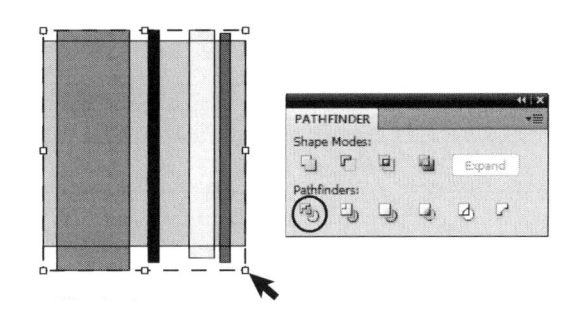

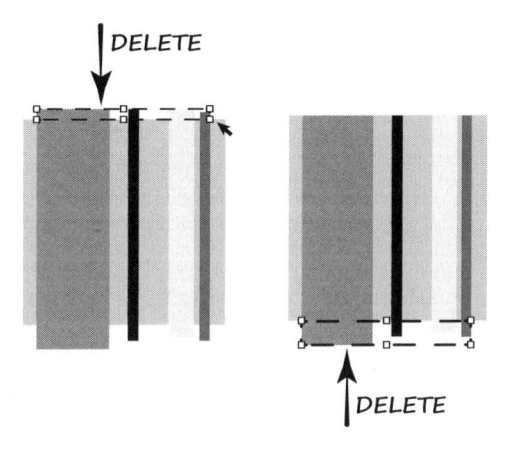

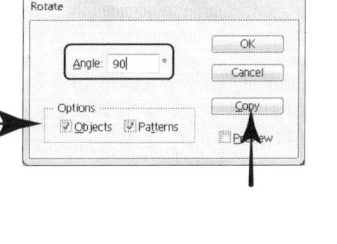

142 | Lesson 8: Patterns

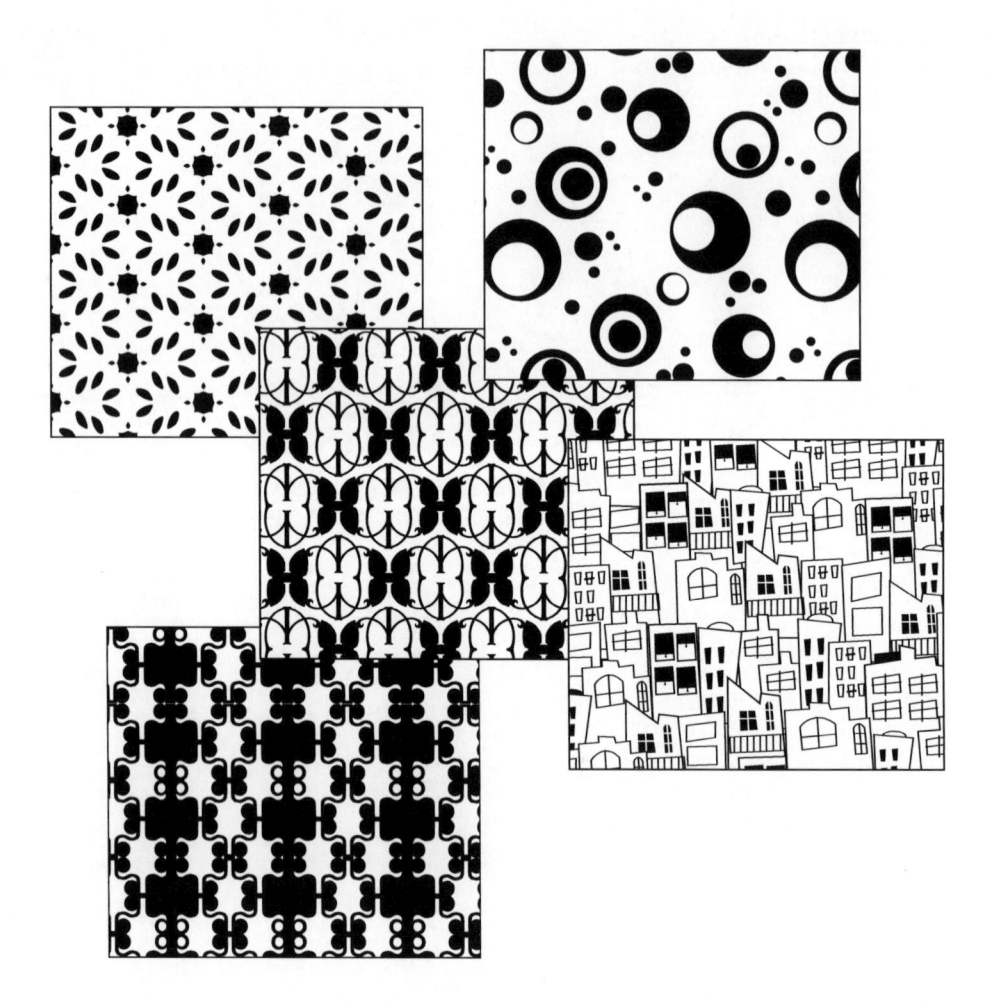

**Patterns from
Black, White & Gray**
Royalty free seamless patterns
by NY Cookie Graphics
Available at:
www.thefashionbookstore.com

adobe® for fashion : illustrator CS5 | **143**

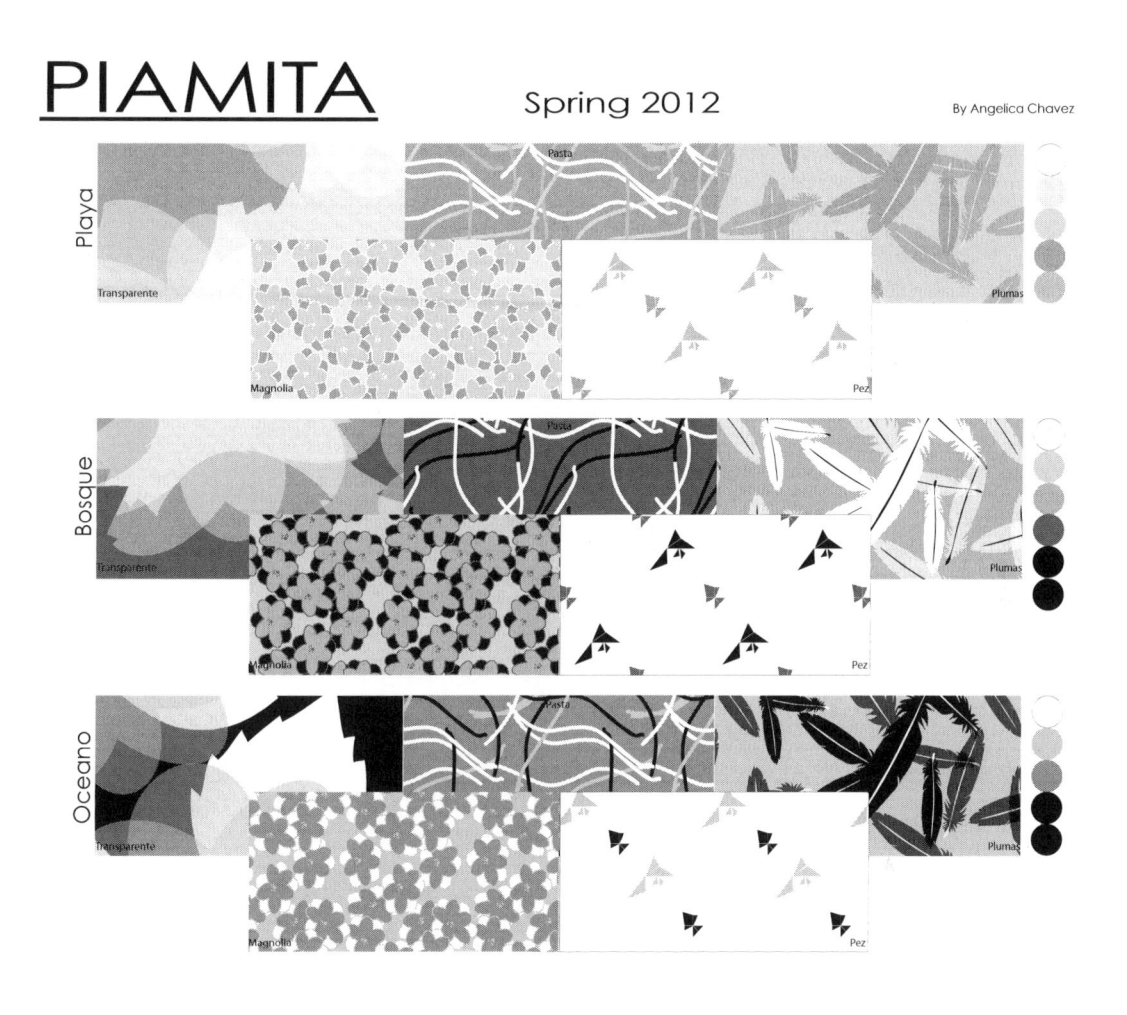

PIAMITA
Spring 2012
By Angelica Chavez

Angelica Chavez
Art Institute of Ca-Hollywood
http://www.coroflot.com/veltimera

Lesson 9: Croqui

lesson nine

DRAWING CROQUI

If you have been practicing all of the lessons in this book you will be pleased to discover that you have been training to use the pen tool from the start. All of that time spent using the convert anchor point tool has prepared you for this next challenge. Tracing a croqui with the **Pen tool**.

I like to start at a corner point, a good spot is where the head meets the neck.
Grab the **Pen tool** and click at this point. Now let go of the mouse button and move the cursor just past the point where the line starts to curve.

Click and drag the handle in the direction of the line you are tracing until the path bends to follow the contour of the croquis.

Continue to **click and drag** each time the line starts to change direction. The goal is to use the fewest number of anchor points possible to achieve a smooth outline.

You can continue on as long as the handles are pointing in the direction you are drawing.

If the handle crosses your path you will need to get rid of it before you continue on. Do this by **clicking once** on the **anchor point**. *(Be careful to click on the anchor point and not the handle you were dragging)*

Continue this process around the entire perimeter of the croquis until you arrive back at the starting point and close the path.

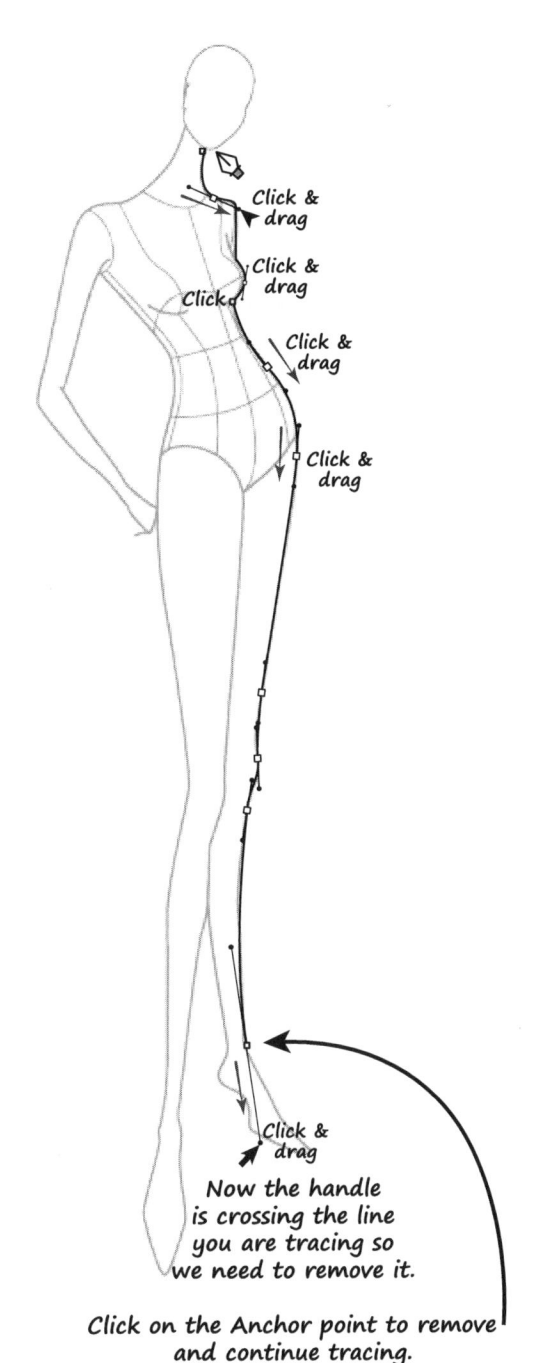

Now the handle is crossing the line you are tracing so we need to remove it.

Click on the Anchor point to remove and continue tracing.

146 | Lesson 9: Croqui

Once you have completed the perimeter you can go back and draw any pieces that need to be punched out. In this case the shape between the arm and the body.

Select everything and open **Pathfinder**. Click on **Exclude** to punch out the hole.

Now you can fill the body with a flesh color.

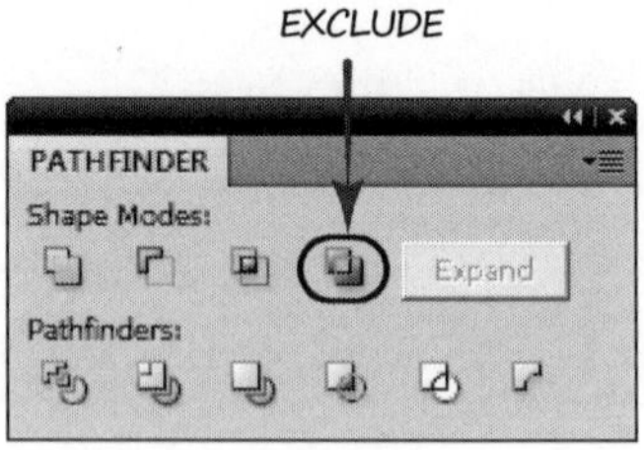

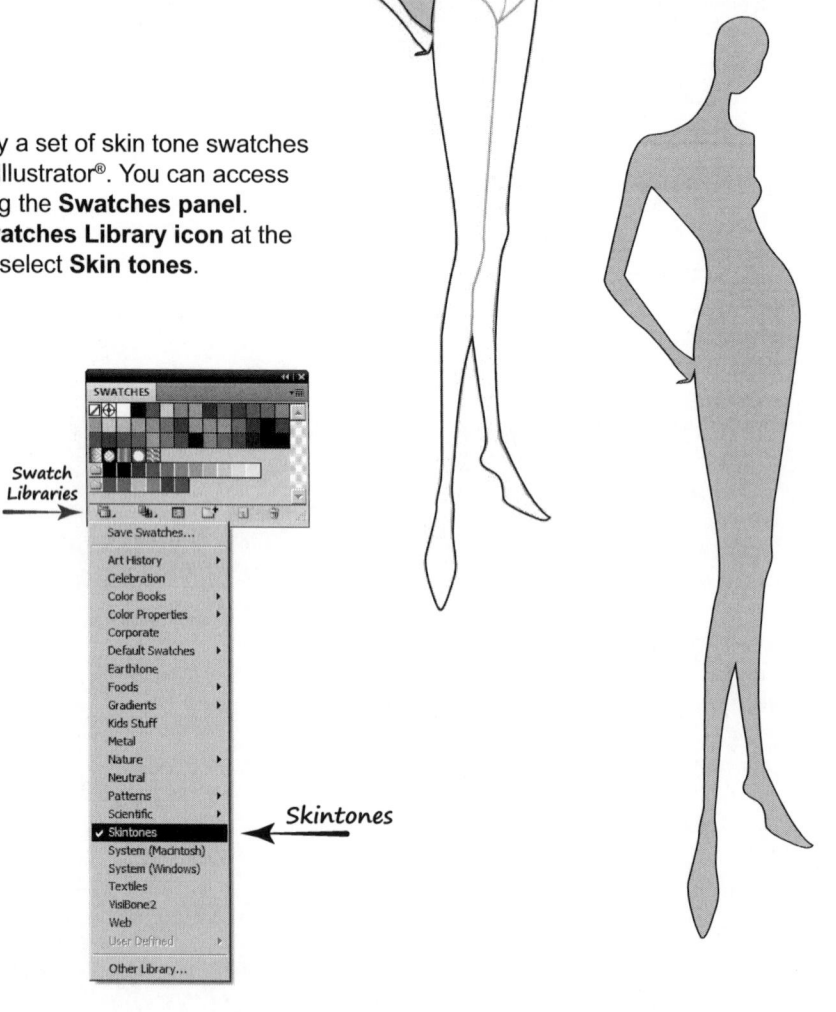

EXCLUDE

SKIN TONES
There is actually a set of skin tone swatches that come with Illustrator®. You can access them by opening the **Swatches panel**. Click on the **Swatches Library icon** at the bottom left and select **Skin tones**.

Swatch Libraries

Skintones

Now for the rest of the detail.

Select the croqui and lower the **Opacity** to **50%**. **Lock** the croquis layer.

Make a **New Layer** above the croquis layer.

In the new layer we are going to draw all of the detail elements.

Using the **Pen Tool** draw details like the line between the legs, chin, hands and ear. When you complete a line use the **Enter (Return)** key to **release the Pen tool** so you can start a new line.

When complete you may want to select all of the details and apply one of the **profiles** at the bottom of the **Stroke panel** for a more hand drawn look.

Unlock the croquis layer, select the croquis and restore the **Opacity to 100%**.

You can soften the look of the croquis by using a dark brown instead of black for the strokes.

For more depth try filling with a Linear Gradient.

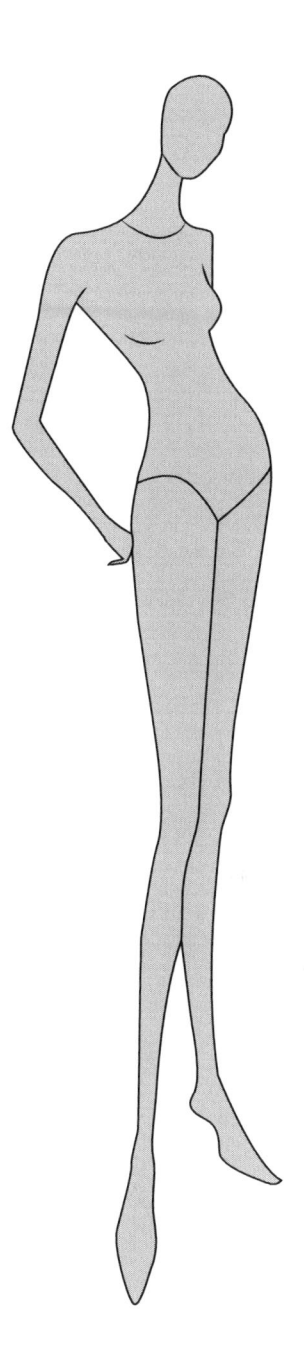

GRADIENTS

Open the **Gradient panel** from the Panel Dock and select **Linear**.

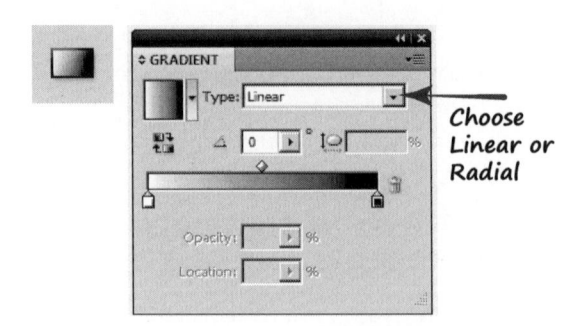

Choose Linear or Radial

CHANGE THE COLOR OF A GRADIENT

Click on a light skin tone swatch and drag it on top of the white swatch in the **Gradient panel**.
Click on a darker skin tone swatch and drag it on top of the black square.

You can add as many additional colors as you want by dragging them in the same way.

Click + Drag

The **diamond** lets you adjust the blend of the colors in the gradient.

To remove colors from a gradient.
Click on the swatch and drag it right out of the **Gradient panel**.

Drag to adjust the amount of each color

Once you have the gradient adjusted the way you want it you can save it.

Click on the **New Swatch** icon in the **Swatches panel** and it will add your gradient swatch. To apply it again just click on the swatch.

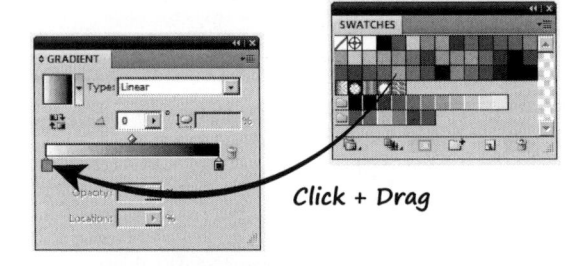

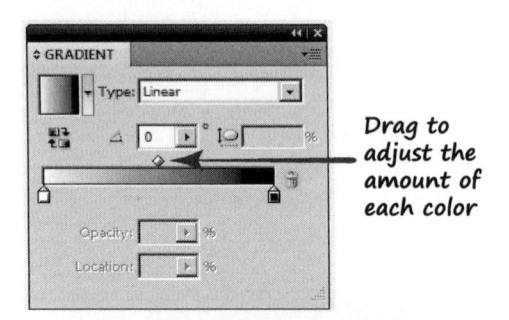

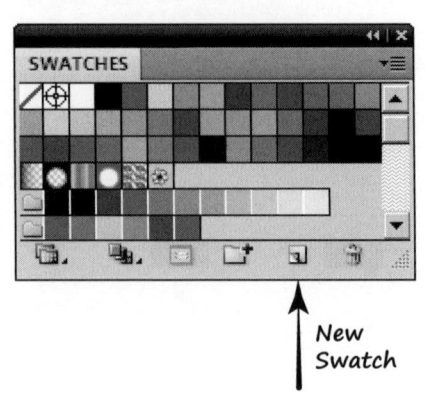

New Swatch

DRAWING FACES

EYES

The eyes are actually pretty easy to draw if you break them down into simple shapes and use a few special brushes. Start by drawing the basic eye shape. If you aren't comfortable free handing it you can always find a head shot on line to use as a guide.

Choose an image, **Copy** and **Paste** it into your Illustrator file. **Lower the Opacity** and **Lock the layer** so it won't move around on you.

Using the **Pen tool** trace the eye and give it a black **Stroke** and white **Fill**.
Now trace the crease and the eyebrow. These should have a black **Stroke** and **No Fill**.

Select the eye and the crease and apply **Width Profile #1** from the **Stroke panel** to add dimension.

Select the eyebrow and apply one of the **Chalk/Charcoal brushes** for a more realistic look. I like **Charcoal-Smooth**. You may need to lower the point size if the brush is too thick.

To access the **Chalk/Charcoal brushes**: **Click** on the **Brush Libraries Menu** in the lower left corner of the **Brushes Panel**. Select **Artistic then Artistic_Chalk/Charcoal** and choose a brush.

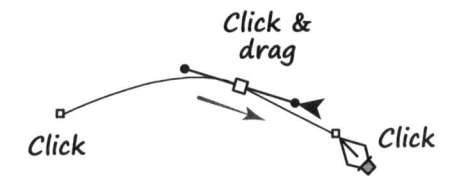

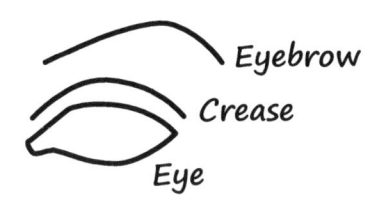

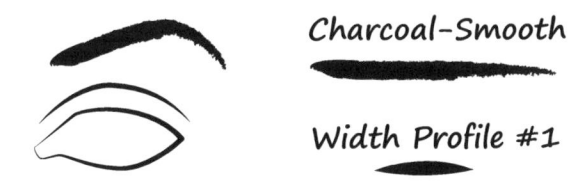

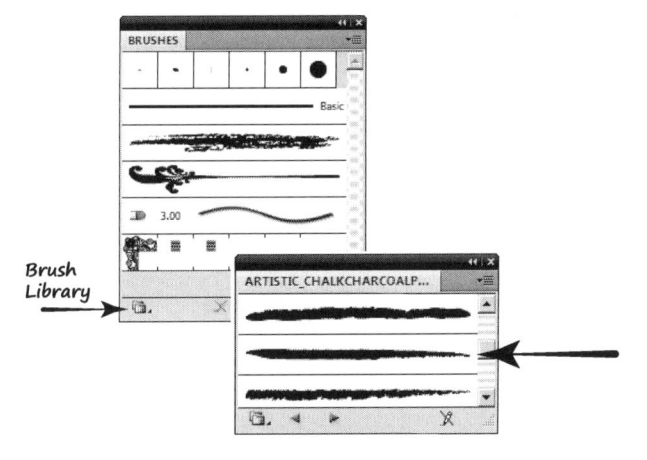

Lesson 9: Croqui

Draw a circle for the iris and fill it with a **Radial gradient**.

Next draw a smaller black circle for the pupil. *(A larger pupil will appear more attractive)*

Add a small white circle for the highlight.

Select them all and **Group**.

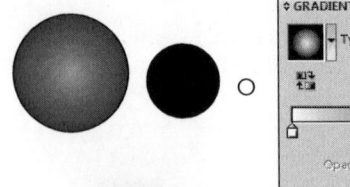

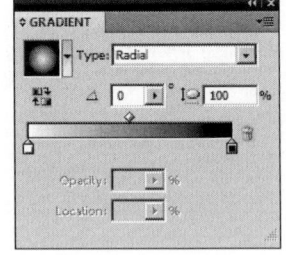

Drag the iris on top of the eye. It should be a bit larger than the eye opening.

Select the iris only and use the **Eraser tool** to remove any areas extending beyond the eye opening.

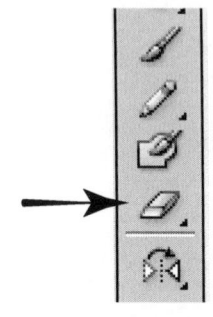

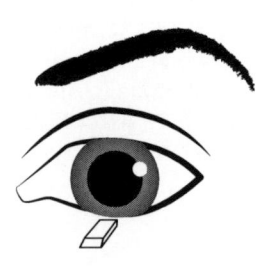

EYE LASHES

EYELASH BRUSH
Using the **Pen tool**, draw an eyelash shape with a **Black Stroke** and **no Fill**.

Change the **Stroke to .5pts** and the Profile to **Width Profile 5**.

Select the lash and open the **Brushes Panel**.
Click on the **New Brush** Icon.
Select **Scatter Brush** and click OK.
When the **Option Box** opens Click OK.

Draw an arched path for the lashes following the contour of your eye.

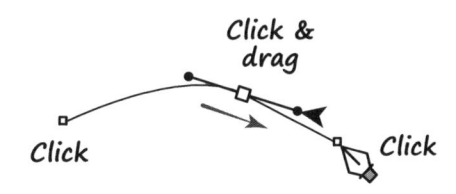

Apply the new **Eyelash Scatter Brush**. *(The scatter brushes are the small squares near the top section of the Brush Panel)*

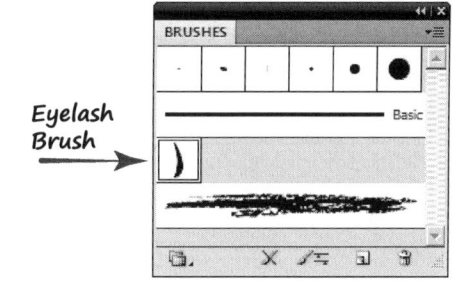

It will look like this.

TO ADJUST THE BRUSH:

Double click on the **eyelash Brush** in the **Brush Panel** to open the options window.

Check the PREVIEW Box so you can see the changes you are making.

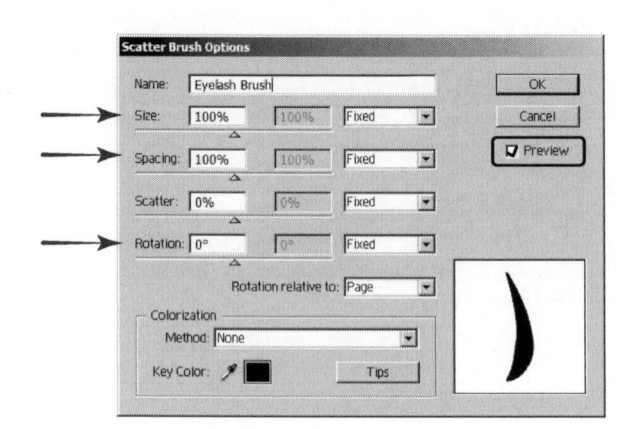

Adjust the **Size Slider** until you like the size of the lashes.

Adjust the **Spacing Slider** so that the lashes touch or over lap.

Adjust the **Rotation Slider** so that the lashes are angling in the correct direction. Click OK.

Place the lashes on top of the eye. Make sure the lashes are covering the top of the pupil to avoid the surprised look.

For lower lashes draw a path along the bottom of the eye and stroke with a thin **Chalk/ Charcoal Brush**.

Save as a symbol for future use.

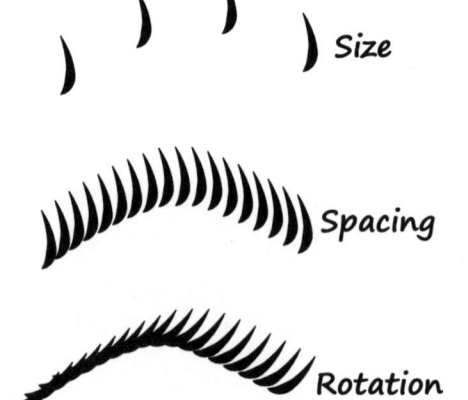

MOUTH

You can use the photo as a guide for the nose and mouth as well.

Start by tracing one side of the mouth.
Select it and **Reflect** it.
Select both sides, **Right click** and **Join**.

Draw a path separating the top and bottom lips and apply **Width Profile #1** or a **Chalk/Charcoal brush** for a rougher look.

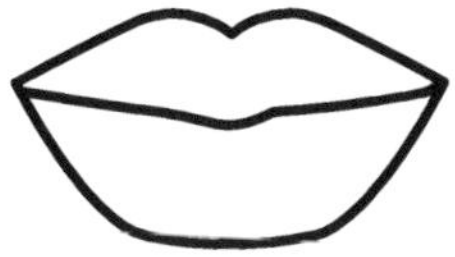

Fill with a **Radial Gradient** to add depth.

Add a few Highlights with a **Chalk/Charcoal brush** and you're done.

Experiment with brushes and profiles to develop your own signature style.

It doesn't need to be anymore detailed than this because it is going to be printed out very small.

Save as a Symbol.

NOSE

Draw the nose the same way we did the mouth.
Trace one side with the **Pen Tool**.
Apply Profiles for a more hand drawn look.
(I used **Width Profile #1**)
Reflect.
Save as a Symbol.

154 Lesson 9: Croqui

BLUSH

To add some Blush to the cheeks draw a shape for the blush.
Give it a **pink Fill** and **No Stroke**.

Select the blush shape and
Effect > Stylize > Feather
Check PREVIEW
Adjust the Radius to taste and Click OK.

You can lower the **Opacity** in the **Control Panel** for a softer look.

I recommend making an assortment of features to save as symbols for future use.

I have a symbols file I call my "Mr. Potato Head file" and it contains facial features for front, profile and 3/4 views. Anytime I make a new eye, nose, mouth, or ear I add it to the file. It's a great time saver when you need to generate some croqui on a deadline.

These faces work nicely in Photoshop® as well. Just Copy and Paste into the Photoshop® file.

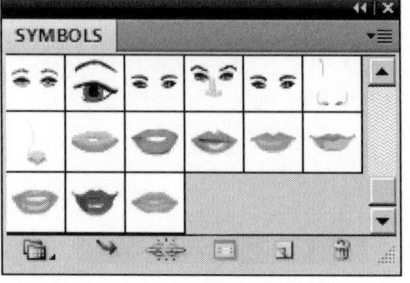

HAIR

Flowing Hair can be drawn freehand using the brush tool.

Note: You will have a much easier time if you lock all the layers and make a new layer just for the hair.

First we need to set the **Pencil Tool Options**.

Double click on the **Pencil Tool** to open the options box.
Un-check Keep selected and **Edit Selected**.
Click OK.

Click on the **Paint Brush Tool**
Select a brush from the **Brushes Panel**
*(I like the **Artistic_Ink Brushes** for hair)*

Set the **Fill to None** and the **Stroke** to your choice of hair color.
Start painting.

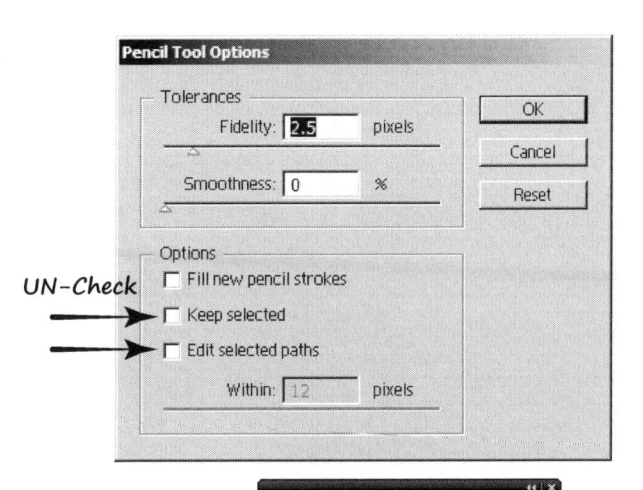

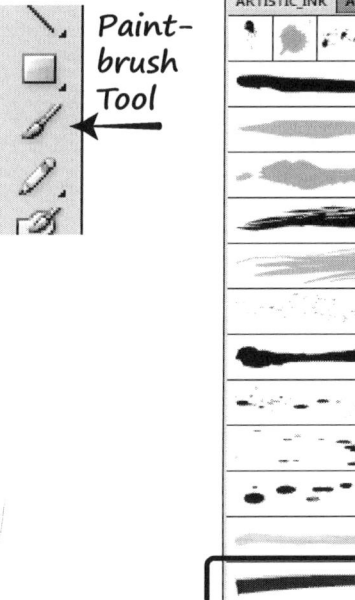

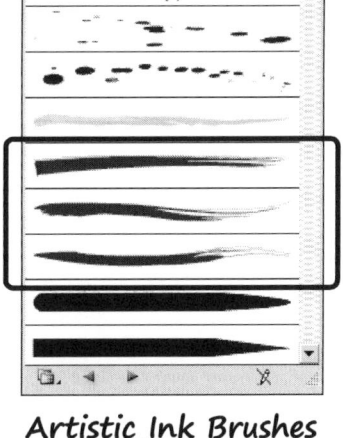

UN-Check

Paint-brush Tool

Artistic_Ink Brushes Good for Hair

Lesson 9: Croqui

Artistic_Scrollpen
Good for Graphic Hair

Tephy Sok
Art Institute of Ca-Hollywood
http://www.coroflot.com/tephism

Keshia Tedjopranoto
Art Institute of Ca-Hollywood
http://www.coroflot.com/Kdaniella

adobe® for fashion : illustrator CS5 | 157

Chalk_Charcoal Brushes
Good for Eyebrows
and lower lashes

Trixie Encomienda
Art Institute of Ca-Hollywood
http://www.coroflot.com/Trixie_Encomienda

158 | Lesson 9: Croqui

Kimberly Hires
Art Institute of Ca-Hollywood
http://www.coroflot.com/
kimberlyhires

adobe® for fashion : illustrator CS5 | 159

Jose Andrade
Art Institute of Ca-Hollywood
http://www.coroflot.com/joseandrade

lesson ten

LAYOUT

The standard size for a fashion portfolio is 14" x 17". The presentation should be neat and professional. There has been a trend, especially in forecasting books to use photographic or patterned backgrounds in layouts. Although acceptable by industry standards they can be distracting. I think a simpler background that highlights your collection and lets the viewer focus on your work is a better choice.

There is a hierarchy to the information on your board and this should be indicated by varying the visual weight.

1. **Flats** -the most important objects on the board. They should stand out.

2. **Croqui** - make them as large as possible for the most visual impact.

3. **Collection title**

4. **Season**

5. **Designer name** - take pride in your work and put your name on it.

6. **Garment descriptions** including fabric type, fiber content, fasteners, and style numbers.

7. **Background** - photographic image, gradient, solid color or border.

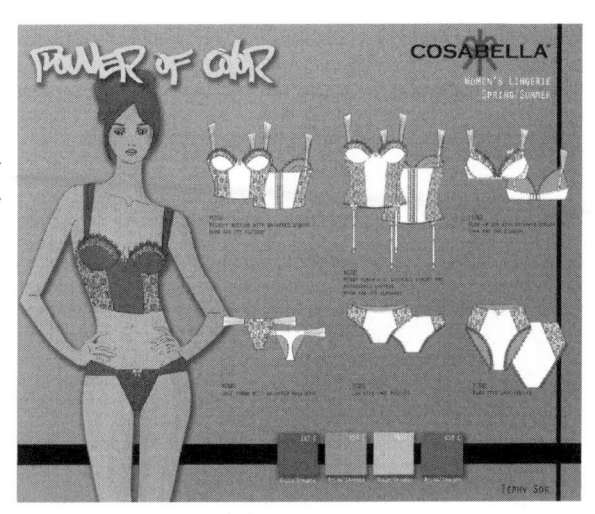

Tephy Sok
Art Institute of Ca-Hollywood
http://www.coroflot.com/tephism

Lesson 10: Layout

Start by opening a new file
select **Print**
      width 17in
      height 14in.
Print will change to custom after you adjust the size.

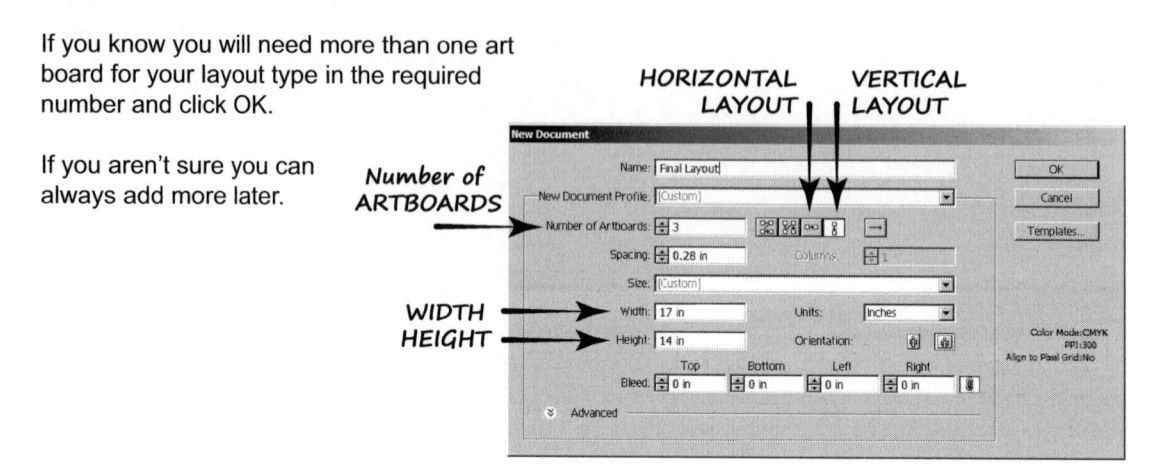

If you know you will need more than one art board for your layout type in the required number and click OK.

If you aren't sure you can always add more later.

Your document with multiple art boards should look something like this:

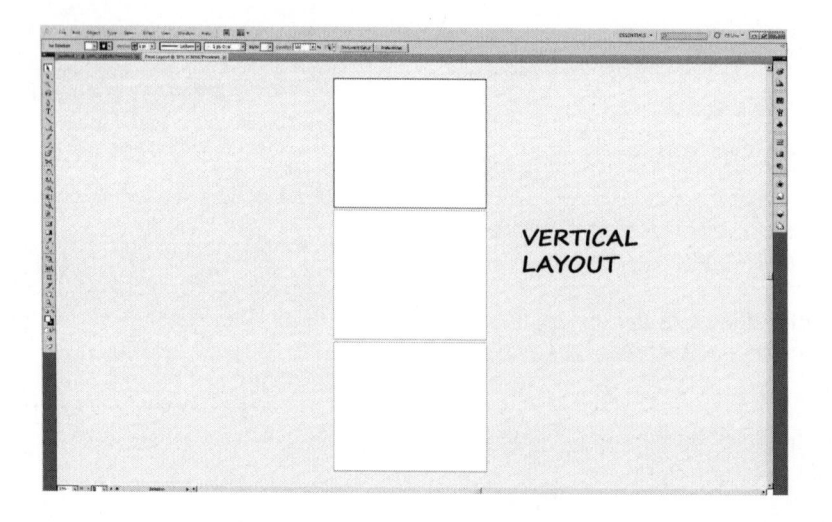

Now you can bring in all of your flats and croqui. I prefer to save the background for last, this will make it easier to see what will best set off the collection.

Open the Illustrator® file containing your flats. Select the flats you want and copy them **Ctrl+C** (*Cmd+C*).

Go back to the **Layout file** and **Paste** (**Ctrl+V** /*Cmd+V*).

Open the file with your croqui and **Copy** and **Paste** them into the **Layout file**.

Now you can arrange all of the elements on the Art boards to create a balanced and pleasing layout.

When arranging flats it is customary to place the back view behind the front view, slightly lower and to the right. Be careful not to cover up too much of the back view.

ADDING TEXT
Next we can start placing the text. The reason for text is to relay information about the collection. If you choose a font that is difficult to read, it defeats the purpose.
Here are some helpful guidelines:

1. **Collection Title** (use 36pt - 72pt type)
This is your chance to use a display font that can add to the visual appeal of your presentation. Select a font that has character but can still be easily read.

DO NOT: Use *Old English*, *Script* or any other elaborate font in **ALL CAPS**. *These fonts were designed to be used in upper/lower case.*

If it's is difficult to read DON'T USE IT!

Lesson 10: Layout

2. **Season** (use 24pt - 48pt type)
This is the next most important piece of information on the presentation. You can use the same font as in the collection title.

Season

Season

3. **Designer name** (use 14pt - 32pt type)
Don't forget to sign your work. You should be proud to put your name on it.

Designer Name

Designer Name

4. **Garment descriptions**, Fabric type, Fiber content (No larger than 10pt -1 2pt type)

This is information that needs to be clear and easy to read. But it should not have as much visual importance as the flats.

Garment Description
Fabric Type
Fiber Content

Garment Description
Fabric Type
Fiber Content

adobe® for fashion : illustrator CS5 | 165

Collection 72pt.
Collection 60pt.
Collection 48pt.
Collection 36pt.
Collection 24pt.
Collection 21pt.
Collection 18pt.
Collection 14pt.
Collection 12 pt.
Collection 10 pt.

ADDING TEXT

To add a title to your board select the **Type tool**. **Click once** on the page and start typing.

Click and drag over the text to highlight it. You can change the font or the point size from the **Control Panel** drop down menus at the top of the screen.

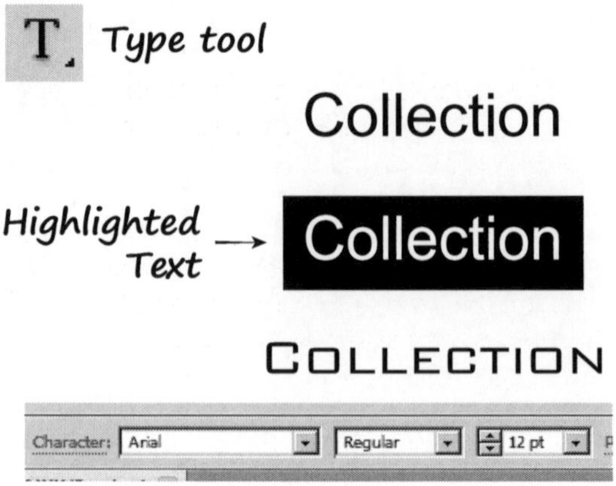

PARAGRAPH TEXT

For **Paragraph text** like garment desriptions select the **Type tool**.
Click and drag out a **text frame** to type in. This will allow you to adjust the height and width of the text block without distorting the type. Just drag the handles.

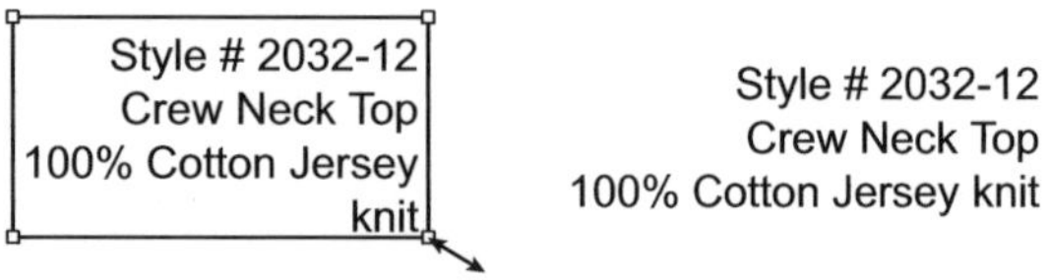

PLACING TEXT ON MULTIPLE ARTBOARDS

Type your text on the first Artboard. Select the font, adjust the size and move into place.

Select the text and **Cut** (**Ctrl +X**/*Cmd+X*)

Edit>Paste on All Artboards

And it will paste your text in the same location on every artboard.

This works for objects as well as text.

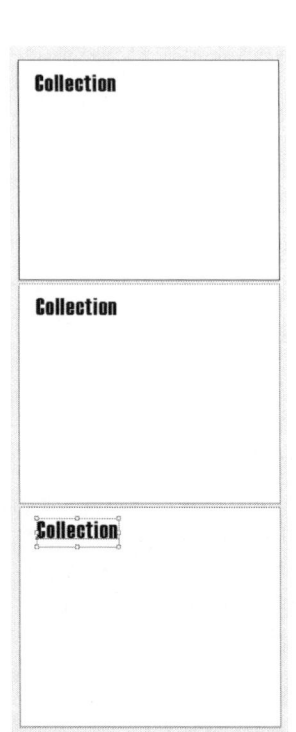

SELECTING FONTS

If you want additional fonts to choose from check out one of my favorite font websites:

www.Dafont.com

It's easy to navigate even for non-fontofiles. Fonts are broken down into very use friendly categories so you can quickly locate the style you are looking for.

You can also type in your own text to see what it will look like in any font before you download it.(*my favorite feature*)

Warning: Scrolling through Dafont.com has been known to cause many a student to lose track of time in the quest for the perfect font. Proceed with caution.

DOWNLOADING FONTS

Once you decide on a font or two click on the **Download button**. You will be asked if you want to **Open** or **Save**.
Click Save. (*I suggest saving to the desktop so you can find it later*)

LOADING FONTS

Locate the font you downloaded on your desktop, it will be in a **Zip file**.
Right Click >Extract All.
Open the file to locate the font with the extension ttf. (true type font)
Select the **Font** and **Copy**.

Start>Control Panel>Fonts
Paste the Font into the font folder.
When you open Illustrator you'll find your font in the drop down.

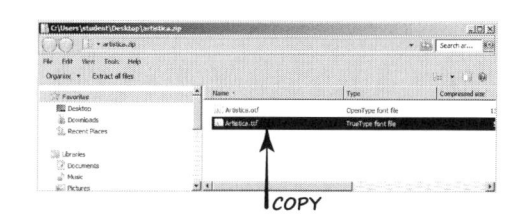

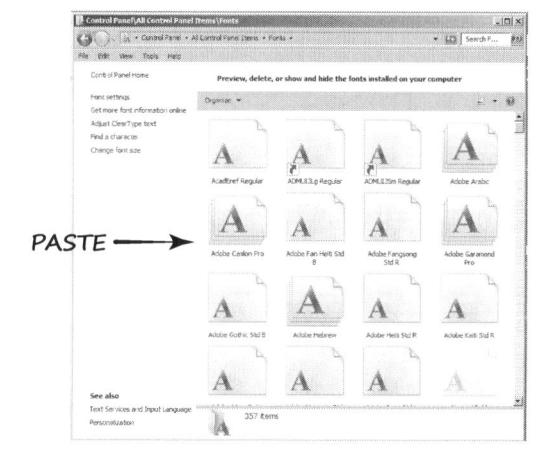

BACKGROUNDS

Backgrounds can be solid, textured, graphic, or filled with a gradient.
Use panels or borders to focus the viewer. Don't let photographic backgrounds over power your work.

Here are a few simple layout styles that will always look professional.

ADD A SOLID BACKGROUND
Make a New Layer.
Draw a **17" x 14" Rectangle** and Fill with the color that will best set off your illustration.
Drag the layer to the Bottom of the Layers Stack. You can also fill it with a Gradient for a different effect.

GRAPHIC PANEL
Select the **Rectangle** and **Scale** it down to create a **Panel**. I usually let the croqui extend beyond the panel to add depth and visual interest.

This can be filled with a gradient as well. **Creating a Gradient** that fades to white can really pop the croquis.

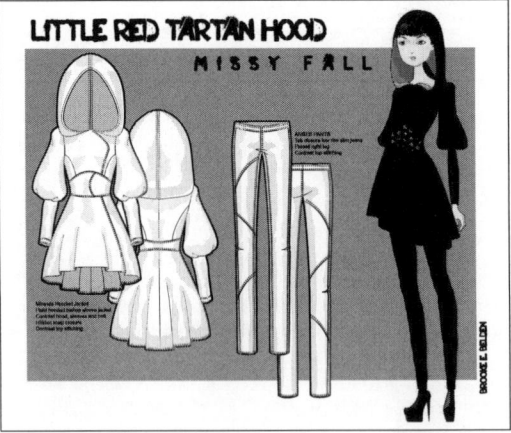

SIMPLE AND ELEGANT

INSET BORDER

Instead of a panel how about a pinstripe? Change the **panel fill to None**. Select a co-ordinating color for the stroke and make the stroke weight heavier.

To make it more sophisticated I usually remove a section of the border and incorporate the type into the empty spot.

Add an anchor point to the panel on either side if the **Collection Title**.
Direct Select the line segment in between and **Delete**. Move the type into place.

Here is a two board layout with a neutral background and an inset boarder.

The boarder was stroked with one of the **Chalk/Charcoal** art brushes for a rougher look.

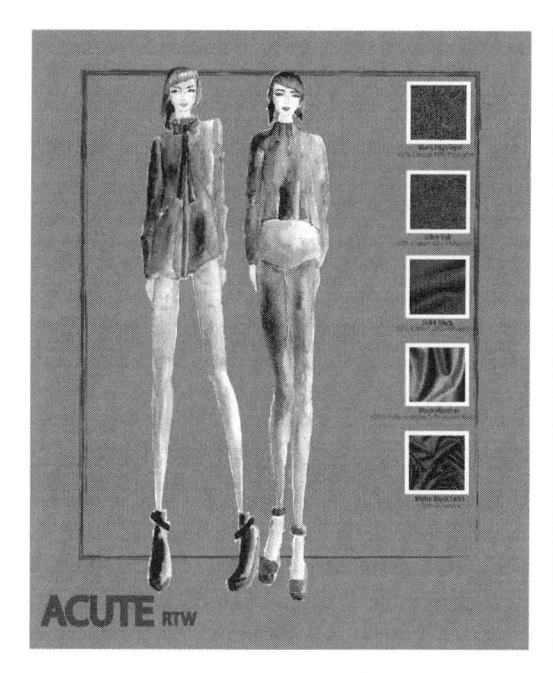

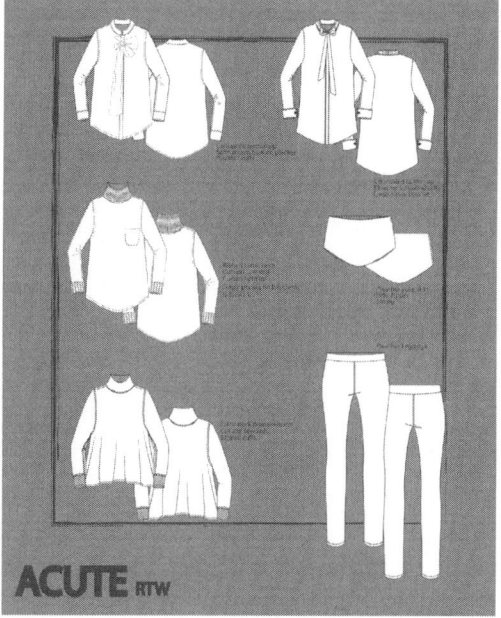

Stella Lee Art Institute of Ca-Hollywood

SAVING FILES FOR PRINT

It is important to save your files as a **Adobe PDF** when you are going to have them printed.

The printer you use may not have access to the version of Illustrator® you are using or to the fonts you have chosen. In order to have all of the elements of your layout print the way you designed them the file must be saved as an **Adobe PDF**. By saving as an **Adobe PDF** all of the necessary information will save with the file so that no matter where you print you can insure the correct output.

File>Save As
Save as Type: **Adobe PDF**
Name and Save.

Trixie Encomienda
Art Institute of Ca-Hollywood
http://www.coroflot.com/Trixie_Encomienda

adobe® for fashion : illustrator CS5 | 171

Trixie Encomienda

172 | Lesson 10: Layout

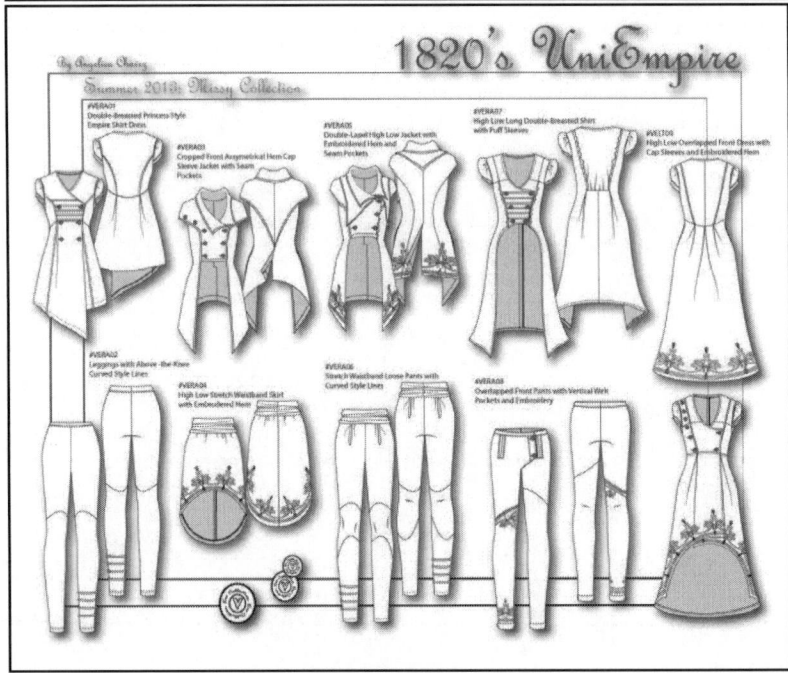

Angelica Chavez
Art Institute of Ca-Hollywood
http://www.coroflot.com/veltimera

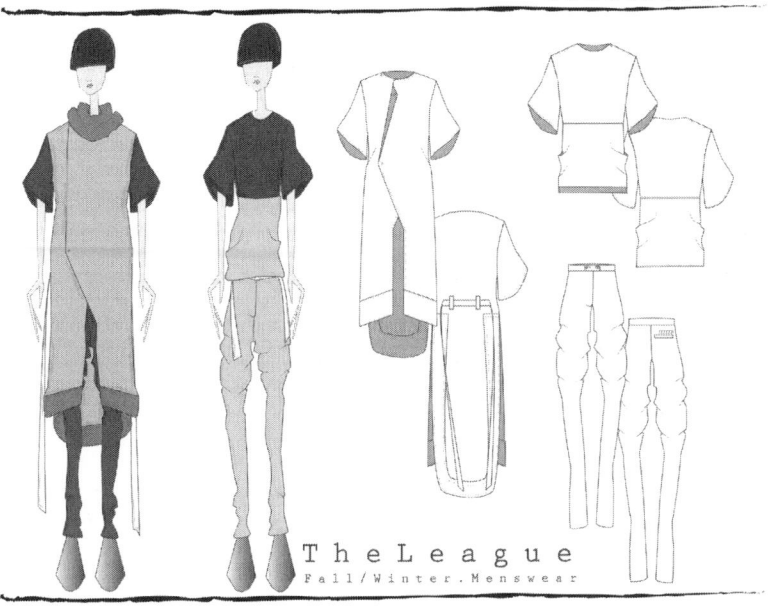

adobe® for fashion : illustrator CS5 | 173

TheLeague
Fall/Winter.Menswear

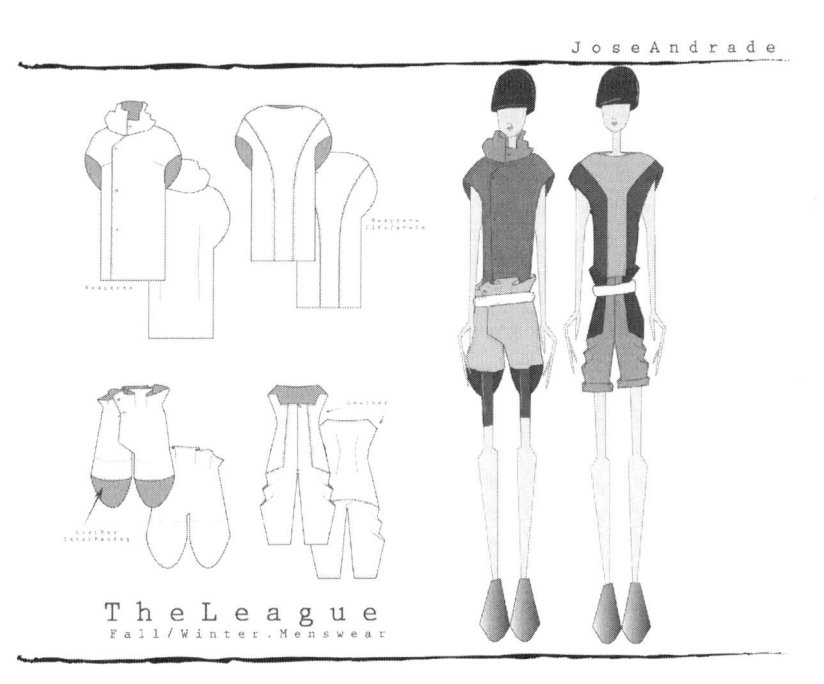

Jose Andrade
Art Institute of Ca-Hollywood
http://www.coroflot.com/joseandrade

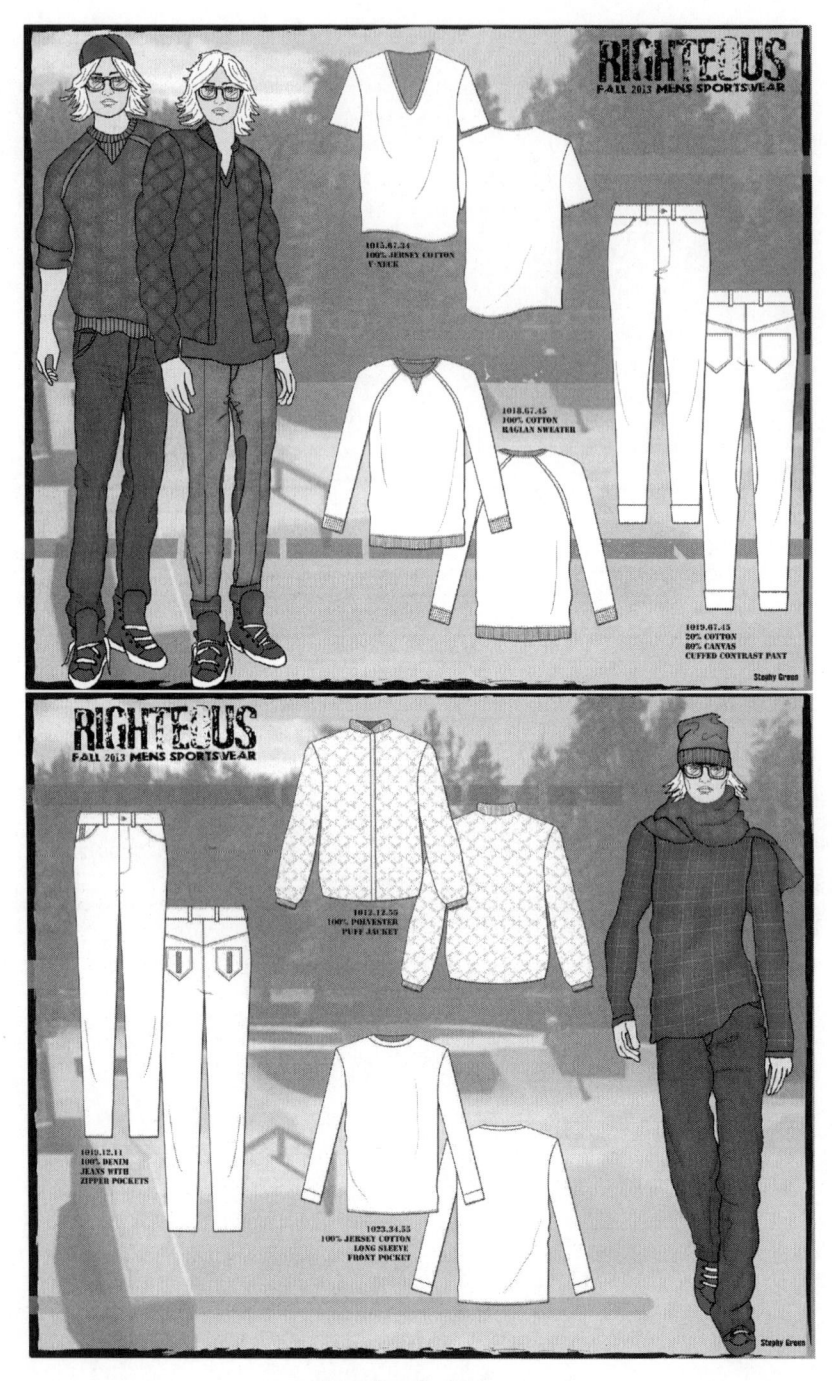

174 | Lesson 10: Layout

Stephanie Green
Art Institute of Ca-Hollywood
http://www.coroflot.com/stephyg

adobe® for fashion : illustrator CS5 | 175

Juan Sim
Art Institute of Ca-Hollywood
http://www.coroflot.com/juan_sim

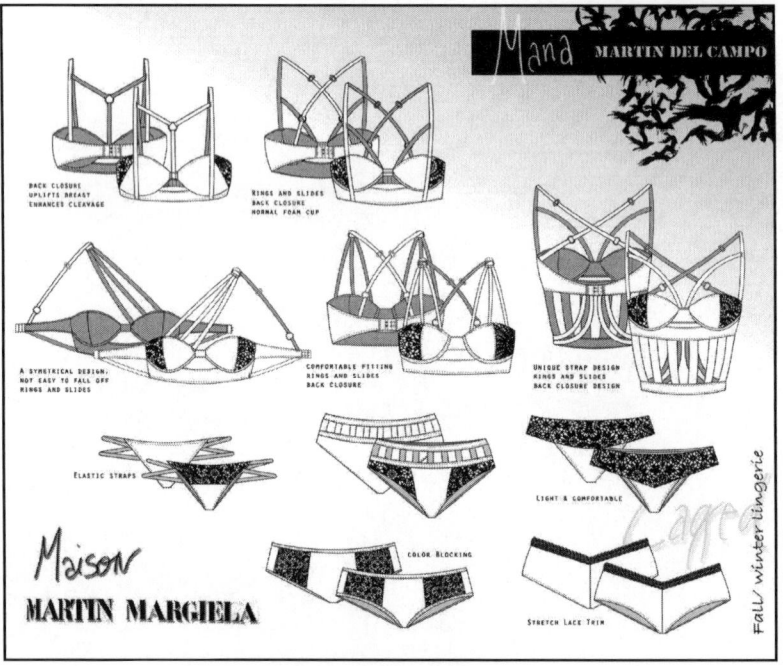

Fernanda Martin Del Campo
Art Institute of Ca-Hollywood
http://www.coroflot.com/fernandamartin

Brooke Belden
Art Institute of Ca-Hollywood
http://www.coroflot.com/brooke_e_belden

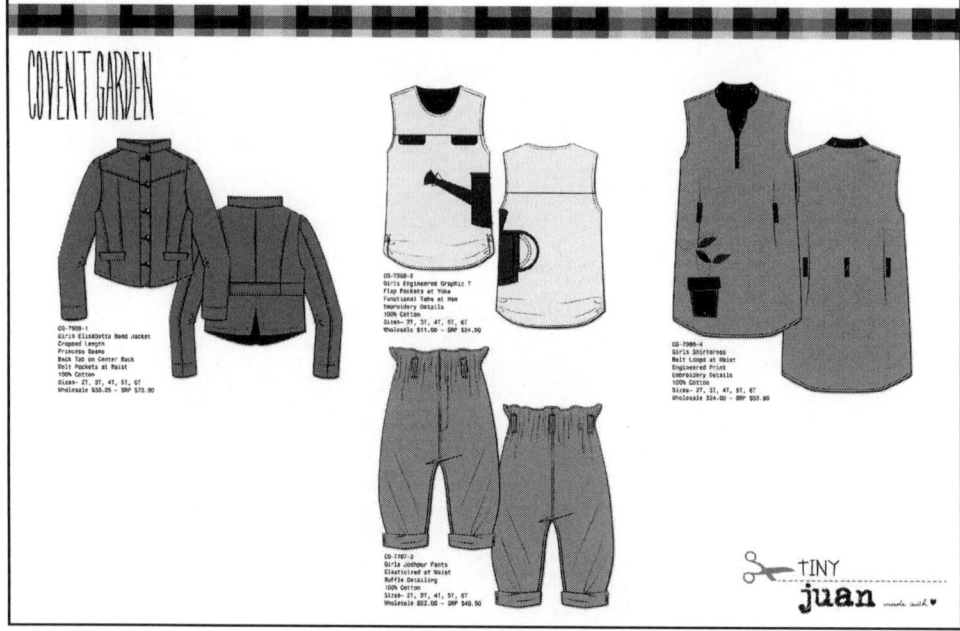

178 Lesson 10: Layout

Juan Sim
Art Institute of Ca-Hollywood
http://www.coroflot.com/juan_sim

adobe® for fashion : illustrator CS5 | 179

: proper citizens :
boys tees : : 7-13

Lauren Diaz
Art Institute of Ca-Hollywood
http://www.coroflot.com/laurendiaz

lesson eleven

ADVANCED SKILLS
USING PROFILES TO ADD FLAIR

In CS5 Adobe introduced Profiles allowing us the ability to vary the width of a stroke at any point along a path. This is a great feature for achieving a more organic hand illustrated look.
Select a path and apply a profile from the stroke panel.

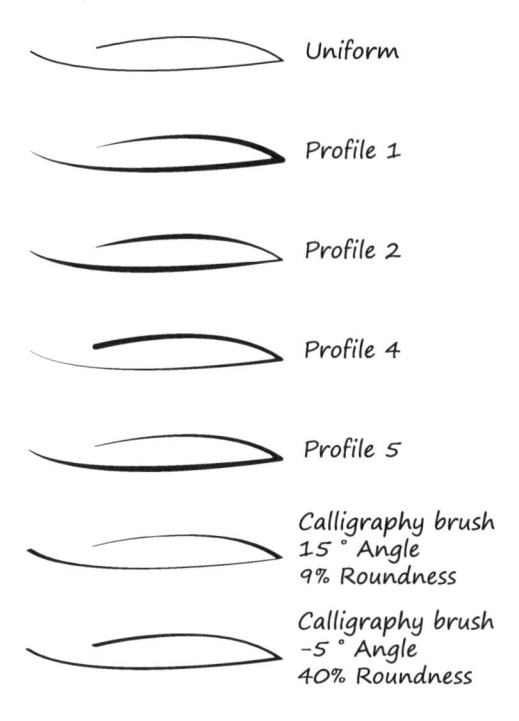

Uniform

Profile 1

Profile 2

Profile 4

Profile 5

Calligraphy brush
15° Angle
9% Roundness

Calligraphy brush
-5° Angle
40% Roundness

VERSION CS4 AND EARLIER
You can get the same effect by drawing the same shapes as these profiles and making a **New Art brush**.

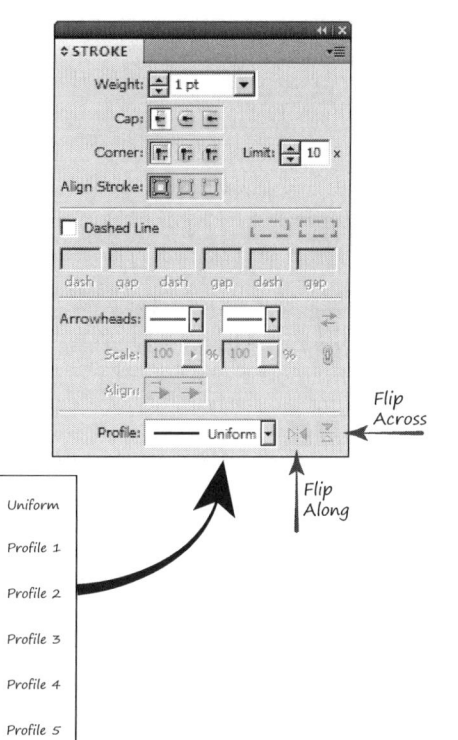

Uniform
Profile 1
Profile 2
Profile 3
Profile 4
Profile 5

Flip Across

Flip Along

QUICK & EASY BOLD OUTLINE

Select the Flat
Copy and **Paste in Back**
Pathfinder Unite to make a silhouette of the flat.
Change the **Stroke to 2 or 3** points for a bold outline.

DROP SHADOW

Select the Flat.
Make sure it is **Grouped** together.
Effect>Stylize>Drop Shadow
- Adjust the **Opacity**
- the **X** and **Y offset**
- and the **Blur**

Be careful not to make the drop shadow too big or too dark. The focus should be on the flat, not the drop shadow.

*To edit go to the **Appearance Panel**
Click on **Drop Shadow** and Edit.*

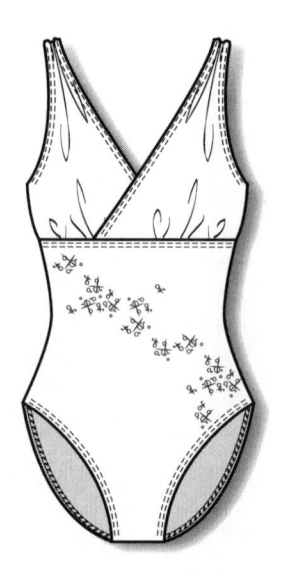

TIME SAVERS

APPEARANCE PANEL

This is like one stop shopping. Instead of having open panels all over your workspace try using the **Appearance Panel**.

From this one panel you can access **Fill Swatches**, **Stroke Swatches**, **Stroke Panel**, **Opacity** and any **Effects** you have applied.
You can even access **Pathfinder** and **Envelope Warp** from the **fx** drop down.

If there is an effect on the object, you can edit it here.

Give it a try It's a great time saver.

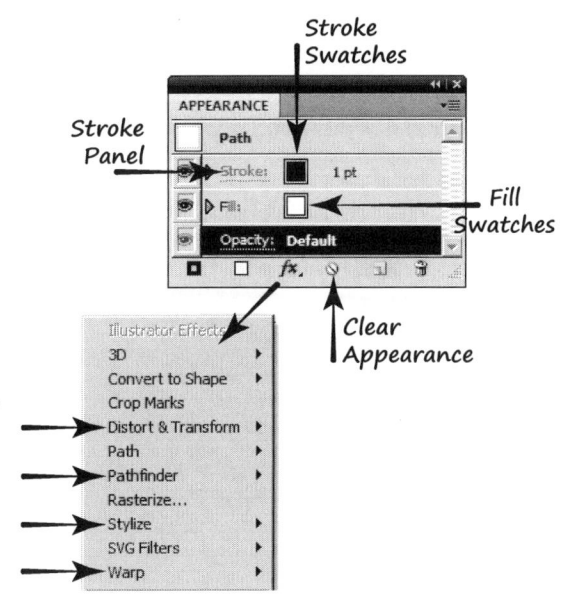

LOCATE OBJECT

Have you ever had so many layers that you had trouble locating an object in the **Layers Panel**?
Don't waste any more of your precious time scrolling through layers.

- **Select** the object or path.
- Click on the **Layers Menu**.
- Select **Locate Object**.

Problem solved!

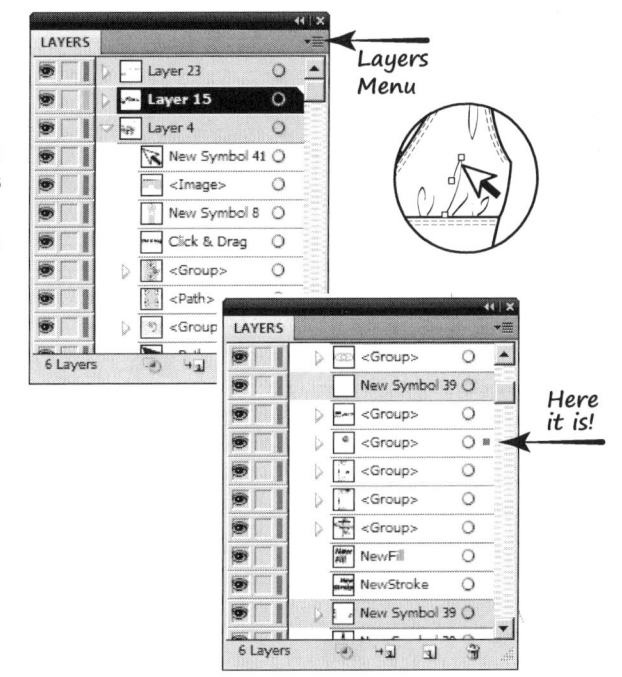

MEASURE TOOL

You can measure objects on the page using the **Measure Tool** *(It's hiding behind the Eye Dropper)*.

Click on an object.
Click on the **Measure Tool**
and it will show you the measurements of the object in the **INFO** window.

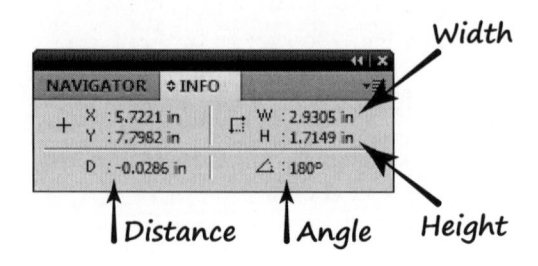

You can also **click and drag** along an object with the **Measure Tool** and you will see the measurements in the **INFO** window.

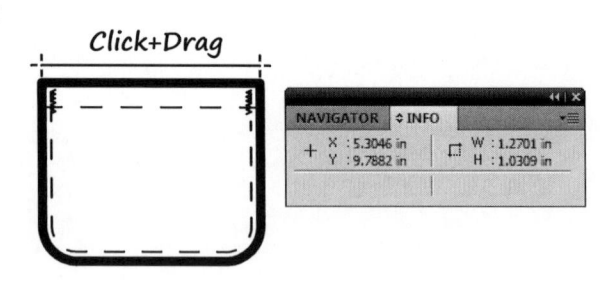

SHAPE BUILDER TOOL

The **Shape Builder Tool** is kind of like Pathfinder on steroids. It is an interactive way of Uniting and Dividing paths.

We need to adjust a few settings in the Options box to get the full benefit of using the **Shape Builder**.

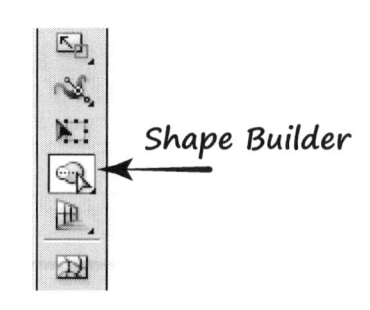

Shape Builder

Double click on **Shape Builder** in the **Tool Bar** to open the **Options Box**.

Un-check:
Consider Open Paths as Closed

Check:
In Merge Mode, Clicking Stroke Splits the Path

Check:
Fill and Highlight Stroke when Editable
Click OK and lets get started.

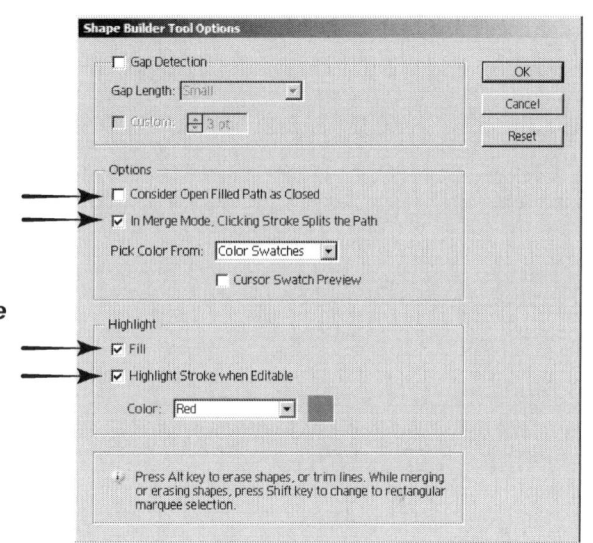

Draw a path to divide with.
This time it doesn't matter if it has a fill or not
It works either way.

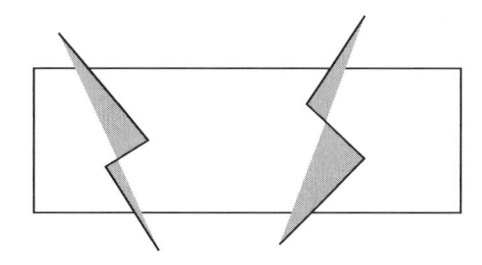

Lesson 11: Advanced Techniques

Use the **Selection Tool** to select all of the objects and paths you want to modify.

With the **Shape Builder tool** **Click once** on a single shape to **Divide**

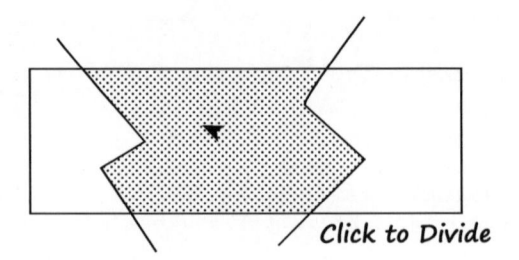

Click to Divide

Click and drag through connecting shapes to **Unite**

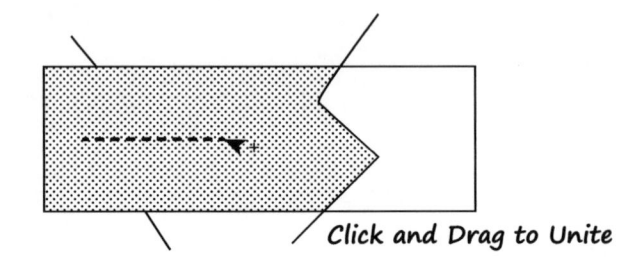

Click and Drag to Unite

Alt+Click(*Opt+Click*) on a path or a shape to **Delete** it.

Alt + Click to Delete

The other time saver is that we don't need to ungroup. Just click once on an empty area of the art board to release, then select a section and fill it.

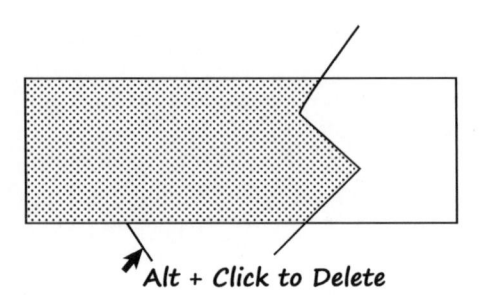

ANIMATED FLATS

THE PENCIL TOOL

Use it to add some movement and flair to your flats. The **Pencil tool** will edit a selected path when you draw over it.

First adjust the settings.
Double click on the **Pencil Tool**
Check - Edit selected paths.

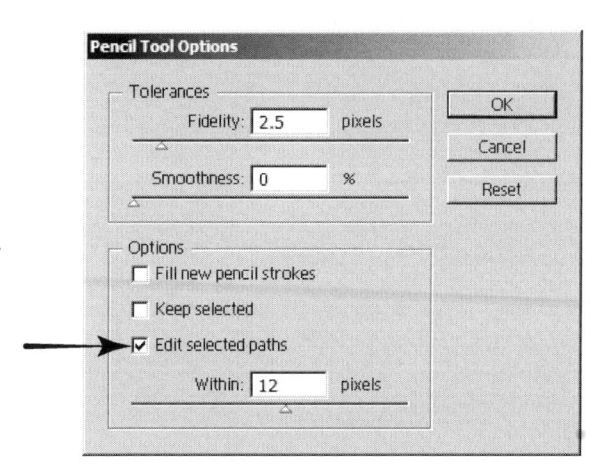

Select the path and draw directly over the path with the **Pencil tool** to make wrinkles and folds in the fabric.

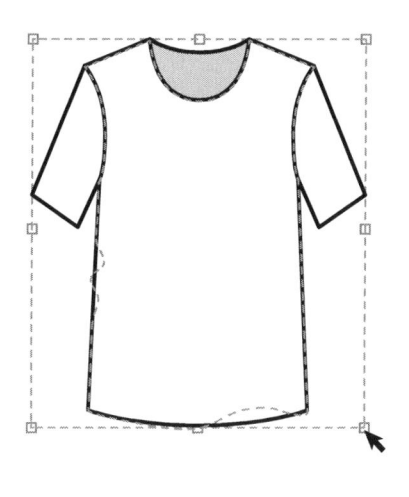

ADDING STITCHING TO BOTH SIDES OF A SEAM

OFFSET STROKE

Select the path.

Object>Path>Offset Stroke
Select 1 or 2 points.

Click OK.

Set the **Stroke to .25pt**.
Dash 2pt - Gap 2pt.

or use your **Stitching Graphic Style**.

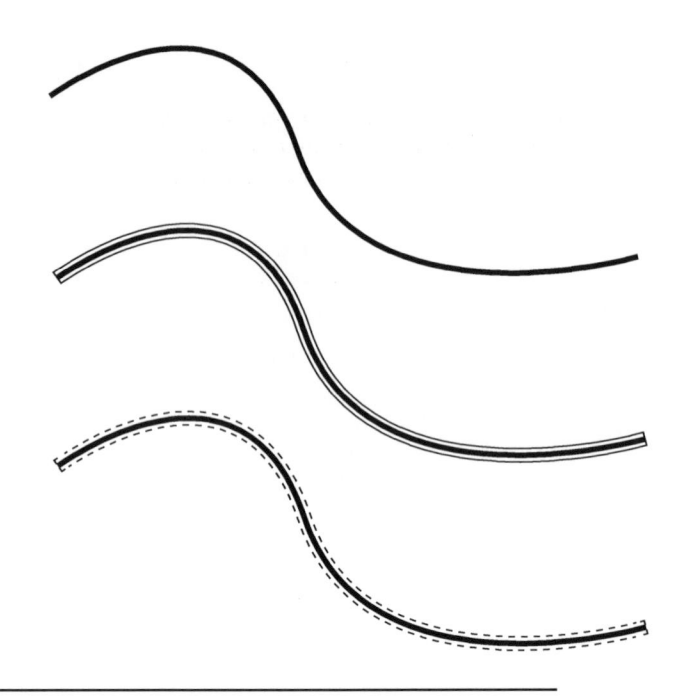

EMBROIDERY

SCRIBBLE

To create the look of an embroidered embellishment you can use the **Scribble effect**.

Draw an object with a fill and no stroke.

Effects > Stylize > Scribble

Select **Tight** and make any other adjustments you like. You can even change the angle by **rotating the radial dial**.
Click OK.

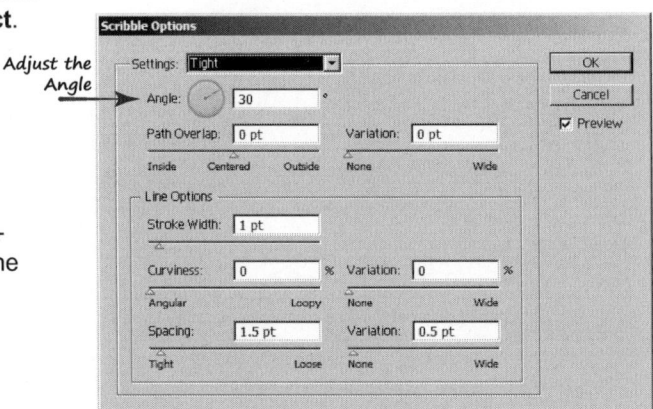

RIBBING

There are three different techniques that can be used to create ribbing. Try them all and use the one that's most appropriate for your particular application.

1. RIBBING BRUSH

Draw a path the height of the ribbing or draw two for a double rib.
Set the **stroke to black**, the **fill to none** and the **line weight to .5 or .25**.
In the case of a double rib you can do one of each.
Select and make a **Pattern Brush** with **Spacing** set to **100%**.

Draw a path and apply the brush.

The benefit of a ribbing brush is that you have control over the style of rib and the ability to bend the ribbing to follow the contour of the garment.

2. RIBBING AS A GRAPHIC STYLE

Draw a path with no fill and set the stroke weight to the height you want the ribbing to be (try 20-40 pts)

Check dashed line
Select **Butt caps**
For single rib set the **dash to .25** and the **space to 1pt**.
For double rib set the **dash to .25, space 1pt. dash .25, dash 2pt**.

Open **Graphic Styles** and make a **New Graphic Style**, name it ribbing. Now you can apply it to any path.

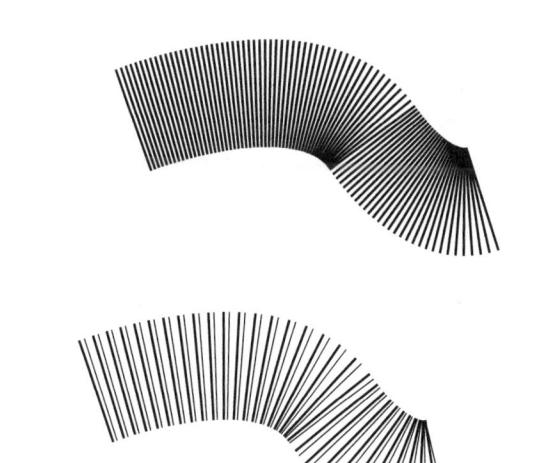

20 points

.25 dash - 1pt gap

.25 dash - 1pt gap - .25 dash - 2pt gap

3. BLEND

For ribbing that needs to curve around a shape use **Blend**.

Draw the turtle neck as a closed path.
With the **Direct selection tool Copy** one side and **Paste in Front** (like we do with the arm holes).

Set the **stroke to .25** and the **fill to none**.
Nudge it over a bit with the **left arrow**.
Draw a **vertical line at center** with the same settings.
Select both paths and **Object>Blend>Make**

Now go to **Object>Blend>Blend Options**.
Set the **Spacing to Specified steps**
Check the Preview box
Adjust the number to your liking and click OK.

Reflect for the other side.

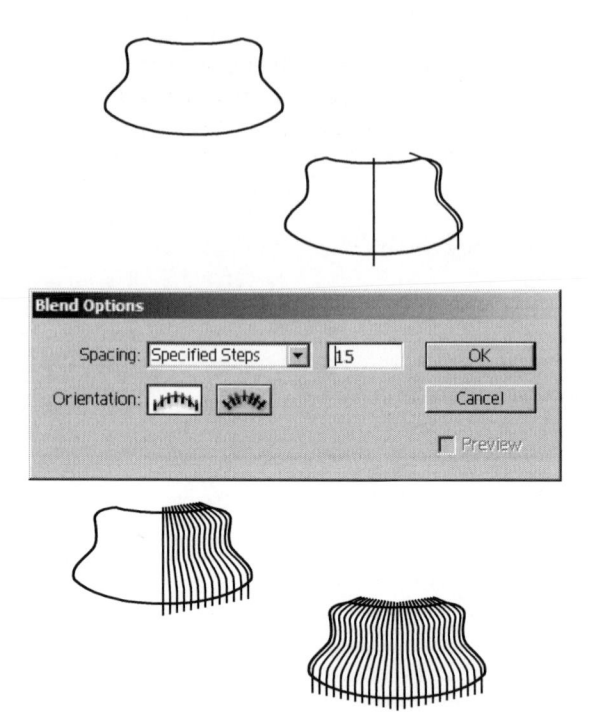

Blend is a great tool with many uses...

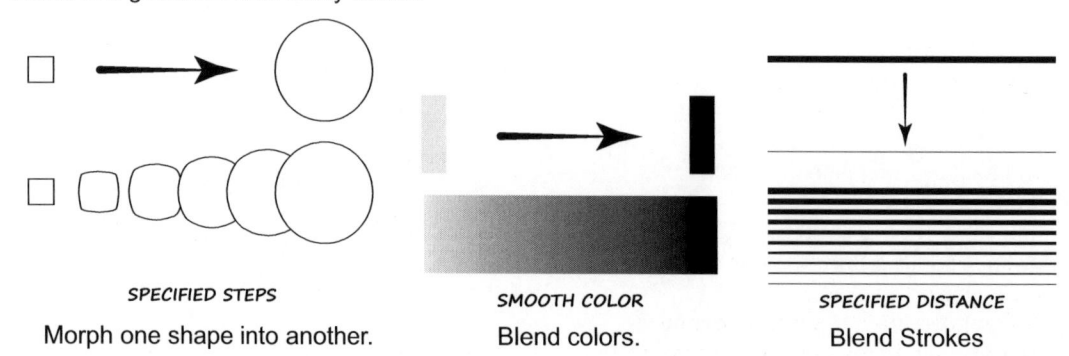

SPECIFIED STEPS
Morph one shape into another.

SMOOTH COLOR
Blend colors.

SPECIFIED DISTANCE
Blend Strokes

CLIPPING MASK

Now that you can create ribbing, lets apply it. To do this we need to use a **Clipping Mask**. Basically that is just a fancy term for putting the ribbing inside the boundary of another shape like a cuff or collar.

Draw a path centered over the turtleneck

Apply the **Ribbing Brush, Graphic Style,** or **Blend**.

Right Click > Arrange > Send to Back
For this to work the ribbing **must be behind** the object being filled.

Select both the turtleneck and ribbing, **Right click > Make Clipping Mask**.

Now the ribbing is correct but the turtleneck outline has disappeared.

Use the **Direct Selection tool** to **reselect the outline**. Set the **Stoke weight** back to 1pt and the fill to white. Tada!!!

EDITING

Editing inside a **Clipping Mask** is just like working in **Isolation mode**.
Double click on the turtleneck to get inside the **Clipping Mask**, make your adjustments and **double click** on the page to release.

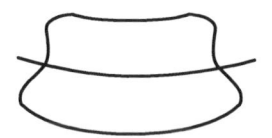

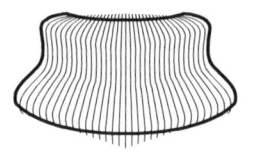

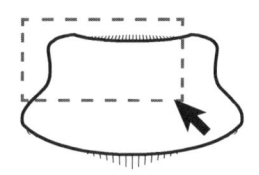

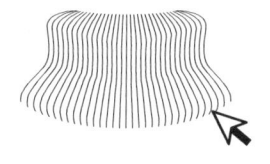

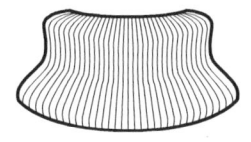

SHADING WITH THE BLOB BRUSH

The **Blob Brush** is a great way to do some fast shading on a flat.

Select the **Blob Brush**.

Adjust the size using the left and right **Bracket keys ([ ])**.

Set the stroke color to black and paint in the shading as if you were using a marker or paint brush. *Don't worry about staying inside the lines.*

Select the shading and lower the **Opacity to 10%**. (*Make a new Graphic Style for future use*)

If you colored outside the lines use the **Eraser** to clean it up. *Adjust the size of the Eraser using the left and right Bracket keys ([ ]).*

Note: Before you add shading to a flat, **lock the layer**. *Make a* **New layer** *for the shading and* **Group** *all of the shading together.*

When the shading is complete, unlock the flat and **Group** *it with the shading. This way the shading will always be easy to edit or remove without disturbing the flat.*

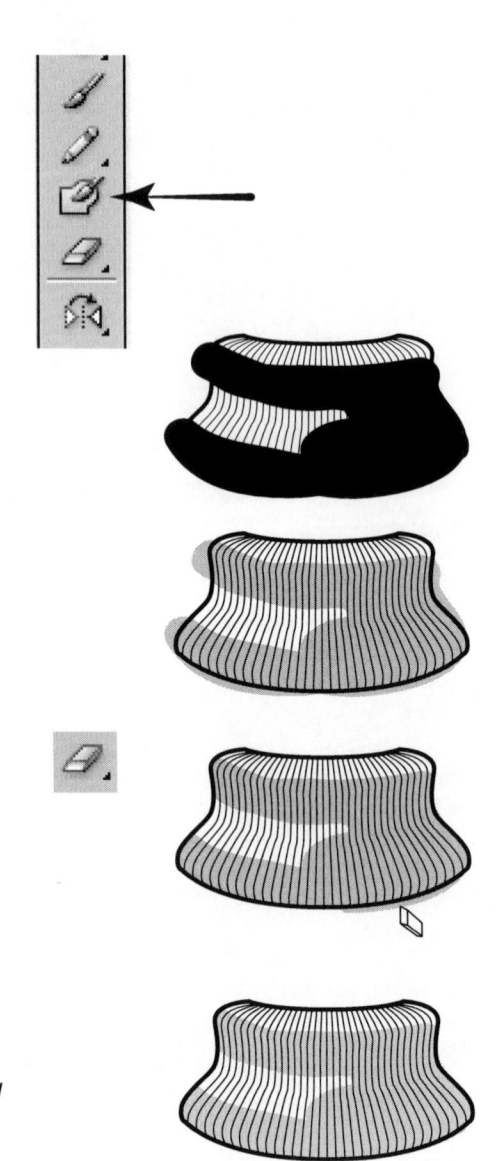

adobe® for fashion : illustrator CS5 | 193

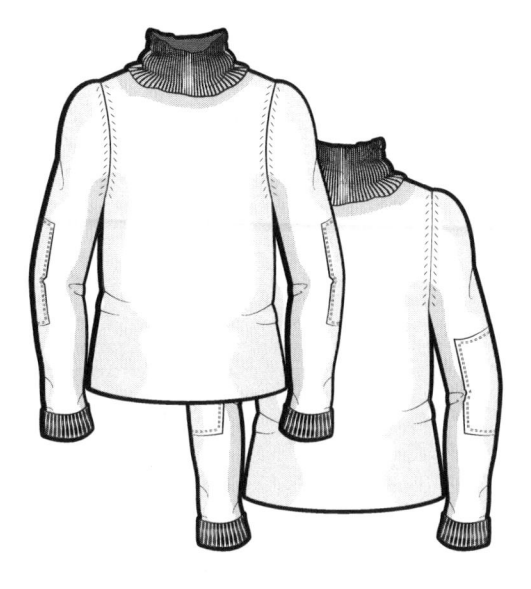

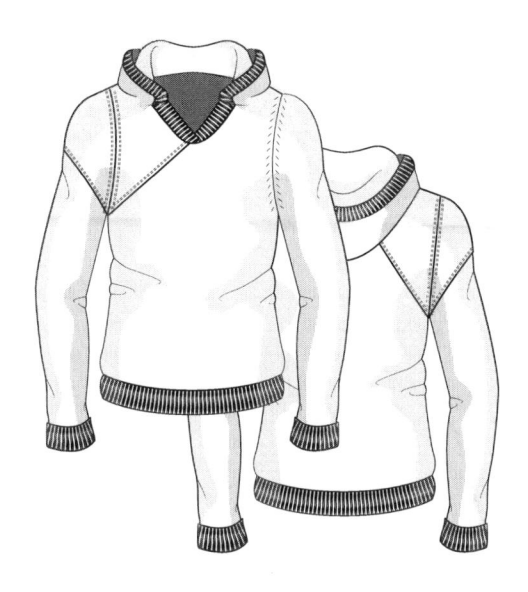

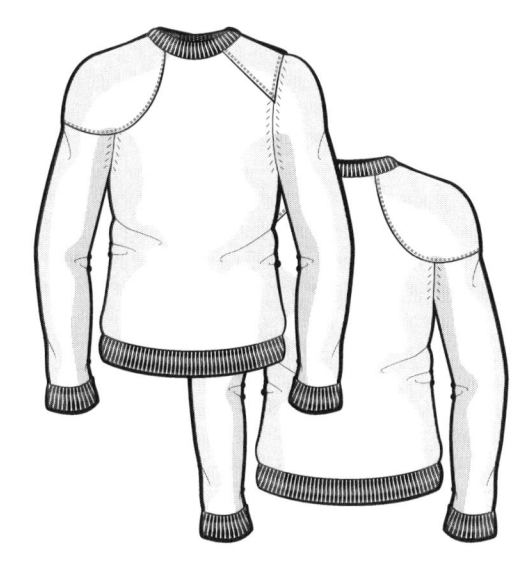

Brooke Belden
Art Institute of Ca-Hollywood
http://www.coroflot.com/brooke_e_belden

ADVANCED BRUSHES

START AND END TILES
First create all of the elements of your brush.

Select the **Left piece**
Edit>Define>Pattern
Name the pattern "**Start**"

Select the **Right piece**
Edit>Define>Pattern
Name the pattern "**End**"

Select the middle section of the brush (this is the section that will repeat)
Open the **Brushes Panel** and click on the **New Brush Icon**.
Select **Pattern Brush** and Click OK.

When **Pattern Brush Options** opens:
Click on the 4th box and select **Start** from the list.

Click on the last box and select **End** from the list.
Click OK.

Draw a path and apply your brush.

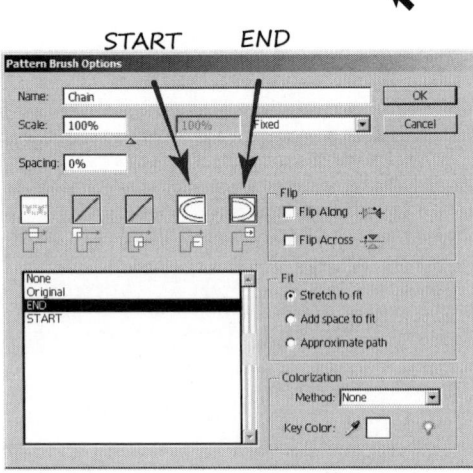

Now it has closed links at both ends. This technique can be used to make all kinds of time saving brushes.

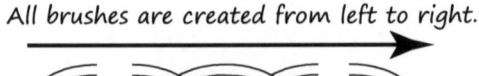

SHOELACE BRUSH

Draw a rectangle.

Duplicate it two times.
Alt(*Opt*) **Drag** and **Ctrl+D**(*Cmd+D*)

Use the **Direct Selection tool** to select and delete the inside line segments.

Shape the ends by adding and nudging the anchor points.

Draw two circles to make the **Eyelet** or use your **Eyelet Symbol**.

Draw a rectangle for the **Aglet**.

Assemble and add details.

Eyelet Start   Aglet End

Select the **Eyelet Start** piece.
Edit>Define pattern.

Select the **Aglet end** piece.
Edit>Define pattern.

Select the center section and make a **New Pattern Brush**.
Select the **Eyelet** for the **Start tile**.
Select the **Aglet** for the **End tile**.
Click **OK**.
Draw a path and apply the brush.

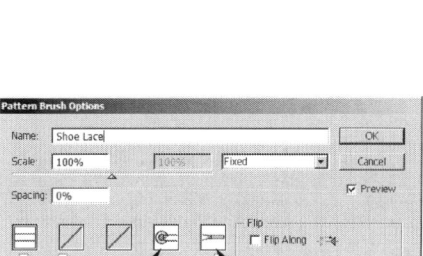

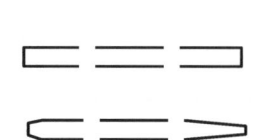

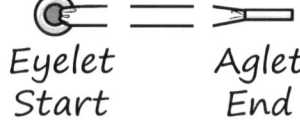

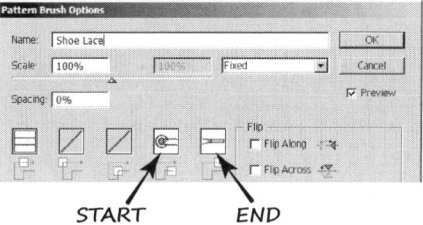

START   END

Lesson 11: Advanced Techniques

EXPOSED ZIPPER BRUSH

Draw **.75pt x 2.85pt Rectangle**.
Set the **fill to white** and the **stroke to .25pt**.

Copy, Nudge over and down and **Group**.

Draw a **1pt stroke** with **Butt Caps** that is exactly the width of the two zipper teeth.
Draw a **.25pt stroke** with **Round Caps** for the stitches.
Select both strokes and **Group**.
Reflect Horizontal.

Draw a **2.5pt x 4pt Rectangle** for the stop.

Extend the **1pt Stroke** to the end of the stop.

Duplicate the **.25pt Stitch** two times.

Drag out your **Zipper Pull Symbol**.
Make a **Copy** of the **Zipper teeth** and duplicate until it is longer than your **Zipper Pull symbol**. Assemble and **Group**.

Select the **Zipper End** and **Edit>Define Pattern**.

Select the **Zipper Pull** and **Edit>Define Pattern**.

Select the **Zipper Teeth** and make a **New Pattern Brush**. Select the **Zipper End** for the **End Tile** and **Zipper Pull** for the **Start Tile**. Click OK.

Draw a path and apply the brush.

A complete zipper with just one click!

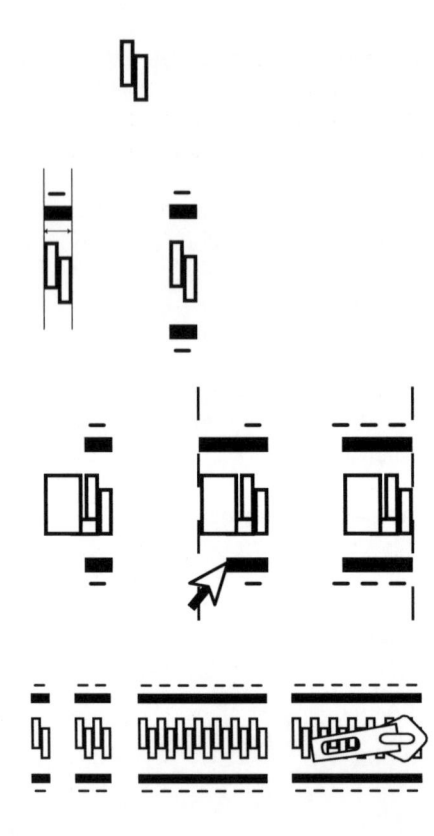

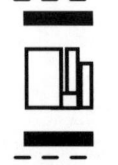

Zipper End Define as a Pattern

Zipper Teeth Make a Pattern Brush

Zipper Pull Define as a Pattern

RUFFLE TRIM BRUSH

Draw a single ruffle with a **black Stroke**, **white Fill** and **Width Profile #1**.
Alt(*Opt*) **Drag** to **Duplicate** three times.
Draw connecting curves with the **Pen tool**.

Select all. **Make** a **Copy** and **Paste** it out of the way for later.

Direct Select and **Delete** the top anchor point of each ruffle.

Select All, **Right click** and **Join**.

With the **Pen tool**
  • Click at point 1
  • Shift Click at 2
  • Shift Click at 3 to close the shape

Change to **white Fil**l, **no stroke**.(*I'm using gray for this illustraton to clearly define the white areas*).

Drag the Ruffles you copied back on top of the shape.

Select the **right end line segment**
Object > Expand.
Select Stroke and click OK.

With the **Direct Selection** tool **align the Anchor Points** with the edge of the white object.

Move the **Upper left corner** of the white piece so that is 90°.Select the single ruffle and **Edit>Define Pattern**.

Select the main piece and make a **New Pattern Brush**.
Assign the **single ruffle** to the **end tile**.

Draw a path and apply the brush.

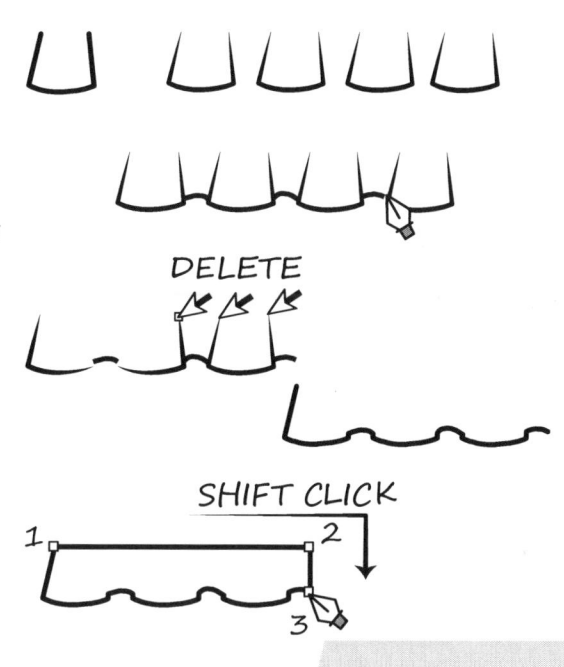

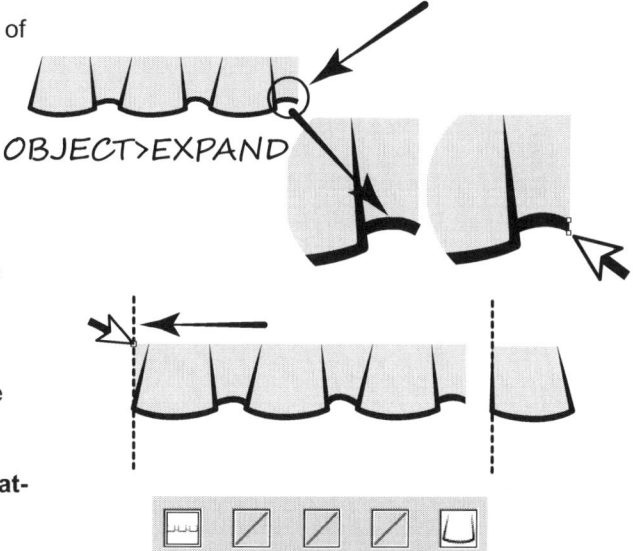

Lesson 11: Advanced Techniques

ELASTIC CASING

Draw a Rectangle.
- **30pts x 4.6pts, white fill, No stroke**
- **Butt Caps and Miter Join**.

Direct Select the top line segment,
Copy and **Paste in Front**
Change to **1pt black stroke, no fill**
Effects>Distort and Transform>Roughen
- Size 2% Check Relative
- Detail 97 Check Smooth
- Click OK.

Object > Expand Appearance
Direct Select the **Anchor point** at each end and **Align Center**.

Select both pieces and **Reflect Horizontal**.

Draw gathers with a **.25 Stroke** and **Width Profile #1**.

Draw a **Line Segment** 9.2pts. and 90°
Black 1pt. Stroke, no Fill and **Round Caps**.

Select the **Line Segment**.
Edit>Define Pattern and name **End**.

Select the **Side Tile** and make a **New Pattern Brush**.
Select **End** for the **Start Tile** and the **End Tile**.
Click OK.
Draw a path and Apply the Brush.

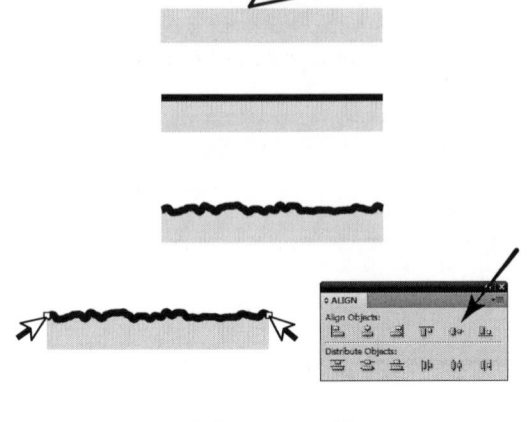

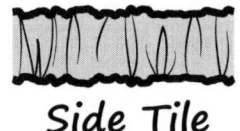

Notice that the Brush is centered on the path. What if you want to align the brush to the bottom or top of the path for easier alignment?

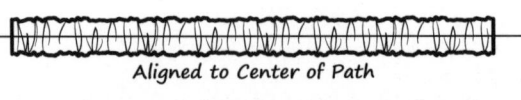

Side Tile

End

Side Tile   Start Tile   End Tile

Aligned to Center of Path

Aligned to Bottom of Path

Drag the Brush out from the **Brushes Panel**.
Right Click and **Ungroup**.

With the **Pen tool Click once** at the top of the **Side tile**. **Set Stroke and Fill to none**.

Click once on **Reflect**
Alt (*Opt*) **click** on the bottom of the **Side Tile**
Select **Horizontal** and click OK.
(*You just added an invisible point below the object*).
Do the Same for the **End Tile**.

Marque Select the **Invisible Point** and the **End** Tile. **Edit >Define Pattern**
Name it **New End** and click OK.

Marque Select the **Invisible Point** and the **Side tile**. Make a **New Pattern Brush**
Add the new **Start** and **End** Tiles
Click OK.
Draw a path and apply the brush.
It will now **Align to the Bottom** of the Path.

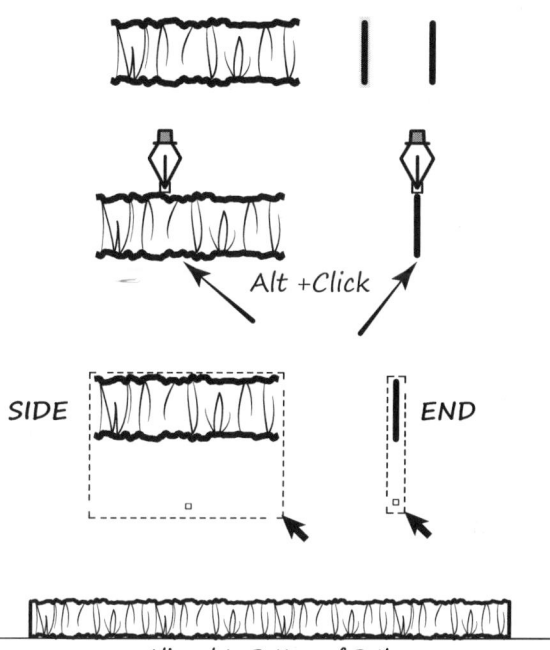

FUR
I've seen a lot of fur done with **Effect >Distort and Transform >Roughen**. It's effective, but I think my **Fur Scatter Brush** knocks it out of the park.

Draw a **Line Segment 5pts, 0°**
Set the **Stroke to .5pts**
Apply **Width Profile 5**

Make a **New Scatter Brush**
- **Size** 100% Fixed
- **Spacing** 12% Fixed
- **Scatter** 52%, -12% Random
- **Rotation** -113°,-45° Random
- **Rotation relative to PATH**
- Click OK

Draw a path and apply your brush.

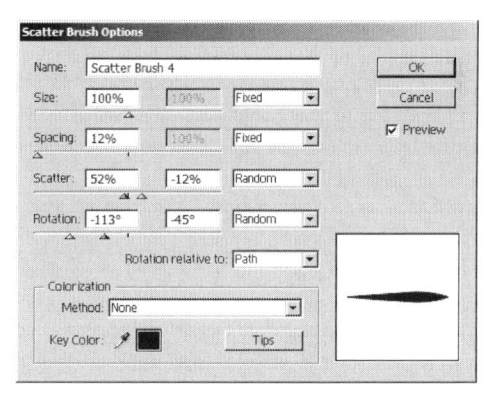

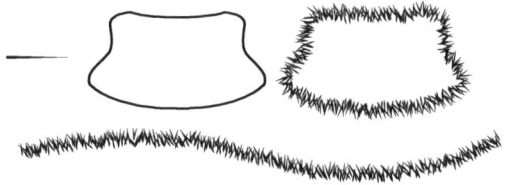

LIVE TRACE

LACE

If you have a swatch of the lace you can scan it and make a **Pattern Brush**.
- Scan the lace into **Photoshop**.
    Image>Adjustments>Desaturate to remove any color.
- **Image >Adjustments >Threshold**
    Drag the slider until you are happy with the image.
- **Image> Adjustments>Invert**
- Crop the image so that you have only one full repeat of the lace motif.
- **Copy** and **Paste** the cropped image into your Illustrator® file.

Full Repeat

When you place a **JPEG** or **PSD** image into Illustrator® you will get the option for **Live Trace** in the **Control Panel**.

Live Trace

Expand

Click on **Live Trace**.
The **Default setting** works great for this.
Click Expand.

With the **Magic Wand** click on the white background and **Delete**.
Select the lace and make a **Pattern Brush**. Setting the **Scale to 12%** should be the correct proportion for the Flat Template I have provided.

Magic Wand

Draw a path and apply the lace brush.

Try different types of lace and apply it to a Circle or Ellipse to create lace embellishments.

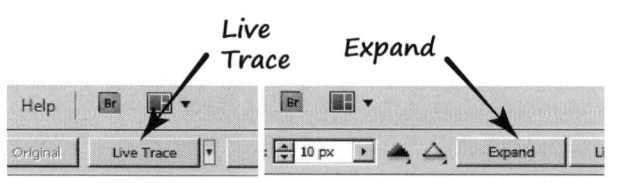

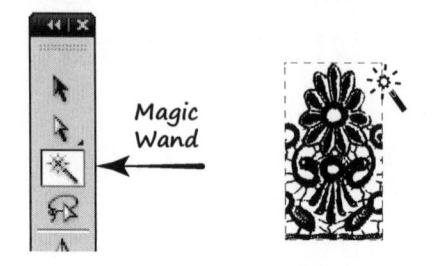

MOCK LACE

PATTERN BRUSH LACE
What if you haven sourced the lace yet? Here is a great trick for making a generic lace brush.
Choose an elaborate font and type a letter with lots of scrolls(I like lowercase y or g)
Switch to the **Selection tool** and
Type >Create outlines
This converts the type into an object.
Rotate the letter about 20°
Reflect > Vertical and **Copy**
Nudge it with the arrow key until there is a small overlap of the two letters.
Select both letters and **Pathfinder>Unite**
Create a new **Pattern brush**.
Draw a path and apply the brush.
Instant Lace!

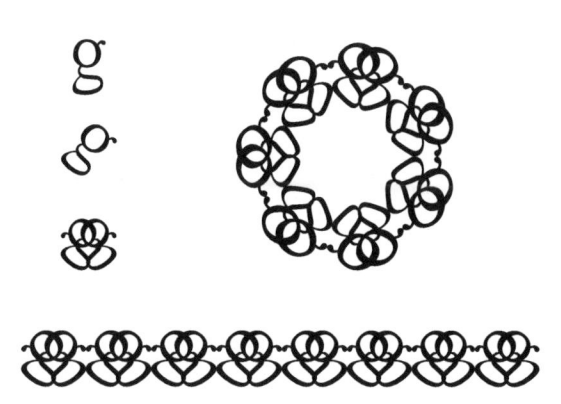

SCATTER BRUSH LACE
For a more intricate lace select both letters and create a new **Scatter brush**.
Draw a path and apply the brush.

To adjust the brush, **double click** on the **Scatter brush** in the **Brush panel**.
- Set the **Rotation Relative to Path**
- Adjust the **Spacing slider** until you like the look of the lace.

Try different letters and a range of fonts to create all types of lace patterns.

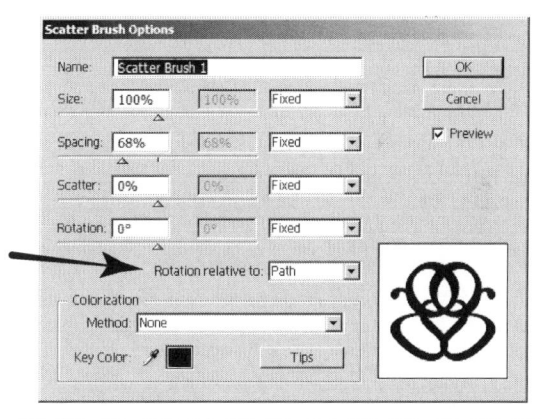

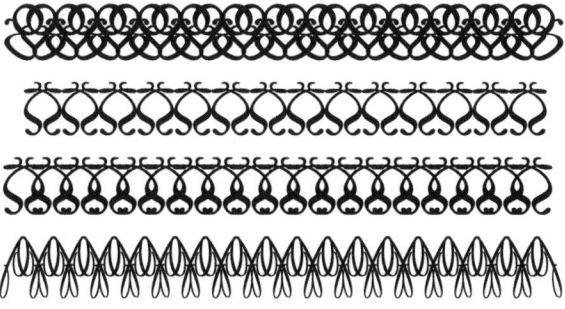

COLORING BRUSHES

If you want to fill your flats with color you may want to change the color of your brushes as well. Here is how the settings work:

If the brush was created with a Black stroke and a white fill:

Colorization set to none -the brush will not change.

Colorization set to Tints - black will change to the stroke color and the fill will remain white.

If the brush was created with a black stroke and a gray fill:

Colorization set to none - the brush will not change.

Colorization set to Tints - black will change to the stroke color and the gray will change to a lighter shade of the stroke color.

Colorization set to Tints and Shades - black will stay black and the gray will change to the stroke color.

ADVANCED PATTERNS

HALF DROP

Start with a **perfect square** tile.
Give it a **Fill but No Stroke**.
Align the Motif to the center of the tile.

To find the tile size, select the tile and you will see Its **Width** and **Height** in the upper right side of the control panel. You don't even need to note the number, just highlight it and **Copy**.

Now we need to set the **Keyboard Increment** to ½ **the tile size**.

Edit > Preferences > General
(**Ctrl+K** /Cmd+K)

Paste the number you copied and then type **forward slash two** (**/2**) to divide by two. *Let Illustrator do the math!*
Click OK.

What you just did was change the nudge amount of the Arrow Keys to ½ the size of the swatch.

Paste and divide by 2

Select only the **Motif**, hold down the **Alt** (*Opt*) Key and **Right Arrow** once to make a copy of the Motif and move it to the right.

ALT+

Release the **Alt** (Opt)Key and **Up Arrow** once to move the motif into the corner.
It should be perfectly aligned.

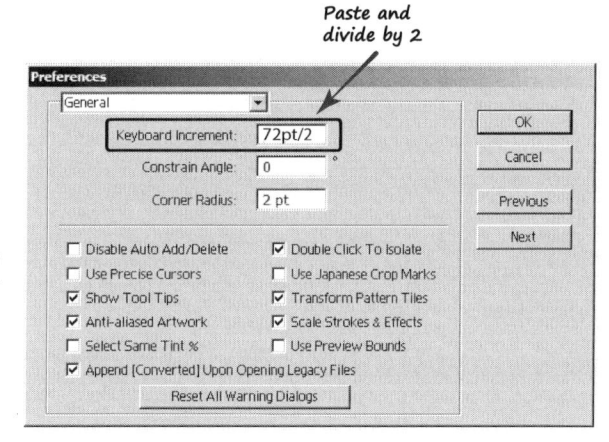

Tap the UP Arrow once to move the motif into the corner

Lesson 11: Advanced Techniques

Hold the **Alt**(*Opt*) Key **Left Arrow** once to **Copy** the motif and move it to the left.

Release the **Alt**(*Opt*) Key and **Left Arrow** once to move the motif into the corner.

Hold the ALT Key and Tap the LEFT Arrow once to copy the motif and move it to the left

Getting the idea?

Continue all the way around the tile.

Select the tile (without the motif) and **Copy (Ctrl +C /***Cmd + C***)**

Paste in Back (Ctrl+B / *Cmd +B***)**

Continue all the way around the tile.

While the tile is still selected change it's **Fill and Stroke to None**.

Marquee Select the entire swatch with the motif.

Edit > Define Pattern
Name swatch and click OK.

Select an object and fill it with the pattern.

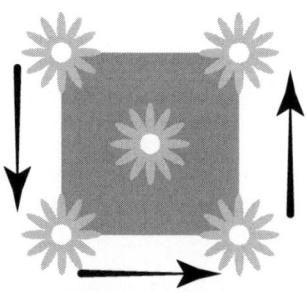

RANDOM OR TOSS REPEATS

The key to creating a perfect tile repeat is making sure that any part of the motif that extends out beyond the edges of the tile is continued on the opposite side of the tile.

Draw a perfect square.
Give it a **Fill but No Stroke**.
Select it and **Copy** the size from the **Control panel**.

To set the **Keyboard increment** click on **Edit>Preferences>General** in the menu bar or (**Ctrl+K** /*Cmd+K*).

Paste the tile size and click OK. *This time we **don't** need to divide by two.*

Start placing Motifs on the tile, any motif that extends beyond the edge of the tile must be copied to the other side.
Select it and **Alt**(*Opt*) + **Arrow** it into place. If a Motif extends beyond a corner you must **Alt**(*Opt*) + **Arrow** it to all four corners.

Now Select the **original tile** and **Copy**, **Paste in Back**.
While the tile is still selected change it's **Fill and Stroke to None**.

Marquee select the entire swatch.
Edit> Define Pattern
Name the swatch and click OK.

Why set the back copy to NONE?
This is how Illustrator understands what size to make the swatch. Remember the stripes in lesson eight?

If the pattern looks like this, you didn't Copy/Paste in Back a tile with no Stroke and no Fill.
Check the layers panel.

MAKING COLOR GROUPS

A **Color Group** is a tool that allows you to group together related color swatches for easier use. You can load existing **Color Groups** from the **Swatch Libraries** menu or make your own. You can even generate a group from existing artwork.

To make a **Color Group** click on **New Color Group** in the **Swatches Panel**. Name the **Group** and click OK.

Now just click on a **Swatch** and drag it into the **Color Group**.

Note: Color Groups may not include Gradients or Pattern Swatches.

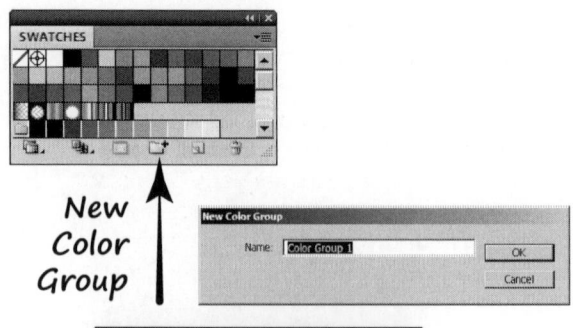

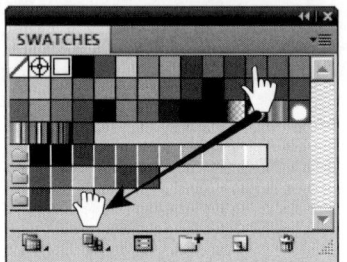

COLOR GROUP FROM ARTWORK

You can also make a **color group** from existing illustrator artwork. This is handy for adding color chips to textile designs.

Draw a **Rectangle** and fill it with a **Pattern**. Click on the **New Color Group Icon**.

When the **New Color Group** Window opens Select "**Create from Selected Artwork**". Click OK.

This will add a **New Color Group** to the **Swatches Panel** with all the colors that are in your pattern.

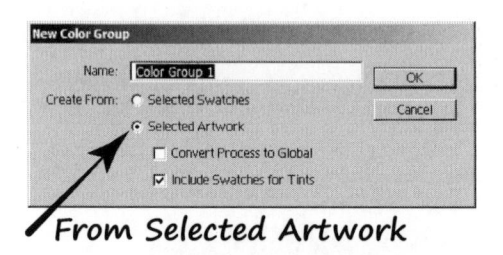

KULER

www.Kuler.adobe.com

Another way to acquire **Color Groups** is to download them from **Kuler**. Kuler is a great website where you can generate color groups or choose from those already created by the Kuler community to inspire your work.

You can access **Kuler** from within Illustrator® as long as you have internet access.

Window>Extensions>Kuler
and the **Kuler panel** will open.

You can search by keyword, newest, most popular, highest rated or random to find color themes.

When you find a group you like select it.

Click on the **Add to swatches** icon and the **Color Group** will be added to the swatches panel.

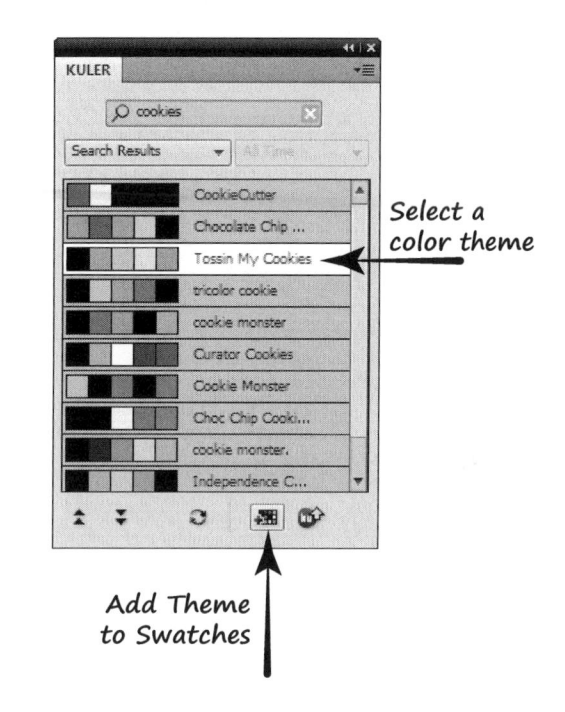

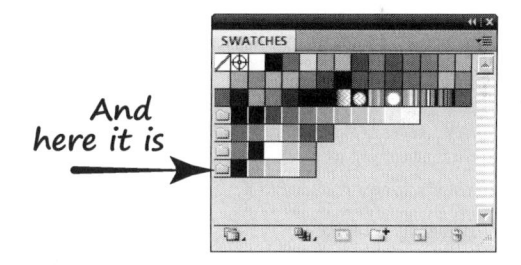

Select a color theme

Add Theme to Swatches

And here it is

RECOLOR ARTWORK

RANDOMLY CHANGE COLOR ORDER

As a textile designer this is one of my favorite features. Now that you have new **Color Groups** to play with and some patterns in your **Swatches Panel** and let's recolor them.

Draw a **rectangle** and fill it with one of your pattern swatches.
Click on **Recolor Artwork** (you can find it in the Control Panel).

Lets start by **randomly changing the color order** of your pattern. By clicking this button you can cycle through all the colors in your color group and get different looks.

When you find one you would like to keep click OK.

RECOLOR ARTWORK

Click to Randomly Change Color Order

The new **Pattern Swatch** will automatically be added to your **Swatches Panel**.
You can randomly change colors as many times as you like.

This is a quick and easy way to generate numerous color versions of the same pattern.

Oh and did I mention it's really fun?

*Tip: Make a **New Color Group From Art** and place color chips next to the pattern swatch. Select both the color chips and the pattern swatch before you click on **Recolor Art work** and it will recolor the chips for you too.*

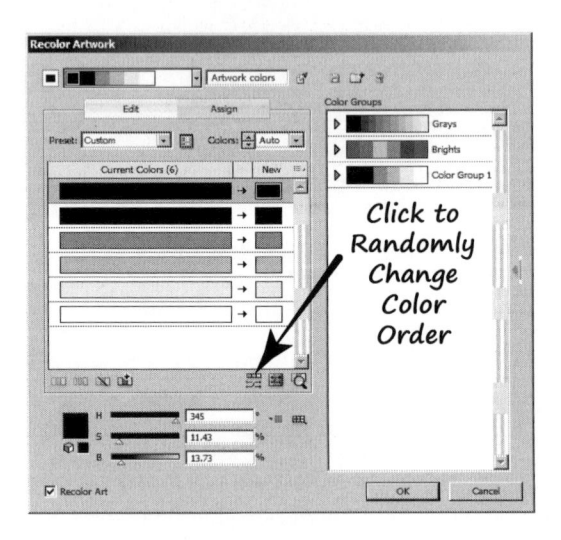

RECOLOR ARTWORK

CHANGE COLOR GROUPS

You can also plug in different color groups. Select the object with your pattern fill.

Click on **Recolor Artwork**

You can click on any color group in the swatch panel to apply that group to your pattern.

You can scroll through the new group to rotate the color placement.

You can **double click** on an **individual Color Chip** to change only that color.

You can **Randomly change Saturation and Brightness**.

You can **Exclude selected colors** so that they won't be recolored. Click on a **Current Color** and click on the **Excludes Selected Color** button.

Recolor Options

Click on a Color Group to Apply

Double Click to change color

Randomly Change Saturation and Brightness

Excludes Selected Color

You have the option of preserving blacks, whites and grays if you need them to stay constant.
Click on the **Recolor Options Button** and check the colors you want to preserve.
Click OK.

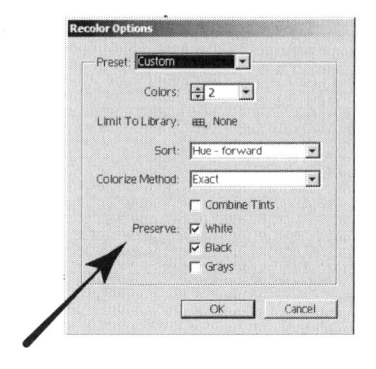

REDUCING COLORS

You can also reduce the number of colors in a pattern.

Shift + click on **Current Colors** to select two or more colors.
Click **Merge colors into a Row**
and the selected colors will be treated as one.

You can Separate them by **Shift + clicking** on each color and clicking the **Separate Colors into Different Rows** button.

Separate Colors into different rows

Merge Colors into a row

It's a great tool, experiment with it and you'll be a wiz at recoloring patterns in no time.

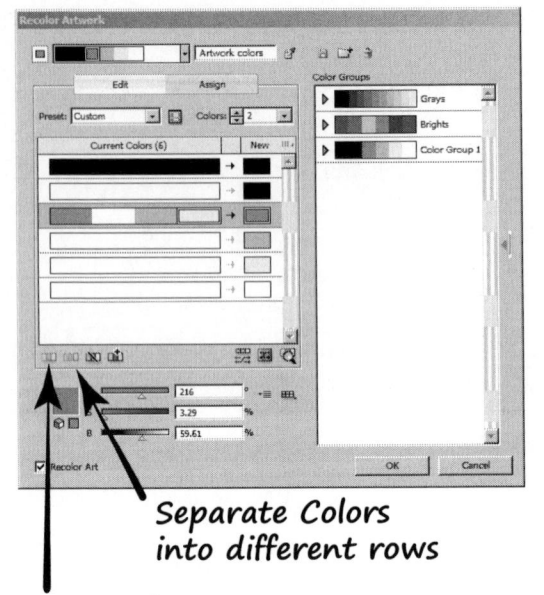

PLEATED SKIRTS

ENVELOPE WARP

KNIFE PLEATS

Draw a rectangle the size of one pleat.
Direct Select the bottom **Left Anchor Point** and nudge it down.

Hold the **Alt**(*Opt*) and **Shift** keys while dragging a copy of the pleat right next to the first one.
Now duplicate this step to create the remainder of the pleats.(**Ctrl+D** / *Cmd+D*)

Select all the pleats.
Object>Envelope Distort>Make with Warp
Select **Shell Lower**

Check the Preview box.
Select **Horizontal radial button**.
Drag the **Bend Slider** to the right until you like the shape.

Object>Envelope Distort>Expand
to remove the envelope mesh.

Experiment with different Warp Styles for different looks.

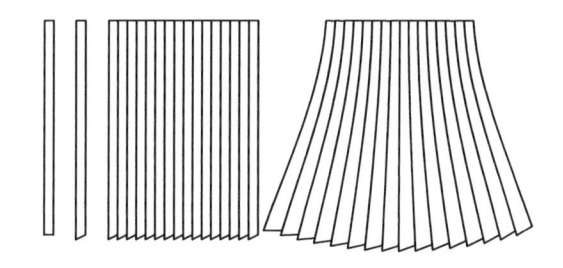

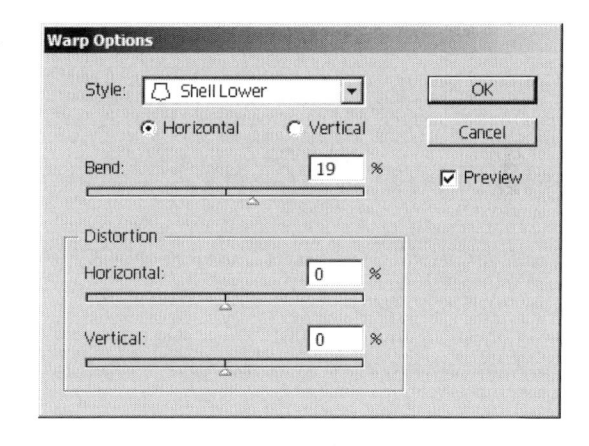

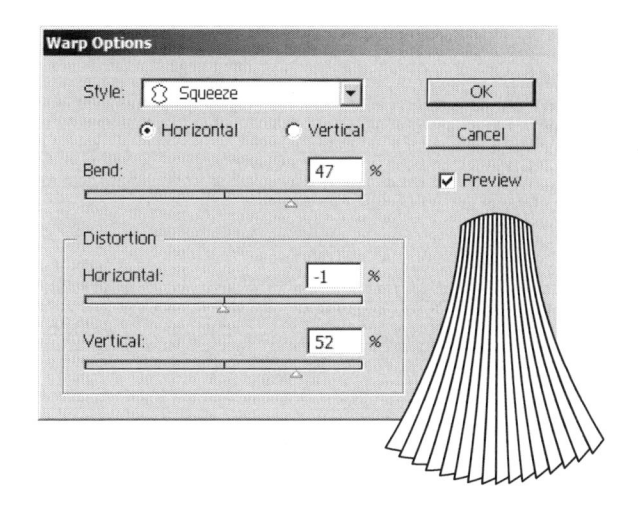

ACCORDION PLEATS

Draw a rectangle the size of one pleat. **Direct Select** the bottom Right **Anchor Point** and nudge it down.

Select it and **Reflect** it to make one pleat.

Hold the **Alt**(*Opt*) and **Shift** keys while dragging a copy of the pleat right next to the first one.

Duplicate this step to create the remainder of the pleats.(**Ctrl+D** / *Cmd+D*)

Select all the pleats.
Object>Envelope Distort>Make with Warp
Select **Arc**

Check the preview box.
Suggested Settings
- Select **Horizontal**
- Set **Bend Slider to -10%**
- Set **Vertical to 23%**

Object>Envelope Distort>Expand
to remove the envelope mesh.

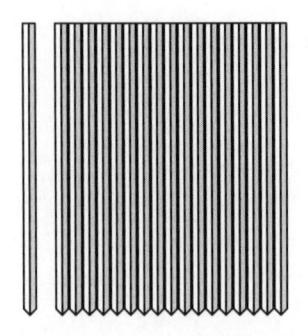

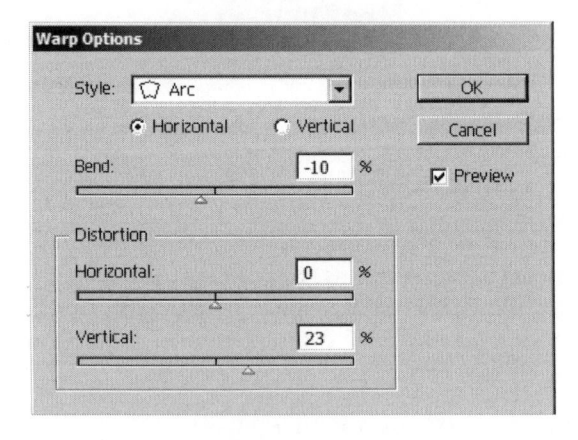

WARPING FABRIC FILLS

ENVELOPE DISTORT

MAKE WITH TOP OBJECT

First check the **Envelope Options** settings.

Object > Envelope Distort > Envelope Options

Check **Distort Pattern Fills** and try again.

Draw a rectangle representing the fabric and fill it with your pattern.
Right Click > Arrange > Send to Back
so that it is behind the piece of the garment you want to fill with it.(**Ctrl+[** / *Cmd +[*)

Select the fabric and the garment piece with the **Group Selection Tool**.

Object > Envelope Distort > Make with Top Object

This will warp the fabric as well as clip it inside the object.

This technique works nicely when the shapes are simple, but you will have no real control over the results. Sometimes you get lucky so I always give this a try first.

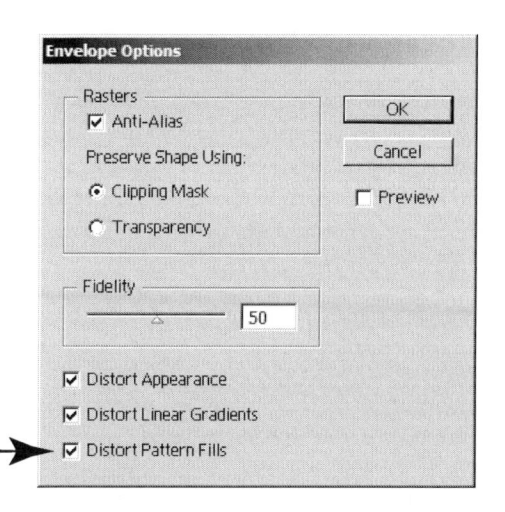

ENVELOPE DISTORT

MAKE WITH MESH

This approach will allow you more control. Draw a rectangle representing the fabric and fill it with your pattern. *Keep it close to the size of the object you are warping it to.*

Select it and **Cut** (**Ctrl+X** / *Cmd+X*).

Double click on the object to go into **Isolation Mode**.
Click on the object and **Paste in Back** (**Ctrl+B** / *Cmd+B*). This will paste the fabric behind the object.

Select the Fabric and go to
Object > Envelope Distort > Make with Mesh.

Check the **Preview box** and select a number of rows and columns you would like to use. *Note: a smaller number is easier to work with. In this case I used only one column and 2 rows.*

Use the **Direct Selection tool** to edit the mesh by **manipulating anchor points** and handles to follow the shape of the garment. The goal is to get the fabric to follow the silhouette of the object as best you can.

Switch to the **Selection tool**.
Select the fabric and the garment piece **Right Click >Make Clipping Mask**.

Now the fabric is inside the garment but the Stroke has disappeared.
To restore the outline of the garment change the **Stroke to 1pt. black**.

You can always go back and edit the Envelope by double clicking on it.

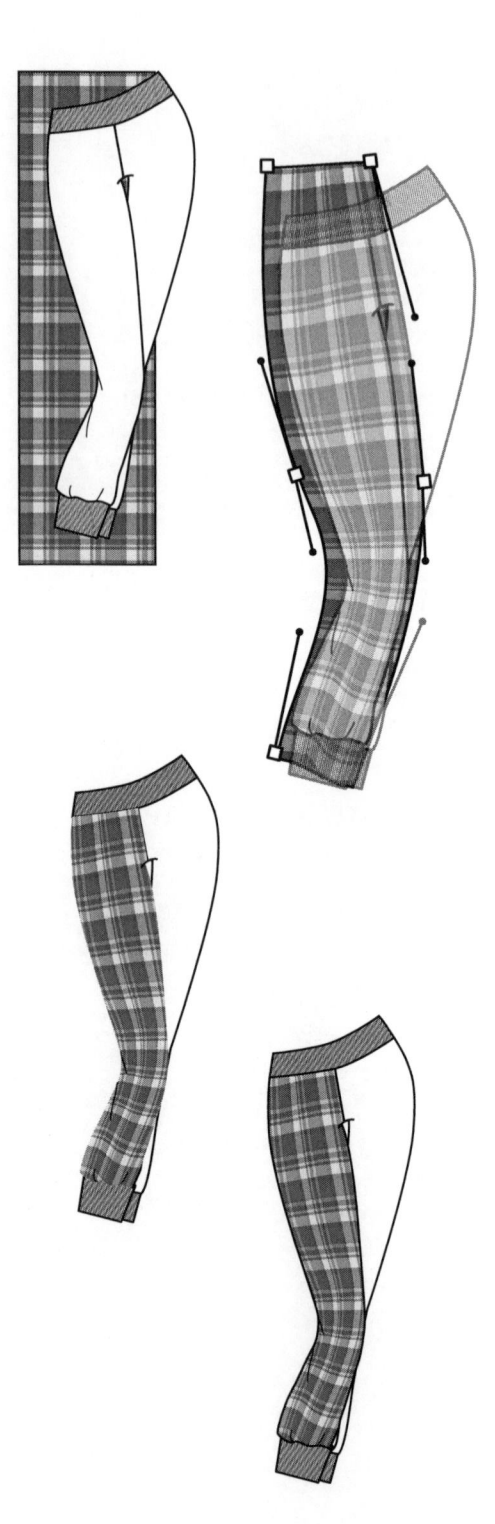

adobe® for fashion : illustrator CS5 | 215

Keshia Tedjopranoto
Art Institute of Ca-Hollywood
http://www.coroflot.com/Kdaniella

my two cents...

I hope that you were able to use the information in this handbook to enhance your flats and improve your efficiency.

The way I see it, a true craftsman can build a house with old fashion hand tools or new fangled power tools. Either way you get a beautifully crafted home.

But only one of them has time to go on a vacation. I like vacations...

Remember the computer is just another power tool. Don't let it get the best of you.

                See you in Maui

                Robin Schneider

Instructors who would like more information about using this book in the classroom can contact me at **Robin@adobeforfashion.com** for exercises and suggested assignments.

student contributors

My deepest thanks to the exceptional students that generously contributed their work as well as their feedback and encouragement.

I invite you to visit their portfolios at Coroflot.com. and I hope you'll be suitably impressed. Most of them are going to be recent graduates when this book is published. They may even be available for work - if someone hasn't already snapped them up.

They come with my highest recommendations.

Robin Schneider

Amber Esparsa 119, 122, 128, 129
http://www.coroflot.com/ale_esparza

Angelica Chavez *172*
http://www.coroflot.com/veltimera

Brooke E. Belden...........57, 91, 117, 177, 193
http://www.coroflot.com/brooke_e_belden

Fernanda Martin Del Campo...................176
http://www.coroflot.com/fernandamartin

Jose Andrade......................159, 173
http://www.coroflot.com/joseandrade

Juan Sim 43, 75, 175, 178
http://www.coroflot.com/juan_sim

Keshia Tedjopranoto........................156, 215
http://www.coroflot.com/Kdaniella

Kimberly Hires.............................158
http://www.coroflot.com/kimberlyhires

Lauren Diaz..................................179
http://www.coroflot.com/laurendiaz

Stella Lee....................................169

Stephanie Green.........................174
http://www.coroflot.com/stephyg

Tephy Sok.............................156,161
http://www.coroflot.com/Tephism

Trixie Encomienda....................157, 170-171
http://www.coroflot.com/Trixie_Encomienda

resources

TUTORIALS & REFERENCE
adobeforfashion.com
adobe.com
kuler.adobe.com
bertmonroy.com
lynda.com
layersmagazine.com
vector.tutsplus.com
designernexus.com
stylesight.com
fashionbizinc.org
illustratorforfashionpros.com

BOOKSTORES
thefashionbookstore.com
indexbook.com

FONTS
dafont.com

CUSTOM FABRIC
spoonflower.com
fabricondemand.com

ONLINE BACKUP
dropbox.com
carbonite.com

PORTFOLIO SITES
coroflot.com
fashionportfolios.com
styleportfolios.com
behance.net
carbonmade.com
krop.com
tumbler.com
divientart.com

BLATANT NEPOTISM
idealchef.com- because it's my brother's site and it's great!
nymoldinspector.com-so my dad won't feel left out.
blogtalkradio.com/divorcedilemma- yep,

BOOKS
Photoshop Studio with Bert Monroy, New Riders Press; ISBN-10: 0321515870

Illustrator CS5 for Windows and Macintosh: Visual QuickStart Guide by Elaine Weinmann and Peter Lourekas; Peachpit Press; ISBN-10: 0321706617

The Adobe Illustrator CS5 Wow! Book by Sharon Steuer, Peachpit Press; ISBN-10: 0321712447

Real World Adobe Illustrator CS5 by Mordy Golding. Peachpit Press; ISBN-10: 0-321-71306-0

9 Heads: A Guide to Drawing Fashion (3rd Edition) by Nancy Riegelman, Prentice Hall; ISBN-10: 0132238446

Fashion Illustration for Designers (2nd Edition) by Kathryn Hagen, Prentice Hall; ISBN-10: 013501557X

Fashion Illustration by Fashion Designers by Laird Borrelli. Chronicle Books; ISBN-10: 0811863360 .

Figure Poses for Fashion Illustrators by Sha Tahmasebi, Barron's Educational Series; ISBN-10: 1438070497

Visit **www.adobeforfashion.com** for updated resources and free downloads.

Questions? Comments?
Send me an e-mail at:
Robin@adobeforfashion.com

index

A

ACCORDION PLEATS 212
ADDING TEXT 163,166
ADVANCED BRUSHES 194
ADVANCED PATTERNS 203, 204
    HALF DROP 203
ALIGN 59
ANIMATED FLATS 187
APPEARANCE PANEL 183
ARROWS 120
    CURVED ARROWS 121
AVERAGE 34

B

BACK VIEW 48
BARTACKS 111
BASIC BLAZER 83
BLAZER FRONT 87
    LAPEL 84
BLEND 190
BLOB BRUSH 192
BOLD OUTLINE 182
BOOKS 219
BOOKSTORES 219
BRUSHES 93
    ART BRUSH 93
    BLOB BRUSH 110
    BRISTLE BRUSH 93
    CALIGRAPHIC BRUSH 93
    CALLIGRAPHIC BRUSH 109
    CALLIGRAPIC BRUSHES 109
    CLOSED ZIPPER 101
    COLORING BRUSHES 199, 202
    CREATING BRUSHES 94, 95
    ZIG ZAG 100, 101
    DOUBLE NEEDLE TOP STITCH 95
    EDITING BRUSHES 97
    ELASTIC CASING 198
    EXPOSED ZIPPER BRUSH 196
    FUR 199
    LACE 200
    LOADING BRUSHES 99
    OPEN ZIPPER 101
    OVERLOCK 100
    PATTERN BRUSH 93, 201
    RUFFLE TRIM BRUSH 197
    SAVING BRUSHES 99
    SCATTER BRUSH 93, 201
    SHOELACE BRUSH 195
    THE BLOB BRUSH 110
    ZIG ZAG 100
BUTTONHOLES 112, 113

BUTTONS 69
BUTTON 105
    FANCY BUTTON 105

C

CLIPPING MASKS 127,191
COLLARS 61
COLOR GROUPS 206
COLOR PICKER 18
SKIN TONES 146
CONTROL PANEL 20
CONVERTING POINTS 26
CREATING CUFFS 67
CROQUI 145
CUFFS 67
CUSTOM FABRIC 219

D

DIRECT SELECTION TOOL 24
DISTRIBUTE 60
DRAWING FACES 149
DRAWING FLATS 38
DROP SHADOW 182

E

EDITING POINTS 24
ELLIPSES 12
EMBROIDERY 188
ENVELOPE DISTORT 213
MAKE WITH MESH 214
MAKE WITH TOP OBJECT 213
ENVELOPE WARP 211
EXPAND 108
EYE DROPPER TOOL 55

F

FACES 149
    BLUSH 154
    EYE LASHES 151
    EYES 149
    HAIR 155
    MOUTH 153
FONTS 167, 219
    DOWNLOADING FONTS 167
    LOADING FONTS 167
FRONT PLACKET 66

G

GRADIENTS 148

GRAPHIC STYLES 123, 124
GROUPS 68
GROUP SELECTION TOOL 68

H

HAND TOOL 25

I

ISOLATION MODE 50

J

JEANS 113
JOIN 33

K

KNIFE PLEATS 211
KULER 207

L

LAYERS 7, 49
    BACKGROUNDS 168
        GRAPHIC PANEL 168
        INSET BORDER 169
LAYOUTS 161, 163
LIVE TRACE 200
LOCATE OBJECT 183

M

MARQUEE SELET 14
MEASURE TOOL 184

N

NECKLINE 45

O

ORGANIZING LAYERS 49

P

PANELS 6

PATHFINDER 35
    DIVIDE 37
    EXCLUDE 36
    UNITE 35
PATHS 21
    CLOSED PATH 21
    COMPOUND PATH 21
    OPEN PATH 21
PATTERNS 131
    APPLYING PATTERNS 132
    CREATING PATTERNS 133
    EDITING A PATTERN 135
    HALF DROP 203
    MOVING PATTERNS 138
    PLAIDS 141
    RANDOM OR TOSS REPEATS 205
    ROTATING PATTERNS 137
    SAVING PATTERNS 134
    SCALING PATTERNS 136
    STRIPES 139
PEN TOOL 22
PENCIL TOOL 187
PLEATED SKIRTS 211
POCKET 107,115
    POCKET FLAP 107
PORTFOLIO SITES 219
PRINCESS LINE 89
PROFILES 82, 181

R

RECOLOR ARTWORK 208
RECTANGLE 10
REDUCING COLORS 210
REFLECT 31
RESOURCES 219
RIBBING 189
ROTATE 29,137

S

SAVING FILES FOR PRINT 170
SAVING FOR EXCEL 122
SCALE TOOL 136
SCRIBBLE 188
SELECTING OBJECTS 14
SELECTION TOOL 14
SHAPE BUILDER TOOL 185
SHAPES 10
SHIRT 46
    BACK NECK 56
    BACK VIEW 48
    SHIRT BACK 70
    SLEEVES 46
        SLEEVE PLACKET 72
SKIRTS 77

STARS 13
STITCHES 53
STRIPES 139
STROKES 51
STUDENT CONTRIBUTORS 217
SWATCHES PANEL 18
SYMBOLS 102
    BAR TACKS 111
    CREATING 104
    BUTTON 105
    DRAWSTRINGS 108
    EYELET 105
    FANCY BUTTON 105
    RIVET 105
    DRAWSTRINGS 108
    EDITING 104
    EYELET 105
    REPLACING SYMBOLS 104
    RIBBONS 109
    RIPS AND TEARS 111
    RIVET 105

T

TECH PACKS 119
TERMINOLOGY 9
TIME SAVERS 183
TOOL BAR 4
T-SHIRT 39
    BACK NECK 56
    BACK NECKLINE 45
    BACK VIEW 48
    SLEEVES 46
TUTORIALS & REFERENCE 219

W

WARPING FABRIC FILLS 213
WELT POCKET 107

Z

ZIPPER PULL 106
ZOOM IN 127
ZOOM TOOL 25

"My crow ate my flash drive"

The best excuse I ever heard for not turning in homework on time.
Of course I had to make shirts-doesn't everyone.

Instructors who would like more information about using this book in the classroom can contact me at **Robin@adobeforfashion.com** for exercises and suggested assignments.